STONE WALLS
—— and ——
River Music
THE COLUMNS OF BOB HILL

Green Thumb Publishing, Inc.

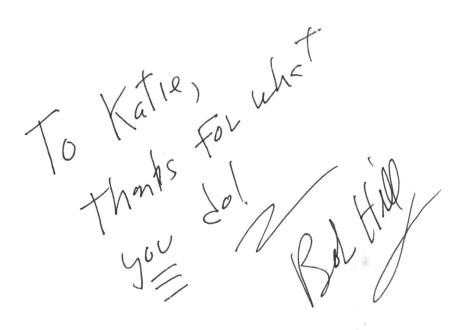

To Katie,
Thanks for what
you do!
Bob Hill

Published by Green Thumb Publishing, Inc.
P.O. Box 3703, Louisville, KY 40201

Cover photograph by Pam Spaulding
Stone wall by Rick Weber

All columns and photographs are reprinted
with the permission of The Courier-Journal,
which holds the exclusive rights to them.

ISBN 1-885379-04-8

STONE WALLS
& RIVER MUSIC

DEDICATION

For Fred
Who has helped us all to grow.

ACKNOWLEDGMENTS

Three months before this book went to publication
it was a yellowing collection of column-sized newsprint
hidden away in manila folders. I thank my wonderful wife,
Janet, who has always herded all that newsprint into folders,
and editor Jena Monahan, a friend and consummate
professional who worked incredibly long and hard hours
on short notice to polish the yellowed prose.
She's the best.
I also thank Courier-Journal photographer
Pam Spaulding, who again gave old photos the light of a new day,
and Mike Covington and Steve Sebree who added
the artist's touch. I don't know where I'd be without
my family and friends.

TABLE OF CONTENTS

GETTING PERSONAL

OUT THERE

SORTA SILLY

PROFILES IN FAST TIME

ENDINGS

Chapter One
GETTING PERSONAL

I most enjoy writing when I can
disappear into a mood, a moment or a
thought and re-emerge an hour or two
later wondering where the time went.
A shorter description of that is:
Don't think, write. The writing process
begins in the conscious mind, but —
when it's going well — magically
heads off in a direction all its own.
Writers need that inner voice,
rejoice in its appearance; we don't
really know how we feel about something — or how to describe what we
feel — until it shows up.
Only then can we get personal.

Like a rock, wall builder links past with present

Old-timers in my neighborhood still talk about the long stone wall that once lined our road, a wall with square-jawed limestone rocks that snaked up and over our hill as if risen from the earth, a wall that nicely repeated itself over and over, then flowed around the bend and disappeared.

Ragged remnants of that wall remain. They are mostly sections that must now rest against the hillside for support or became unearthed when I dug out some tree stumps, but I can always picture that wall whole and healthy in my mind. One of my dreams is to rebuild the wall, to find enough time and rock to re-create it, to pay homage to its makers, to restore its symmetry to our neighborhood, to leave my mark.

That, in large part, is what rock-building is all about; leaving some sort of mark. I am not a man good at tiny and precise detail; the molding under a bathroom sink installed 10 years ago has never been fully nailed to the floor. I am not a man who can plumb or wire a new addition; I've watched a half-dozen experts do it and can never remember a single turn or splice.

I like to deal with the larger, more permanent things. I like to work with rock.

There are easier hobbies. You'll never get a hernia lifiting a stamp. You don't need hammers, chisels, goggles and large pry bars to trade two Mickey Mantle baseball cards for a Willie Mays. Nor are rock walls really forever; most of my stone comes from other walls or from the foundations of old houses and barns; it's just my turn to use the rock before someone else comes to get it.

I built my first rock wall — actually a rock garden — about 25 years ago. The farmhouse we had bought had the foundation of an old outbuilding buried under its driveway. I pried loose about 25 heavy rocks — one at a time — and hauled them across our lawn in a wheelbarrow, weaving like a drunk, my legs bowed like the curve of a fiddle.

It was fun — a nice mix of work, play and spatial relationships, something new and something very atavistic. I felt good doing it. I like to work hard, to sweat, to step back and admire what I've done, then plunge in again. My rock garden looked good; the gratification was instant. I felt a link with the men who had quarried those old rocks. I felt they would be pleased.

Our present home, another old farmhouse, produced more rock gardens — a dozen at last count. None of them are very original — just three or four layers of rocks built into a slope, against tree stumps, or free-standing creations mothered over by flowering crabs.

In retrospect some of these gardens do not blend into my landscape. They are too obvious, too intrusive, and must be torn down or rearranged. Nature displays its well-worn rocks with a certain grace or character; a few of my man-made creations have the unsubtle charm of a walrus in a wading pool.

Until recently, I never paid for a single rock. I've been given rock by generous neighbors, stolen rocks from construction sites, scouted them out in weekend travels along the back roads and once rented a Hertz truck with a tailgate lift to haul home a friend's gift of a dozen interesting-looking rocks that were twice the size of seat cushions. If you like rocks, you will understand that. If you don't, there's no explaining it.

My freebie days ended voluntarily early this year with a marvelous find; a neighbor had a long rock wall at the very back of his property, an old, raggedy wall that stretched into a dense thicket of worthless trees and shrubs. I bought the wall on the spot. Then we had to haul it home.

My 23-year-old son and I did it, a father-son expedition of some weight, eight ... 10 ... 12 slow trips in a short-bed pickup. The wall looked to be at least 75 to 100 years old, some of it covered with a vivid-green moss that I knew would die in the sunlight of my open field. Part of the wall had slipped and fallen, but part remained proud and strong, as solid as the day it was locked into place.

You cannot move such a wall without thinking about who build it, at what cost, and what they were trying to fence in — or out. I would pause at times, looking at the wall's shadows, crevices and dark hollows, knowing I could never fully restore its aged charm, feeling a little bad I had disturbed its silence

I wanted to rebuild the wall near my barn, another large and rustic project that friends and I had built of old timbers and graying oak siding. It is a barn whose windows — which require that tiny and precise detail work — are as loose and floppy as the day I installed them 12 years ago.

Last month I took a two-week vacation, in part to find time to rebuild my new-found stone wall, a vacation that was about the equivalent of staying home to carry the family washing machine up and down the basement stairs 100 times a day.

The trick in wall-building with limestone is to construct a good foundation by using the flat, mostly rectangular, 50- to 100-pound rock on the bottom. That done — and I counted a total of about 300 rocks in each 60-foot section of wall — the idea was to "tie in" each succeeding layer, overlapping the stones to prevent one joint from running vertically up the wall's face. Unless you are on a steep hill, it's always best to keep the top layer of rock parallel to the bottom. Beyond that, it's all trial and error.

Once you get the rocks home — I had a great litter of rocks strewn along the new fence line in descending order of size — raw strength is not all that important. Rocks can be tipped, levered and nudged fairly easily, and working on your knees can help prevent too much bending of the back.

The joy of construction is in finding just the right rock for the right place, in turning it over, then around, then over again, matching its rough texture and shape against the mother rock below it, brother and sister rocks next to it.

The right rock will just "click" into place. If you're lucky, three rocks in a row will go "click, click, click." Then you'll have to hunt 15 minutes to find the fourth, often using a hammer or chisel to pound off a protruding corner or knob. I never use mortar; my chief allies are gravity and patience; the latter a commodity in very short supply in almost everything else I do.

It's always best to have a hundred smaller rocks on hand to chink the spaces, to keep the bigger, uneven rocks from tipping, to run a capstone along the top to give the wall flow and symmetry. It's always fun to stop and look at the fossils etched in the limestone, the incredibly delicate outlines of sea creatures that died 300 million years ago, their engravings looking as fresh as yesterday.

A good rock wall can be taken in with one sweep of the eye, or enjoyed in small sections, in intricate detail, the eye finding the individual patterns that pull the whole together. I never did like too much perfection in rock walls; they look like capped teeth. I will check my walls once or twice a year for spillage, but the fallout is always minor. What's a year to a rock?

One day I worked six straight hours on my new wall, lost in thought and concentration, forgetting everything but the task at hand. Those are the periods I enjoy the most, the most restful, relaxing and peaceful hours I can find.

That was short-term. The long-term reward was a new section of wall that looked as if it had been in place 60 years, my link to the past, something good and lasting I had built with my hands, something to look forward to when I get home.

Dec. 4, 1992

Nashville take note: Columbia is fickle, may not stay long

In the first few weeks of my freshman year in college our dormitory bulletin board became littered with the poignant, painful debris of true love suddenly gone south — "Dear John" letters.

Longtime girlfriends who had pledged eternal love in August had found replacement males by Labor Day. When their subsequent Dear John letters were compared for literary style — and bitter, disillusioned, occasionally drunken freshman would gather three deep in their underwear for loud discussions on syntax, sincerity and merit — the letters were remarkably consistent.

They always recounted good times together and contained a litany of reasons why the relationship would no longer work. They always ended with the wish: I hope we can remain friends.

I have the feeling Columbia/HCA President Richard Scott is going to be writing somebody Dear John letters for the rest of his life.

Certainly his full-page "Dear Louisville" letter in yesterday's Courier-Journal explaining why he was moving company headquarters to Nashville after its 10 stormy months of professed love, legislative manipulation, lies, deceit, public rancor and unfaithful behavior was a classic of the Dear John genre. Let me please explain; don't forget the good things; Louisville will always be important to us.

"Louisville is a special city and the Commonwealth of Kentucky is a special state," he wrote. "The people are generous and caring. This is a place that will always be important to us."

All that was missing from this tender relationship was money. I was struck while watching Scott's press conference announcing the move Tuesday in Nashville by the way he said the company was moving immediately. He had that same portable, likable, little-boy smile he'd brought to Louisville. But he bit off the word "immediately" as if he couldn't say it fast enough, or strong enough.

He followed with three quick reasons: office space, airport facilities, quality of life, leaving the distinct impression Louisville had none of the above. I guess that was no time to remind Scott that Kentucky Gov. Brereton Jones had been led to believe Columbia/HCA was willing to build facilities in Louisville, that an expanded airport is almost at hand, that Columbia/HCA headquarters is now moving to the Rhinestone Cowboy capital of the world.

At least there remains the possibility that Columbia/HCA will leave behind a $10 million engagement ring; its apparent pledge for the new University of Louisville football stadium — which would be named for the company and be built in the shape of a 50,000-seat hospital gurney.

I did feel a sense of loss when I heard Columbia/HCA was leaving; could the city survive both that and Howard Schnellenberger in a two-week period? I got over both losses quickly; both were essentially business decisions we couldn't do much about.

Columbia/HCA officials said the company was headed south even if Kentucky had repealed the hated — and perhaps soon to be repealed — provider tax. While they were at it, the company also had complaints about Kentucky's intangible property, income and occupational taxes. Gee, where does the line form for that list? Kentucky tax codes need some examination — and it was being done — but why didn't that silly old state legislature just roll over and hand Columbia/HCA the keys to the whole medicine cabinet?

From a strictly business point of view — and what's love got to do with that? — what Columbia/HCA did makes perfect sense; the majority of its corporate operations are, or will be, in Nashville. Corporate loyalty to any one community is almost a thing of the past; corporations are all for sale to the highest bidder; economic blackmail is the name of the game, deceit and deception the playing rules.

I had hoped — a little naively — that perhaps Scott and Columbia/HCA might stick around and try to make a real difference instead of just trying to make real money.

Chalk it up as another personal — and community — learning

experience. So long, Rick, thanks for writing. Don't let a banjo hit you in the butt when you leave Nashville.

Jan. 12, 1995

Touch of humanity free with purchase of burger and Coke

If I ever did know her name, I've forgotten it. It doesn't matter much. She was the girl — a young woman, really — who worked behind the counter at McDonald's. I was the guy who always ordered two cheeseburgers and a Coke — more recently amended to two hamburgers and a Diet Coke — to go.

This went on, sometimes three or four times a week, for months. By then, of course, dialogue wasn't necessary. She'd almost have the stuff waiting by the time I walked in the door. I'd have my $1.75 in hand. Rarely has commerce been more swift or satisfactory.

Well, you know how it is with people you meet almost every day in a store or fast-food restaurant. They become familiar. Conversation becomes easy. In a way, they become friends, even if you don't know their names. You care about them. You begin to look forward to seeing them. More important, you notice when they are not around.

Alas, a few months ago McDonald's moved her from working behind the walk-in counter to handing hamburgers and french fries out the drive-in window as the public rolled past.

Whatever she had to say after that she would toss over her shoulder while passing white sacks out the window.

Usually the public was backed up bumper to bumper and nearly out into the street.

You do wonder what America did for lunch before the invention of drive-in windows.

She was amazingly cheerful almost every time I saw her. I know it is not always possible to be that way when a hungry America is continually rolling past your window asking for more ketchup or dropping its change onto the drive.

There must be moments when french fries are best delivered through an open window and into the face of a screaming child at about 40 miles per hour, cold soft drink to follow.

Indeed, the next generation of saints might come from young men and women who spent 5, 10, even 15 uncomplaining years handing round breakfast muffins through rectangular windows.

Imagine, if you can, saying a short prayer to St. Buffy, the patron saint of scrambled eggs.

Yet, and through it all, Our Lady of the Window at least appeared to be happy in her work, even if she wasn't. That's close enough for me. Optimism is often its own reward.

Yesterday, for the first time, we were able to talk a little longer. She had to catch a bus home and had to walk a few blocks to meet it. She was even more cheerful than usual. She said she is getting married in a big ceremony in May. She said she plans on being married for a long, long time.

There was something so appealing and optimistic about that, even from a young woman whose name I did not know, whose fiance I had never seen, whose family I had never met.

Somehow you never think about all those people behind a counter at McDonald's getting married, raising families and then lining up, bumper to bumper, for dinner at a fast-food restaurant.

I know the statistics about the number of marriages that survive. I know it is not easy. But I would be willing to bet three weeks' worth of lunch that they make it.

April 10, 1984

Baby's father deserves compassion, not righteous indignation

When our daughter was about a year old, I made a quick trip to visit her maternal grandfather — one of the few trips we ever made without my wife. Her father was a farmer, a small, wiry, interesting man given to hard work and tall stories — the latter always sprinkled with just enough facts to lend them credibility, but not quite credence.

It was January, the temperature well below zero; cold, but not the type of weather to keep people indoors in Northern Illinois, where frigid weather comes with the corn-stubble. On the way to the farm I spotted my father-in-law's car at the local coffee shop, a favorite haunt for him and his neighbors, especially when the winter winds blew in from Iowa.

By then I had spent days listening to my father-in-law's coffee-shop stories, his eternal claims of poverty, his tales of wandering the country during the Great Depression, working the Kansas wheat fields and the Montana sheep ranches. I could recite many of his stories — as could his audience — but this was a funny, gregarious, story-loving bunch that would invariably indulge him — and thus, themselves. What else was there to do in Northern Illinois in January?

I pulled into the crowded parking lot near the gas station — my daughter in a car seat sound asleep, well-bundled in several layers of snowsuit. I didn't want to wake her, or take her inside.

And I was afraid to leave the car's motor running for fear of engine fumes. I decided I would turn off the engine, run inside to tell her grandfather we had arrived, then come back out.

What I did next has haunted me — if I let myself think about it — for 30 years. I went inside the coffee shop, somehow got to listening to the farm stories, and forgot about my daughter. I don't know how long it was — 10 minutes, 15 minutes, 20 minutes — before the name *Jennifer* suddenly flashed in my mind. I ran outside, opened the car door, and there she was: awake, grinning at me, none the worse for the experience, although her eyes did have a puzzled edge to them. Today, even as I write this sentence, terrible feelings of guilt wash over me.

Those feelings were even more powerful last weekend as I read the tragic story of Brian Swett, the University of Louisville employee whose 5-month-old daughter died, apparently of heat prostration, after he went inside to work, forgetting she was in the car.

How could that have happened? How could somebody forget a child in a car, forget to take her to a day-care center? Was it some distraction, a preoccupation, a change of domestic routine that had not yet become habit? All I know is that we are human; it can happen; I did it. I love my children more than life itself, but I once left my daughter alone in a car on a frozen January morning.

I was disappointed — but not surprised — at the level of righteous indignation, if not hatred, aimed at Swett by a few callers to local talk shows. We can all be so good at raising other people's children, at pointing fingers, at being judgmental. Swett's friends and co-workers have nothing but praise, sympathy and respect for the man and his family. The murder charge against him — are we worried about another Susan Smith episode here? — is absurd, ludicrous, cruel.

We all — if we are honest — can remember moments when we accidentally placed our children at risk, were not as careful as we should have been, got busy and forgot them.

We can all look back and shudder. How can any parent examine a lifetime of raising children and not feel empathy, compassion and aching sorrow for Brian Swett and his family?

I was lucky; our daughter recently graduated from a fine university; our son breezed home last weekend to leave a gift of what he does best — photo images. Our family remains intact. Brian Swett will never again know that feeling. Isn't that burden enough?

July 18, 1995

Where were you, Great Daffodil?

It is 12:06 a.m. Wednesday. I am sitting in the fog and darkness of my backyard. I am facing east toward a distant sun and the dented, galvanized beauty of my half-dozen garbage cans.

I am waiting for spring.

And maybe, so help me Linus, The Great Daffodil.

Good grief!

Spring is due in at 12:22 a.m. I had never waited her in before, just accepting on faith she would show up unescorted some time after "Laverne and Shirley" and before "The Star-Spangled Banner" sign-off.

But this year is different. I have been particularly tired of this winter. A simple yet elegant greeting for spring is in order.

So I am sitting alone on my children's basketball court. My children claim it is their father's basketball court, but that is another story.

I am sitting in a lawn chair, a dubious contraption of tubular aluminum and green and white plastic — all in all the absolute essence of modern spring.

I am wearing my best sport coat, a daring, V-necked T-shirt, jeans that have been washed to the color of wood ashes and red basketball shoes, Chuck Taylor Converse All-Stars.

I am holding a crystalline glass of white wine in one hand. I am taking notes (carefully interviewing myself) with the other. I am feeling a little stupid about the whole thing.

I am wondering if The Great Daffodil will arrive by gardener's wheelbarrow or just will simply push up through the ground and slam-dunk me through my children's basketball goal. I am wondering what I am doing here. I am wondering what the neighbors might be thinking.

My wife accepts my greeting of spring with the normal calm of a journalist's wife. She is in bed asleep. She wouldn't even pour the wine.

It is 12:17 a.m. Wednesday. Night sounds, pressed close to the ground by the heavy fog, carry clearly to my backyard.

A towboat beats heavily up the Ohio River a half-mile away. A farmer's geese stir, cry angrily into the night, tuck their graceful necks under smooth white wings and settle back to sleep.

A jet airplane, a young calf and a distant dog, undoubtedly a denter of garbage cans, perform in turn, a cappella, and the night closes in again.

Our yard light throws long shadows across the back field. Dark shadows from my split-rail fence angle crazily into my tiny patch of woods. The deep shadow of my lawn chair could easily hold The Great Daffodil, lock, stock and stamen.

Advance public-relations types for The Great Daffodil already have been at work. My crocuses, clumped thickly in purple and white patches, arrived last week on slender green feet.

My fairy's circle of tiny daffodils bloomed yellow on dark green for the first time Tuesday. My irises and lilies are stirring light green. My poppies have put on star-shaped leaves and, faithful Republicans that they are, are out looking for more real estate to control.

It is 12:21 a.m. Wednesday. I remain a solitary nut in a lawn chair looking glumly around a fog-filled yard for a great spring flower, my vigil lighted solely by a yard light and Public Service Indiana.

I don't even have a decent speech prepared if The Great Daffodil does show up. I am a man who dislikes speaking before Kiwanis and Lions clubs. What am I supposed to say to a 12-foot green and yellow flower?

Good grief!

So, as the countdown toward spring continues, I am gazing anxiously around my backyard. I am beginning to believe in The Great Daffodil. I am continuing to wonder how a yard that is so friendly by day can be so mysterious at night.

It is 12:22 a.m. Wednesday. Spring has arrived. I lift my crystalline wine glass in the general direction of my dented garbage cans. There is no response. There is no Great Daffodil.

It is 12:28 a.m. Wednesday. I can see my biggest mistake was not bringing the wine bottle out with me. I shift uneasily in my lawn chair. The fog presses in: I am thinking of my favorite "Peanuts" cartoon strip. I have searched for years for a copy of it. Charlie Brown is pitching in a baseball game. He is, of course, being shelled. The next-to-the-last cartoon box shows a disgusted Charlie saying:

"Good grief, 184 to 0."

In the last box, a forlorn Charlie asks, "How can we lose when we're so sincere?"

It is 12:34 a.m. Wednesday. I am back in the house. But I leave the lawn chair outside on my children's basketball court. You can never tell who might need it.

March 24, 1979

It was an unfair(way) trap — and no 'Bones' about it

Unlike today's lazy, spoiled and generally irresponsible students, I worked hard, very hard, in college earning spending money.

I stole golf balls.

Since the golf balls were appropriated from the bottom of lakes at a nearby fat cat country club, the legality of the deed was never considered.

To me it was merely a redistribution of wealth.

They were rich Republicans with lousy swings.

I was a latter-day Robin Hood with a Titleist fetish.

My partner in sociology was Kendall Lee "Bones" Rhine, my prewife roommate. When I first met Bones, he stood 6 feet 10 inches tall, but had to cover it all with only 185 pounds.

If the wind rose to more than 15 mph, we had to mail him to class in a manila envelope.

Bones eventually gained 60 pounds and played professional basketball in Louisville with the original Kentucky Colonels.

Stealing golf balls may have been easier, if not more honest.

The name of the fat cat country club escapes me, but it was on the outskirts of Houston, Texas. Bones was the wheel man. I was tail gunner and keeper of the dormitory pillow cases, which doubled as golf ball sacks.

We would dress in black clothes straight out of "Assignment in Zanzibar," tucking the white pillow cases under our shirts. Bones always parked about 50 yards up a lane across from the club, and we'd hoof it in from there.

We tried to pick moonless nights and were always very careful. I don't care how you dress, it is very hard to hide on a golf course when you are 6 feet 10 inches tall and weigh 185 pounds.

It was always a nervous walk, but it had its rewards. One night an Angus steer loomed up in the darkness near us, and Bones and I learned how to fly.

We usually went out on Sunday nights, particularly after a weekend tournament. On a good night, we would each half-fill a pillow case with $1.25 balls, then sell them for 35 to 50 cents each, plus overhead.

Alas, our golfing customers, many who did not fully understand the historical and sociological importance of our businesss, began to horn into the act.

The lane across from the country club became so crowded with cars on Sunday nights that a guy needed a reserved parking space. The business went to the dogs, golf course security doubled and Bones and I went hungry on weekends.

And Bones was not a man who could well afford to go hungry on weekends.

We laid off the country club for a few months, then returned one inky night in late summer for a final try. By then the market was glutted with cheap golf balls, and we had the lane to ourselves.

We hiked to the lake free from bovine intervention and waded in. There was nothing scientific about our search, particularly at night. All we could do was slop around the pond, hoping to strike golf balls with our hands or feet.

Bones got the deep end.

The night proved to be one of our best, and in an hour's time the bank was littered with hail-sized golf balls. We were so busy we didn't even look up until the country club security guard rose magically from a sand trap, flashlight in hand, signaling an abrupt end to our merchandising career.

Bones took off like a startled crane, covering three fairways in about 15 seconds. I cleverly tried to disguise myself as a sand trap, failing miserably.

It was the detail that struck home after that: the size of the guard's dog; the anger on his face; the even, round hole at the business end of his .22 rifle.

He did not appear to be a man well-versed in the legend of Robin Hood.

By then Bones was two-thirds of the way to Oklahoma and I didn't feel so hungry anymore. The guard shouted for his partner while I silently called for The Great Sand Wedge Goddess to get me out of this one.

I am certain I still hold the record for the most "Hail Marys" uttered in 30 seconds in a Houston country club sand trap after 11 p.m. on a Sunday night.

Happily, the guard did not call the law but just marched me off the course toward Bones and his fast-idling car.

The guard stayed behind me every step of the way, his rifle only a few feet from my back, its business end looming like a sewer pipe in my mind.

Even some 15 years later I would forgive the guard his little forced march, but the thief kept our golf balls.

July 31, 1980

Change from supporter to foe of death penalty took time

Sometime this spring — after a lifetime of believing in it and long before Timothy McVeigh or Harold McQueen were in the news — I became opposed to the death penalty. It was not a sudden change; I've been moving in that direction for several years.

One day, as if being eased over the top of a hill after a lifetime of pushing against it, I found myself on a new path: It's wrong for the state to take a life no matter how heinous the crime.

I've given the death penalty a lot of thought because about 15 years ago I was foreman on a jury that recommended death for a man who had brutally murdered a young mother, left her nude body dangling from a belt fastened to the top drawer of a dresser. The woman's young daughter found her there, an image she surely would carry to her grave, an image that made it easier for me to recommend the killer should die.

He didn't. The case was appealed based on a supposed error made in the sentencing portion of the trial by the court-appointed defense attorney. As a result, the death sentence was reduced to about 40 years in prison.

For several years after his original sentencing, the murderer would call me about once a year. He'd always say he had no hard feelings; the jury hadn't understood all the evidence. Then he would ask for copies of photographs made of him being led off to jail.

I don't believe I ever hated him on a personal level. The image we jurors had of him was presented through legal filters: courtroom maneuvers, police and expert-witness testimony, a judge's discretion of what was admissable. But at that time, I thought he should die for what he did.

I don't feel any guilt about that. I'm not the same person I was when we recommended death. I can't go back and change what I believed then, what we the jury did. But if asked now to serve in a case where the death sentence was a possibility, I would express my opposition to it and surely be dismissed by the prosecution.

The cases of McVeigh, who murdered 168 innocent victims, and McQueen, who murdered a helpless store clerk, have heightened my thinking on the death penalty. The polls I've seen indicate about two-thirds of us favor it, one-third oppose it. The numbers surprised me. I thought about 80 percent would favor death; a violent society seeks violent ends.

It is our societal violence — random, senseless, brutal and crippling — that more than anything has led me to change my mind on state-sanctioned execution, and only then over a period of 15 years.

I don't believe the death penalty is a deterrent to crime. Most murders are committed in rage, in moments when a murderer has little time to think about the consequences. The way the death penalty is administered is neither swift, nor sure, nor fair. Appeals take many years. Historically, the poor and minorities are executed in much greater numbers than the rich and powerful.

Fifteen years ago I did not care much about the validity of those arguments. I wanted equal punishment. I saw one execution balancing out another; eye for eye, tooth for tooth, death for death.

It was an often-used biblical phrase quoted from larger text. I had heard it all my life as a rationale for the death penalty. More recent investigation showed it's a part of Exodus that also gives how-to instructions for a father selling his daughter into slavery, establishes the rules allowing a master to beat his female servants, to keep the children born to his servants and to assign conjugal rights to his wife.

If you must quote the biblical "eye for eye" as a defense of capital punishment, please use what you will from the other Exodus instructions also. It's all, as we say, in interpretation.

The violence on our nation's streets — and Louisville's streets — is appalling. It leads our newscasts, brings endless stories from grieving parents talking about their children caught up in a maelstrom. What hope can we have as a nation to end our seething violence when the state takes lives too?

For a while during my metamorphosis I believed execution was best in some cases, not in others. It can't work that way. If execution is wrong once, then it is always wrong. My role models in this change have been the parents of victims of the Oklahoma City bombings who have steadfastly opposed the death penalty for McVeigh.

They are certainly in the minority but have held true to their values. I'm just now beginning to understand how difficult that can be.

June 14, 1997

Birds of a feeder flock with critters

We've always fed the birds, of course. A half-dozen feeders dangle outside our kitchen window like some bizarre housing development. The feeders come as plastic houses, translucent silos, wooden platforms and metal suet cages, offering a comic skyline as if it were amply funded by the National Endowment for Bird Feeders. The birds must be laughing. Our plastic feeders hang from a heavy metal merry-go-round contraption anchored in concrete. The wooden feeder — with plastic windows — is nailed atop a cedar pole. Something for everybody, including — and I'll get to this later — a pair of squirrels, a barn cat, two dogs and one of Curtis Hooper's chickens.

When I look at our wind-whipped collection of avian feed troughs I think of a friend who lived in Columbia, Md., one of those highly planned human communities that offers something in housing and recreation for all interests and pocketbooks. Columbia is so planned, so nicely balanced, so relentlessly civil that speed bumps there — and I wish I were making this up — are labeled "traffic calmers."

We have unconsciously copied Columbia in bird feeders. Our motto: Where egalitarian utility meets thistle seeds. We try to feed finches, chickadees, cardinals, woodpeckers and hated starlings alike. The bigger birds are such messy eaters they scatter cracked corn and sunflower seeds all over the ground, keeping the ground-feeding doves in fine feather.

In the spring, when all the birds can find their own food, we allow the fallen sunflower seeds to bloom into flowers — and more seeds — keeping the cycle turning. I worry that our feeding efforts smack too much of fatty socialism — are we not encouraging woodpecker welfare? — but my bleeding-heart wife keeps lugging home the suet and 50-pound bags of sunflower seeds.

Our little experiment in community living worked well for a few years, but then we began noticing a gray barn cat lurking beneath the contorted filbert bush near the bird feeders. Then we began noticing little piles of feathers near the bush. Hmmm . . .

Not that the balance of power changed dramatically. The birds kept dropping by in large numbers, occasionaly thumping off our kitchen window in confused flight. Two of the neighborhood's stray dogs would keep the cat occupied often enough to maintain an uneasy truce. We decided to keep an eye on the area but not send in armed militia; speak softly and carry a big sunflower.

Our first squirrel showed up two or three years ago. Agile and aggressive, it would scamper up the cedar pole and defiantly perch on the wooden feeder like the school yard bully. It sat on its haunches, held sunflower seeds in its paws and dribbled crumbs all over the feeder.

Something about the squirrel was humanlike, endearing. At first it paid some attention to our frantic, get-the-heck-off-our-feeder pounding on the kitchen window. Then it just looked at us, squirrel eyes in sharp focus, sizing up the situation, basically a no-brainer. It was outside in the cold, we were inside in the warm; we weren't going outside; let us pound that window.

The companion squirrel began showing up last year; two raiders for the spoils. We didn't want to fool with a squirrel security thing, so we opened the feed store a little wider, bought more sunflower seeds. The squirrels usually dined together, one on each side of the feeder, sometimes with a bird or two dodging their bushy tails.

Early Sunday morning one of Curtis Hooper's chickens showed up. Curtis Hooper is the best neighbor anyone has ever had, but sometimes his chickens wander. When I looked out the window the chicken was feeding on cracked corn that had spilled from one feeder, and the two squirrels were eating the sunflower seed. I didn't see the barn cat, but maybe that's because the two neighborhood dogs had wandered close, casting a hungry eye on the chicken.

This is what happens around our house when you set out to feed birds. Of which we had none early Sunday morning. Go figure.

Dec 17, 1996

Flooding violated the right to know that you can go home

The contrast was startling; I had just spoken to a cheerful group of Louisville Water Co. employees inside the elegant Kentucky Derby Museum; I stepped outside to a world gone mad.

Thick rain pelted the museum parking lot. Everything familiar had been turned around. Central Avenue was a black lake shimmering in the street lights. A car plowed through the water, its headlights barely above the surface, looking sinister, threatening, a giant, glistening bug on the prowl.

I circled the parking lot, trying to find a safe exit. I took Central to Taylor Boulevard, angled right toward Winkler Avenue.

A Metropolitan Sewer District truck blocked the road, floodwater lapping at its door.

A half-dozen cars tried to turn around at once. We were soon engaged in an elaborate, back-and-forth dance of turns and twists, barely missing one another, each driver a ghostly figure behind a windshield made nearly opaque by rain.

I headed south on Taylor toward the Watterson Expressway. My thinking was to abandon flooded surface streets, take the Watterson east to Interstate 65 north, and make it home to Indiana the longer, safer way.

The entrance ramp to the Watterson was under water. Two cars ahead of me skirted this lake by driving up the exit ramp about 100 feet, then cutting across the grass to the "on" ramp. I hesitated briefly, then followed; I wanted to get home.

I drove east on the Watterson, hugging the right-hand lane, looking for the signs to I-65, windshield wipers beating desperately. A half-mile ahead — near my exit — red and blue police lights flashed in the night; a string of cars was coming down the "on" ramp; there was no way for me to go up.

For the first time I felt doubt, a flash of panic: *What if I couldn't get home.* My wife was alone, feeding a thin layer of water into our basement sump pump with a broom. I knew she had been at it for hours and was worried about me, our house. *I had to get home.*

I continued east on the Watterson, made a U-turn at the Poplar Level Road exit, headed back toward I-65 north. I was hurried, worried; little in my middle-class existence had prepared me for the possibility that I might not be able to get home.

A car full of teen-agers was parked where the Watterson exit forks north toward I-65. They were screaming something into the rain, pointing out their car windows as if there was danger ahead on I-65. Several cars in front of me heeded the warning and swerved back on the Watterson. I had about three seconds to make a decision. I saw no immediate danger and angled north onto I-65.

I peered anxiously ahead, fearing a sudden current of water that would slam me off the road, toss me into a guardrail, trap me under water. Traffic was steady, and I saw no police lights, no danger. Hunched over the wheel, peering into the night, I saw traffic bunch at Arthur Street; floodwater had covered the road. By then I easily accepted what normally seemed impossible. Nothing in this night, this storm, made any sense; why not water across I-65 at Arthur Street?

Traffic squeezed left into one lane. A huge tractor-trailer loomed to my left. The next driver let me cut left. I, in turn, let someone else cut left. Flood courtesy prevailed; we all escaped the deeper water.

Ahead was the Kennedy Bridge, Indiana, a telephone. I called my wife, who was still pushing water. I promised to be home in 20 minutes, but couldn't find a way through Jeffersonville; deep water blocked me at corners where rain had never gathered before.

"Honey," I told wife when I got back to a phone, "I may not get home."

There was nothing else for either of us to say. I took I-65 north to I-265 and then made my way east. I passed a string of fire trucks and police cars stopped to pull a water-filled car from a cornfield ditch. I skirted the floodwater and stalled cars, and pulled into my driveway 90 minutes after leaving Churchill Downs.

My wife was sitting at the kitchen table, exhausted. We held each other tightly for a few seconds, then went down to the basement to sweep water.

March 4, 1997

Forest visit triggered a range of emotions

This has been the most marvelous autumn I can remember; warm, sweet, evocative, almost caressable; a leaf show worthy of Zeus; a slow-motion lingering of time and season.

Yet, it was soon to be over; those lovely leaves stuffed into plastic bags or blown like confetti through 10,000 mulching mowers; the misty autumn mornings turned sodden in cold rain. I wanted a place to enjoy autumn's final moments. I chose the Clark State Forest near Henryville, a favorite retreat, though it's been several years since I had been there.

The forest entrance off U.S. 31 led past grassy fields. A father was throwing a football to his son, short-armed passes that wobbled like a bent wheel. A man and woman were casting fishing line into a small lake. Most of the main roads are now paved — a far cry from the more adventurous times of slippery gravel. The roads led up and over the forested knobs, stately oaks glowing white above a carpet of brown leaves.

My immediate goal was the fire tower, long a landmark in several incarnations; thousands of Hoosiers hold fond memories of climbing it, on the good days seeing downtown Louisville. Tourists are twice warned the climb can be hazardous to their health. The most noticeable words include: "must be 18," "use extreme caution," "falls" and "death." This was surgeon general stuff — read our lips: "If your heart doesn't get you, gravity will."

Still, who can resist climbing a fire tower, especially one perched on a hill that offers the finest view south of Brown County. The first few steps were coated with a relevant social message: "Becky Sanders LUVS Josh Levthart." It was dated 1-2-94, however, and both may have gone on to more sustaining relationships.

The steps beyond the first level — there are nine — carried a message with a more poignant tone: "For my Son, Christian. Love Always. Your Daddy."

The tower quivered a little on ascent, not dangerously so, but enough to add relevance to words like "falls" and "death." The railings were low, but thoughtfully covered with hog wire — a nice Hoosier touch. At the fifth level a comic named Alice Natkhsuka had written "High" by her name — a personal greeting mixed with an altitude notification. At the top — I counted 99 steps — was this message: "Hank Jr. Rules." You can run from the excesses of country music, but you can't hide.

The view from the top offered a 360-degree sweep of russet hills accented with dying flares of red and orange leaves, the clean smell of pine; the wind whooshing through conifer boughs. But I had a sense of urgency. I wanted to get to Bowen Lake, a placid, seven-acre jewel at the back of the forest. I like to sit on its bank and think Thoreau-like thoughts, primarily: Beware any enterprise that requires new clothes.

I knew something had changed when I saw a sign along the road: "Caution. Gun range below hill. Do not stand on embankment." I had heard muted booms from the top of the tower and thought them some kind of construction work. It soon became obvious the war zone noises were more sinister. My treasured spot was now next to a shooting range; the natural amphitheater formed by the lake echoed and re-echoed with the crackling boom of rifle fire.

I soon learned that the range has been there three years and is heavily used by grateful state police, hunters and recreational shooters. Forest manager Walt Zak has received one complaint about the noise; a schoolteacher. The range is closed Sundays to allow silence to return to the hills.

I could stay only a few minutes; the reverberating gunfire drove me away. I have nothing against hunting, legally done. I knew the target shooters had as much right to be there as I did; hunting is allowed; it's a state forest, not a state park.

But I felt a loss, a melancholy, the sharp disappointment of a child who had just learned the salient details of Santa Claus. I had set out to say goodbye to autumn and ended up losing a lot more — something almost impossible to articulate. The thought of it ran over and over through my mind like the sad ending to a good song.

Nov. 11, 1994

Hang tough!
Mother Nature will solve it

Help me out here. The plan was to hang a better purple-martin house in the back yard, lure in those family-oriented beauties from wherever they go during football season, then watch them eat 56 quadrillion mosquitoes a day.

It was a good plan, almost a romantic plan, with one flaw. Except for the man who sold me the three-story, 14-apartment, $120 birdhouse, I don't know a single person who's actually lured in purple martins.

Nor, in five years of trying, have I been able to regularly lure hummingbirds to their feeder, although I can package and sell all the ants you can handle. I'm so disgusted I didn't even take the bluebird house out of the garage.

The purple-martin concept had stirred my soul, that feel-good place where easy environmentalism meets $120 birdhouses; yuppie-like summer nights spent watching nuclear families turned into mosquito-eating machines.

Then a spring storm and shoddy pole construction — mine — conspired to push my three-story birdhouse about 42 degrees in a

north by northwest direction.

I lashed the pole to a garden shade house, applied for federal bird-house wind relief, notified my Allstate Insurance agent — ho, ho, ho — and sat back waiting for the money to pour in.

Meanwhile, a few sparrow-like birds poured in and began nesting. It was too late to change the birdhouse tilt; like it or not I was a landlord.

I didn't really mind the winged interlopers. From what little I know of ornithology, the purple-martin window of opportunity opens sometime in mid-March, slamming shut about two weeks later. After that it's either chase the other birds away with a 30-foot stick, or just accept whatever or whoever shows up.

I will draw the line at grackles, but I don't think it ever hurts to allow sparrows into $120 birdhouses. It gives them a chance to see how the other half flocks — think Republican — maybe even listen to Rush Limbaugh. That's what bird brains are for.

I've become accustomed to the tilt of our birdhouse, perhaps best viewed standing on one foot while falling over. I don't see the birds often, but I know they are in there, probably doing all sorts of stuff that would anger Jerry Falwell. Anything done in the warm darkness and privacy of their birdhouse is fine with me.

I did worry, however, about their children. I felt responsible that their first view of the outside world would be 42 degrees off-center. Or their nests would be level and their nursery ceilings would be 42 degrees off-center. Either way, the dysfunctional-child possibilities were endless.

I knew what the politicians would do about this. The Republicans would meet in Miami and call for a capital-gains tax cut for birdhouse builders, the Democrats would meet in Chicago, praise children and complain about the Republicans.

One option was to slowly ratchet the purple-martin pole into a more upright position, meanwhile offering vertical-support grief counseling to the youngsters. Another was to form a parents support group — Taking In Lost Toddlers (TILT) — raise money, petition Congress and don bird feathers. A third option was to open a pre-flight bird nursery school, preparing the little nestlings for the mixed-bag world that awaits them by reading to them of Audubon and the Sierra Club.

After some thought I've decided on a more radical course: Do nothing; good ol' tough love; let Mother Nature work it out.

It wasn't an easy decision; that is the future of the world out there in that 14-unit, $120 bird complex. But I've known kids tilted a lot more than 42 degrees who eventually learned to fly without smashing into the garage. I've got a strong feeling it's all going to work out.

May 22, 1993

Bay window opens up new vistas and gives one a fresh perspective on life

We recently had a bay window built into our kitchen wall, a three-sided wonder lovingly fitted into place by craftsmen who care. It has already made such a difference in our lives.

The bay window replaced a standard rectangular window — a flat, one-dimensional window that offered a flat, one-dimensional view of the world, a view gone stale with time.

We were ready for a change. It was time for new perspectives, to peek around new corners. Now I can look a little to the left and see the arching limbs of my weeping white pine, the gnarly silhouette of our Kentucky coffee tree, the pale green leaves of our tulip poplar.

Beyond them is our weeping Norway spruce, its deep-green older branches decorated with the bluish-green flares of new growth. I love that spruce; it was only 6 inches tall when planted and now its limbs curl and twist at eye level. It can measure me as I measure it.

I can better see my rock walls. They were built from stones my son and I hauled home in a pickup truck, fossil-coated rocks moved to a new place and butted up against the faded oak siding of our new-old barn, good relationships all around.

I had hoped the window would bring some changes, a new way of looking at things, but I was surprised at how big a difference it made. We do tend to stand in one spot too long. We fear change. We cling to the comfortable, the familiar, the easy. Most of us see only what we want to see from one narrow perspective.

I have two new treasures in my sideyard — a pair of budding Franklinia trees. They are American natives, fall-coloring trees with a funky history; not one has been found growing in the wild since 1790. It's always good to have a little history at work outside the kitchen window.

My new view is framed beneath the stout gray limbs of a sugar maple, a tree I'd liberated from a crowded patch of woods 15 years ago. The tree now repays me with dense summer shade on hot afternoons.

My lacy green arborvitae stand silently in formation, support troops for the feather reed grass, purple rhododendron, pink-flowering crabapples and white serviceberry.

I can better see my witch hazel, a risk taker all its own, a shrub that blooms in February and March when few others will dare. I planted a clematis at the feet of the witch hazel this spring. The two can prosper together, the clinging vine and the shrub, blooming at different times, one dependent on the other.

Sometimes even a subtle shift in attitude, in being willing to look at an old situation from a fresh perspective, can make a difference. I like the view past our barn down the gentle green sweep of the pasture, a view I've seen a thousand times.

One day, when some friends were over, we climbed to the loft of the barn and viewed the pasture from there, a higher and better place. The angles were all different, the flow of the land altered; another kind of beauty that had been there all along had I bothered to climb the ladder.

I accumulate shrubs, ornamental grasses and trees the way street people collect aluminum cans, peering into odd places, taking almost everything that comes without enough thought or planning, half-way convinced that someday they'll stop making aluminum cans.

I can see from my bay window it may be time to slow down a little, try to figure out what's most important, then proceed from there.

Easier seen than done.

There's a winter king hawthorne straight out from the bay window, the crown piece of a setting that includes a pink-flowering almond, a red-berried deciduous holly, an explosion of yellow day lilies, a cascading red rose and another stone wall. That's the view that's always been there. I take comfort in that too. People who are always seeking new perspectives can be as lost as those who never look for any.

My view to the right — a direction rarely traveled — has also been broadened. Our yellowwood tree seems ready to make a move; with some luck I'll see its lily-white, wisteria-like blooms. We've also added a new perennial garden, trying to scale it to our natural landscape and away from the self-serving interests of the maple-tree roots.

My only disappointment with our bay window is that I didn't make it wider. Another foot or two and I could have seen that much more, an even broader picture of life and limb, more vistas to peruse and ponder.

Or maybe I would have just fallen out the window.

May 15, 1993

From my father's chair, a glimpse of genes and generations

I am sitting in my father's chair in my parents' home. The chair is at a corner of the room near the kitchen alcove, a bookcase on its right, a floor lamp by its side. The chair is stiffly upright, more comfortable than it looks, brown in color, with flecks of white.

My father is in the hospital recovering from a heart attack; the prognosis is good, but he is 75 years old. Most of the family has gathered to be with my mother, to visit my father, to wrap our arms around this moment and make it go away.

I've become so accustomed to seeing my father in his chair that
I can see his image there even when the chair is empty. He sits in a
certain way, his fingers folded prayer-like against the front of his
nose, or with his arms at his side, unconsciously rubbing his
thumbs against his forefingers, lost in thought.

He will leap into the conversation for a time, then sit back,
watch from a distance.

What's odd is that I now find myself doing the same things.
Often when I write, pausing between thoughts, I find my fingers
rubbing against my face, or folded on top of each other. Often
when I am watching television or lost in thought, I will find
myself unconsciously rubbing my thumbs against my forefingers.
I will argue for a time — our family gatherings are often closer to
group encounter sessions than anything you might see on "The
Partridge Family" — then sit back and listen.

These are obviously hereditary echoes, pulses of my father
passed on to me, which I may have passed on to my son or daughter.

They are as easily identifiable as our other similar traits: personality, creativity, work ethic, sense of humor.

It is interesting to think about how far back some of these characteristics might go. Did our great-great-great-grandfather sit
around on a bushel of potatoes in Ireland unconsciously rubbing
his thumbs against his forefingers?

Did a great-great-great-grandmother in France press her fingers
against her face while staring off in thought?

Are men more likely to inherit the unconscious traits and habits
of their fathers, daughters the mannerisms of their mothers? It
seems to me my wife has more of the gestures, mannerisms and
expressions of her mother than her father. Or perhaps I am just
more conscious of how I imitate my father's acts, especially now.

Nor do many of these mannerisms seem especially unique to
our family. What is it in the human genes that makes us press our
fingers against our lips when in thought, or unconsciously rub fingers together?

What is it about humans that collectively make us throw our
arms up in disgust, shake our fists in anger, cover our faces in
shame? Why do we purse our lips in thought, scratch our heads
when lost for an answer, shrug our shoulders in dismay?

Did we learn those things watching others, or did cave men and
women first shake their fists at the inconsiderate heavens and the

futile gesture has been passed down to us ever since? Where do the new mannerisms jump on, the old jump off? Maybe there is a common genetic pool only 10 characteristics deep, and all of us are swimming around in it.

What's odd is that I find myself imitating my father's mannerisms more and more as I get older. Or perhaps I am just more conscious of them. One of my favorite essays — it was written by E. B. White — described a father and son walking together, and for just a moment the father could not remember if he were the boy, or the man. He remembered taking walks with his father in the same fashion, and time and genes had begun playing tricks on him. It all seemed so familiar that the generations didn't seem to matter.

I find comfort in this genetic mirroring, the generations forming a tunnel of imagery that reflect forward through time. That feeling is surely heightened because I am sitting in my father's chair and he is in a hospital bed, thoroughly irritated at being there, curious to know the full details of the medical technique aimed at making him well, uncomfortable with his thoughts of mortality.

I like to sit in his chair, although I would prefer that he were in it. It's a good chair from which to think, argue, rub my fingers against my face, rub my thumbs against my forefingers and think about time, family and life.

March 12, 1994

The sounds of silence remind one we all like to share things with others

I've been home alone all week while my wife has been visiting friends. It sure has been another of life's learning experiences. Normally the situation is reversed. Normally I am the one getting on an airplane, my wife is left standing at the airport and I soon become too engrossed in my work to think about the sounds of the almost empty house I've left behind.

This time I was left standing at the airport. This time I had to walk through the front door alone. This time my house greeted me as more of a stranger, half of a whole, a life out of sync.

I felt as if I was inside a drum, every sound magnified, every thought reverberating against itself. I felt hollow and empty, a visitor in an art gallery of everything we had collected over the years: furniture and dishes, family photographs and bath towels. All of it looked familiar, but I kept asking myself: Why isn't someone else here?

Many years ago a woman asked me to write something about what it was like to be left a widow, to abruptly lose a partner after 40 or 50 years of marriage, to know that the loss was irreplaceable, irrevocable, forever.

I couldn't do it then and I don't want to do it now. I can't presume to know that depth of pain. But I got a glimpse of it this week. Our house wasn't the same place. It wasn't a home.

I've always thought "home" to be the most powerful word in our language. It's so evocative, so emotionally loaded. "I'll be *home* for Christmas"; "It's so good to be *home* again"; "Hi son. We love you. When are you coming *home*?"

I sat around the house at night very conscious of the fact I was alone. I would watch the World Series, my eyes on the television, my other senses aware of a larger picture. I could see a man seated on a couch watching baseball, feeling dwarfed by his surroundings, slopping popcorn all over the fabric. Part of me was watching the game; part of me was watching me watch the game.

All of me had to pick up the popcorn — another change in my lifestyle.

My inner thoughts seemed somehow louder, more like public address announcements from the cerebral cortex, muffled messages from the mind:

"Yer attention ... Yer attention, pleeease ... Bob Hill's next thought now arriving on track 11. It's not much of a thought, but he's been very distracted lately and it's the best he can do at this time. We apologize for any inconvenience or delays ...."

None of this approached personal depression. It was, after all, only a week. There are couples who are separated much longer on a regular basis; some even come to enjoy their time apart. Often it serves to heighten the pleasure of time spent together. There are people who like being alone, or at least learn to deal with it, make the best of it. There are people who find being alone to be the worst thing that could ever happen.

Our house, built about 130 years ago, gives off a loud "creeech" from time to time as timbers shift in the roof. A few years ago we added a floor-to-ceiling bookshelf in the front hall, making room for several tons of volumes, always an impressive sight even if most haven't been opened since the Carter administration.

I worry a little about that bookshelf because the added weight seems to have increased the frequency and loudness of our "creeech." Or maybe it was just being alone that made it sound more ominous. It would be a little awkward to welcome back my wife to a house broken in half like a saltine cracker, hundreds of unread books spilling into the fault.

What bothers me most about being alone is total silence. It's welcome at first, a peaceful emptiness that requires no work; no sounds to decipher. But soon there are sounds and sensations I need — the murmur of someone breathing beside me, a stirring in the bed, a rustle of sheets, being able to reach over and touch somebody you love.

I like the morning sounds of people, footsteps along the hallway floor, the gurgle of the coffee maker, even the liquid rumble of our computerized furnace as it goes about its programmed chores.

I like the feel of heat filling our house, pleasant to touch and smell, and a little mystical, too; the stuff just oozes into our lives when we most need it.

I like the cheerful frenzy of the mockingbird outside our window, the mournful bellow of a towboat down on the Ohio River, the sight of the ruby-tipped dogwoods outside our bedroom window.

But mostly I like having someone to share it with.

Oct. 23, 1993

Author/columnist revisits Ignatow case on 'Geraldo'

The cabdriver's name — apparently shortened by several vowels for economy of presentation — read GRGO JUKIC. He was piloting his Yellow Cab through New York City traffic, making a broken-field run from LaGuardia Airport to the William Morrow Publishing Co. in midtown Manhattan.

Morrow had published my book, "Double Jeopardy," the story of how Mel Ignatow, a Louisville salesman, murdered his girlfriend, Brenda Schaefer, and was acquitted of the crime.

I was going to Morrow to meet with two publicists who would

escort me to West 57th Street to make a TV appearance on
"Geraldo." Mike and Tom Schaefer, Brenda's brothers, also were to
appear on the TV show, as was Brenda's sister, Carolyn Coop.

I had mixed feelings about the trip. I had worked very hard on
"Double Jeopardy" and was proud of it. It had been a best seller in
Louisville all summer.

Morrow had first thought it only a local interest book, but as
sales expanded into the Midwest, the book went into three more
printings. "Geraldo" is syndicated across the United States,
Canada and Europe. "Geraldo" provided a chance to push the
sales envelope a little farther. "Geraldo" also was . . . well . . .
Geraldo.

As we wormed our way through Manhattan traffic, I could see
the cabdriver's face in the rear-view mirror; broad, furrowed, ani-
mated.

"Geraldo," he said as we discussed my eventual destination.
"Maybe he's good, maybe bad. Who knows?"

Exactly.

The taping of the show was to begin at 1 p.m. We arrived at the
CBS studio about noon, were escorted past audience members
lined up on the sidewalk into the "green room." Here was a surprise: The room was packed; obviously there were more people
going on this show than we had been led to believe.

The Schaefers were there, also a little nervous and uncertain.

Ten months after Ignatow was acquitted on charges of murder

ing their sister, photographs taken by Ignatow's female accomplice as he brutalized and tortured Schaefer before killing her were found in his home.

Even with those photographs, Ignatow could not be retried for the murder. The Fifth Amendment provision on "double jeopardy" guarantees that no one can be prosecuted twice for the same crime. Ignatow eventually was sentenced to jail on perjury charges for lying to a federal grand jury. He could be released in November 1997 after serving only five years.

Also backstage at "Geraldo" was a man named Jack Levin, a college professor who has become Geraldo's hired gun, his "go-to guy" on all manner of crime. Levin was an amiable man with a doctorate in sociology and a slight resignation to his fate.

"I've been on 'Geraldo' about 25 times," he said. "I've written books on all sorts of things, but nobody cares.... Everybody wants to talk about crime."

Other panelists waiting in the room included experts and authors involved in Canada's infamous "Ken and Barbie" murders, crimes similar to those in the Schaefer case in which an accountant and his wife videotaped the sexual assault on two teen-age girls before killing them. Unexpectedly, a late entry was added to the "Geraldo" milieu: seven relatives or friends of a family of five blown up in a car in a horrible multiple-murder-suicide in Maryland. There would be 20 people on the show.

What was it that cabdriver had said?

Following an energized pep talk to "be spontaneous" by a show producer who said he hadn't slept in three nights, we were led into the studio. The room was cool, almost chilly, the tightly packed audience in place. There were so many participants on the show that the five authors/experts on the various crimes had to sit in chairs in front of the audience. Like nervous debaters — so little time, so much to say — we all shook hands, wished each other good luck.

Geraldo Rivera appeared stage left to rising, well-coached applause. He was a smaller man than I expected, crisply dressed in gray and black, his lips tightly pursed, his body stiff, erect. The sign to his left announced the theme of this show: "Murder Most Foul."

Outside of a handshake, there was no personal contact with him at all.

"Why is it," Geraldo asked dramatically, "that a man would kill himself, his wife and three children?"

We were off.

Remarkably unself-conscious — we are a TV nation — the seven relatives and friends of the five dead people told a horrible tale of jealousy, rage and madness. Apparently the bomber had given hints he might blow up the family; Geraldo zeroed in on lingering feelings of guilt. Two of the crime experts seated next to me quickly jumped in, saying that the survivors should not feel guilt, that the bombing was not their fault.

None of this seemed quite real, but there was some visceral appeal to it, a terrible fascination with the tragedy of others. The audience was transfixed, pulled into the emotions — if not soap opera — of the moment. Geraldo would linger when necessary, then suddenly move on when the pace slowed. The Maryland segment took up the first half-hour of the hourlong show. I was not feeling good about the next half-hour.

Tom and Mike Schaefer took their places onstage. Carolyn Coop sat in the front row of the audience. The Schaefer family is good, strong and stoic. It has had a lot of practice being stoic; not only was Brenda murdered, but another sibling — Louisville police Officer Jack Schaefer — was murdered in the line of duty in 1971.

I was worried about the Schaefers; I did not want them embarrassed for the sake of the book. My fears were misplaced. They helped turn the focus of the show. They talked of healing, of the need to allow others to help; the dead are gone, the criminals often in jail; it's the families that live with the pain.

My task was to very briefly outline the book — the proverbial TV soundbite. I wasn't on the air three minutes, even that could end up on the cutting-room floor. The Schaefers handled the bigger picture.

"I thought I was strong enough to get through this alone," said Tom Schaefer, looking directly at the Maryland family, "but I was wrong. You have to get help."

The Schaefers talked about a support group to which they belong — Kentuckians' Voice for Crime Victims.

The group's members are the real experts on crime, tragedy and the best ways to seek healing. The rest of us just write books about it.

Oct. 9, 1995

Nature's fragility and tenacity lure us to webs of intrigue

I vaguely remember reading a story out of Boston a few years ago about some bird — perhaps a rare hawk — that had set up housekeeping on a ledge of some tall, downtown building.

Whatever the bird, its perch didn't qualify as your normal avian maternity ward — at least not the antiseptic, big-limbed berth we humans expect. Somehow — hey, if I got all excited about details I would have become an accountant — this bird nest ended up being the constant focus of a nearby television camera. Much of Boston got caught up in watching a family take flight. It was sort of like watching "The Brady Bunch" on aviation fuel.

Eavesdropping on nature without leaving the sofa has its advantages. You can pay your respects without paying any price; you can feel warm and fuzzy inside no matter the temperature outside; you can turn it off, make it go away.

There's something deeply appealing about adaptability — and sheer stubbornness — in nature. The bad side is that we humans force the changes, rip and ruin the native habitats, then cozy up to the television to marvel at nature's damage control.

Thus the appealing story this week of the seven peregrine falcons that have set up house near Kentucky Utilities' E. W. Brown power plant in Mercer County. The seven are the known survivors of the 13 birds released this summer by state biologists in an attempt to revive a species nearly wiped out by pesticides and loss of natural habitat.

The birds have adapted to their new home because power plants and skyscrapers resemble high cliffs, their natural habitat. To me, this would be like asking a bear to hibernate in the basement of the Humana Building because it's cool and dark down there, but I've never been pushed from my natural home.

Any parent who has happily sent a child off to college or a new job only to see said child return home for additional nurturing can relate to this: All seven power-plant falcons are relying on hand-outs from the biologists; their hunter-gatherer skills need some fine-tuning.

The nurturers are more than willing. Scores of Kentucky Utilities employees stick around after work to help locate falcons.

Our external packaging — feathers or not — might differ, but internal nursing instincts are a constant.

One of the falcons, Wild One, has a strong Louisville connection: She might be the daughter of a pair of peregrine falcons that have made Kentuckiana home. Wild One was found last month wandering around near the Kennedy Bridge — haven't we all? — and was later released near the power plant. If that's all it takes to get an all-expenses-paid home in Mercer County, then let's all meet near the Kennedy about 9 a.m. some Saturday.

Closer to home, I've been dealing with the stubbornness of nature in another form: spiders. I like to come to work before sunrise, when neither people nor peregrines are wandering the bridge and the phone is not ringing. I like stepping out my door in the morning when my yard is crisscrossed in soft shadows made mysterious by deep pockets of darkness and while the morning air is still as church.

I walk along the edge of the house, pass beneath a small, columned entranceway, brush against a gangly rhododendron, step out onto dew-soaked grass. But about a week ago — just as I passed beneath the dark entranceway where almost nothing can be seen — I felt a spider's web against my face.

It was an unpleasant feeling, sticky and intrusive. Fearing its creator might be lurking, I quickly slapped at it, tearing it to shreds, brushing its silky presence from my hair and face. "Stupid spider," I thought. "What a dumb place to build a web."

The spider obviously thought otherwise. The war of wills was on: my daily routine vs. the spider's web.

On Day Two I remembered where the web had been, held one arm up in front of me in the classic tomahawk-chop position. I felt the web — faintly — and pushed through. Day Three was the same. As were Day Four and Day Five. On Day Six, a Saturday, I rested.

The spider, ever ambitious, did not, would not.

In all of that time I never saw it, nor did I ever have the sense that the spider had anything personal against me. It just was declaring some sort of territorial imperative, some right or need to my well-mortgaged space.

Thursday morning the web wasn't there. I can't say I missed it, but I did feel a faint sense of regret. Where had it gone? Then early yesterday morning as I brushed past the rhododendron, I thought I felt the web.   *Aug. 12, 1995*

Thinking big cuts news down to size

Being an early riser, I usually walk down our long, long drive-way in the dark to get the morning paper. We have always been blessed with good paper-delivery people, so the journey almost always reaches a successful conclusion; The Courier-Journal waits, curled like a sleeping cat, in our white, plastic paper box.

The very few times in the past 20 years it hasn't been there, I've reacted with an anger far disproportionate to the crime. The sad lot of the diligent paper-delivery person is that you can do some-thing exactly right in all sorts of weather 99 times out of 100, and the one discrepancy looms all the larger by comparison. Life, as John F. Kennedy told us, is not fair.

Call me boring, but I like the bringing-in-of-the-morning-paper thing. I'm a newspaper junkie. I look forward to reading it, antici-pate its musings, always wonder what fate befell us while sleep-ing. Bringing in the paper is often the closest modern man can get to his hunter-gatherer mode — with coffee. I feel pity for the poor city folk who merely have to peek out the front door in their bathrobes, finding the day's news only a few feet away.

The big sissies.

Unless a blizzard is roaring in, I most enjoy bringing in the paper in the winter. The air is still, brittle and clean, the gravel crunchy, the dogwoods bare silhouettes, the Big Dipper bullet holes in black velvet.

One of the few things I've remembered about astronomy is that two of the stars composing the Big Dipper point directly to the North Star. I can vouch for that. I've never failed to return safely to my north-south driveway. I've gotten the newspaper all the way home every time. It is in those moments that my sense of kinship with the ancient mariners, biblical sheepherders and Odysseus is almost palpable.

Actually, the Big Dipper hangs directly over my neighbor Curtis Hooper's house all winter — about 70 degrees up and many light-years away. It's not there in the humid summers, but then neither is any sense of sky. The Big Dipper probably summers in Minnesota.

Astronomy has been much with us lately, what with the apparent discovery of ancient, teeny-tiny life on Mars and the delayed successes of the Hubble telescope. Humility is running rampant in the whole astronomy business as new information makes it evident that Galileo may have been as close to the truth as some of his modern brethren.

The statistics are numbing. The Milky Way — of which Earth is a dues-paying member — is a spiral galaxy of about 100 billion stars. There are billions of galaxies in the universe, all formed billions of years ago. Multiply it out: Billions times billions times billions. Go buy a lottery ticket.

I get to thinking about that stuff, and I don't know how astronomers can get out of bed in the morning. Where to begin? How many galaxies to count today? Where else to find life? What else is the Hubble going to tell us to wipe out 50 years of research and theory?

Perhaps I'm being a little too dramatic, if not hysterical. As I read it, astronomers know practically all they need to know about galaxies except for two things: How did they form and how did they get the way they are today?

The main theories on those questions are that the galaxies occurred either top-down, bottom-up or both; i.e., the subgalactic clumps could have been created by top-down condensation and then assembled through bottom-up mergers.

Maybe you already knew that, but it's the kind of stuff I like to think about while walking down my driveway in the mornings. It pretty much whittles down to size anything the newspaper has to offer.

Nov. 12, 1996

Karla can't take this no more! News people should do more than ask why

Memo to all area high school journalism teachers and advisers, journalism professors at the University of Louisville, University of Kentucky, Western Kentucky University, Indiana University, et al.

Assignment: Please lead your classes in serious, thoughtful,

wide-ranging discussions of the radio, TV and newspaper coverage of the 13-year-old girl from Eastern Kentucky who wore black
lipstick to school.

Don't spend too much time on the who, what, when and where.
Please concentrate on the why. I hold little hope for success, but
maybe with some thoughtful discussion the next generation of editors and reporters will be able to distinguish cheap, shallow, inva-
sive, knee-jerk sensationalism from legitimate news.

I'll begin the discussion with the obvious: Karla Chapman —
who's been all but buried alive in media coverage after being suspended from school for wearing black lipstick — is a very trou-
bled 13-year-old. She doesn't need TV stations and news services
sending reporters and photographers hundreds of miles to watch
her apply black lipstick before her bedroom mirror. She may be
crying for attention, but what she really needs is help. She needs
counseling. She needs a friend, someone to talk to, someone who
understands being 13.

I watched the TV coverage of the kid being hounded all the way
into her *elementary* school by a pack of rabid newshounds, and I
wanted to throw a brick through my TV set.

Doesn't any assignment editor out there have a 13-year-old
daughter? Don't they remember what an awful, confused, terrible
time that was for all of us? Can't they see Karla has been out of
school for weeks because her parents have used her to fight a
pitched battle over a doubtful cause?

How can you watch that kind of coverage, read all the stories,
and not have sympathy for the girl for what's she's been through?
She's so young, so vulnerable, so incapable of understanding all
this. What did you understand — what could you process — at
her age?

Karla Chapman has had center media stage for weeks, but what
do we really know about her except her choice of lipstick? Where
are the things we need to know to give meaning and reason to this
story? Do we know her hobbies, her friends, her likes and dislikes?
Do we know her grade-point average? Do we know if she's had
problems in school before?

Shouldn't we see her for what she is — a confused teen-ager —
or must we shape her to fit our narrow needs, make her a desig-
nated media symbol of all that's wrong with our schools, ourselves, our society?

Do we know anything about her parents or her stepmother's

educational background, or must we settle for knowing only she's being charged with harassment over the incident?

Do we know anything about her father except he's been charged with terroristic threatening and abuse of a teacher resulting from a confrontation at his daughter's elementary school? What type of education did he have? What's he done with his life? Is this issue about his daughter, or is it about him?

If the Pike County case is supposed to be a newsworthy challenge to blind school authority — to some hard-line school administrator drawing a line in lipstick at her school door — then Karla's parents seem poorly equipped to carry the banner. They haven't made their case to me; could they state it any differently for Montel Williams?

School discipline is a valid issue, but this story — as presented — wasn't up to the task. It needed context. That's the major discussion point: Do we think enough about this? Have time, space and bottom-line constraints become a rationale for shoddy journalism? Do media indulge — as the public complains — in too much blood-lust, copycat journalism: We have to do it because other newspeople are doing it? Aren't we getting worse?

Yesterday's media onslaught provided an even more tragic story line. Karla's mother said Karla locked herself in her bathroom and threatened to slash her wrists. The parents said they had to break down the bathroom door to stop her.

Television obligingly showed Karla being led away to a mental-health center. She'd told her stepmother — in adolescent tears — "I can't take this no more. I can't take this no more."

Who could? Why should she have to? Let's get Karla some help, then please, please, leave her alone.

Dec. 7, 1996

Pardon our French,
but the kid was *trés* perfect too

Uncertain of the best approach, I carried a hand-lettered sign to Standiford Field that said *bonjour*. Our guest, Severin Sejournet, was a 16-year-old relative from France. His English was weak; my French, comatose. Severin's mother had sent a small photograph, so we knew whom to look for. I was hoping *bonjour* would do the same for him. It did.

Many years ago my parents had been guests of Severin's grand-parents in France. More recently Severin's sister had stayed at my parents' house. This was my first opportunity to meet my interna-tional family. We all wanted to keep the fragile relationship alive.

Until Severin arrived I'd given very little thought to our French family, the descendants of two brothers of my great-grandfather who stayed in Europe while he emigrated to America. They were so distant, both in miles and genealogy, that I felt none of the nor-mal bonds of flesh and blood. I discussed them in the abstract, if at all. Severin was to be with us for almost a month. His mother had said he was very quiet and shy. With our children in college, and no one in our neighborhood Severin's age, we worried about keep-ing him entertained; we wanted him to be comfortable; we wanted him to feel at home. So I took him to River Falls Mall, a place were teen-agers cluster like pea gravel. I thought he might be interested in the electronic games, the arcade toys. Twenty-four hours in the country and he headed directly for a New York Yankees baseball cap, "Chucks" basketball shoes and Levis.

Severin took an instant liking to baseball. He already was a big sports fan; tennis, golf and soccer, and the World Cup kept him entertained some of the time. But often when I'd peek in to see how he was doing he'd have a baseball game on television, a sport he rarely saw in France. That intrigued me, pleased me; my young French cousin was so interested in my favorite American game. Some friends of ours took him to one Louisville Redbirds game; I took him to another; he collected a free baseball cap, ate Cracker Jack, rooted for the home team.

On another night I had a softball game. It was a league for men on the far side of 50, an amiable collection of old jocks and walk-ing wounded. Severin sat alone in the dim bleachers, chin resting on palms, enduring it all.

"Your game was lovely," he said when it ended, further proof his English was in need of fine tuning.

Our son took him to Chicago for a few days; Sears Tower, Navy Pier, the movie "Forrest Gump." When we left on our two-week vacation we stayed with friends outside Chicago — who wanted to see "Forrest Gump."

"That's what we do in America," I explained to Severin as we headed into the theater. "We drive from town to town and watch 'Forrest Gump.'"

Our journey led through Minneapolis, home of Mall of America, a retail monster so ravenous it has an amusement park in its belly. Severin had his first roller-coaster ride, indoors; his grin was much more eloquent than his English. In Upper Michigan he stayed in a cabin on a lake with his American family, a group thoroughly representative of this country: loud, loving, opinionated, gregarious, generous, close-minded, cranky and buoyant. During the day Severin learned to shoot pool; he could explain that one to his mother. At night we played Crazy-Eights — 10 players, two decks of cards. Severin won two of them. He was beginning to fit right in.

This was fun, an awakening. Severin was always polite, on time, picked up his clothes and did his own dishes. My wife began negotiating a trade.

Disaster almost hit on the way home. Severin left his passport and airline tickets in Illinois. After two hours of phone calls, our friends tracked us down to a family reunion near Indianapolis, 250 miles away. Severin was to leave the next day. We backtracked, met in the middle, solved the crisis.

We said a temporary goodbye at the same airport gate where we met. Severin was going home with a dozen gift T-shirts, baseball caps, pennants, basketball shoes and Levis. We were going home as part of a larger family. "This was very perfect," Severin said.

Close enough.

Aug. 8, 1994

Primal feelings flow from glaciers

One of my firm rules about the first day back from vacation says I get to inflict a glacier story on people. That's especially important because glaciers from 500 to 2,000 feet thick were within 60 miles of Louisville only 10,000 to 12,000 years ago, a mere flick of ink in geological history.

The glaciers did hang around long enough to help create the Ohio River Valley, then obligingly filled it with meltwater on the way out of town, headed north toward Alaska. If only Louisville's waterfront development — even a bridge or two — could be completed in the same time frame.

I've always enjoyed thinking about glacier stuff, the ebb and flow of the various ice ages over millions of years. Speed was never the glacier's forte — most cranked along at about one foot a day, coming or going. They clung to much of North America like frozen cake icing, stretching in huge, frosty sheets from what is now Washington state to Nova Scotia, dipping down into Illinois and Southern Indiana. Glaciers were the big erasers that wiped the earth clean, rearranged the furniture, allowed other forms of life to live there, to try something new and exciting.

Speaking of which, our vacation was spent in Alaska, in a rented van, rolling past some of the finest scenery on God's glaciated earth. The problem was I kept thinking I was in a man-made theme park. I couldn't shake the feeling our tour would be over in a few hours, that our car was outside in the parking lot, that I was within one souvenir T-shirt of heading home. I was looking at reality, feeling virtual reality and thinking Six Flags Over Fairbanks. The wild caribou, bear and mountain sheep were just outside the window, but I just couldn't get fully with the program.

That worried me. I've not spent that much time in theme parks; we may be the only family in the United States that's never visited Disney World, Disneyland and/or Dollywood. I do spend some time watching the Discovery Channel and have always been a little partial to travelogues, but not to the point — I thought — where they have co-opted my thought process.

Am I alone on this? Do you now drive across Montana, visit Yellowstone, do Yosemite and have trouble believing it's real? Are the wild animals too domesticated, turned into pitiful beggars by obliging tourists? Have we spent so much time in front of the television, watching movies or looking at life from behind clean windows that the senses are baffled by the real thing?

We're seeing the country, but we're not touching it. We're out there, but living in air-conditioned comfort, parking side-by-side in Winnebagos, moving on luxury liners, tour boats and domed rail cars, sleeping in pricey lodges, lining up on cue for meals, wheels and seals. We see what we're expected to see, what we're *supposed* to see, but is that the real deal?

Well listen, sport, I can hear you saying, just remove your posterior from the van, find a backpack, head at right angles from the paved road onto the road less traveled by. That could make all the difference.

Not that easy to do, at least not the first time in a new land when you're trying to get the lay of the place, where paved roads are best for rented vans and the bears have occasionally taken to gnawing the feet of tourists. But certainly the thing to do the next time in Seward, Homer, Denali National Park and Preserve and, perhaps, Nome.

But on the last day in Alaska — the last *afternoon* in Alaska — we did drive down a road less traveled by and it did make a difference. We saw a huge glacier reaching out like a frosted lion's paw from the base of a gray mountain. The road — and $6.50 fee — took us to the glacier's edge.

We walked a quarter-mile around a moonscape of black rocks, some polished, some buried in ice in a million shards. We walked out onto blue-white ice, felt the glacier's icy breath, watched meltwater plunge into deep crevices.

The feeling was raw and primal; a distant kinship with ice ages past; a valley filled with meltwater 12,000 years ago. I raised both my arms over my head, shook my fists and looked up at the gray mountain from which ice flowed like a river.

July 22, 1997

Chapter Two

OUT THERE

While sifting through more than 20
years of columns for this book the
largest stack quickly became the one
labeled "Out There." It was my
catchall place for everything wacky,
funny, bizarre, quixotic, interesting,
sad, poignant or terrifyingly human
that didn't quite fit anywhere else.
But the more I thought about it the
more I realized we all live Out There.
We sit inside and look out on occasion,
but most of the time we're right
Out There too. Good thing.

The Beverly Hillbillies — what's next?

The truth be known, I always liked "The Beverly Hillbillies" TV show. Perhaps it was because of the show's opening song, redolent with mountain imagery, savage wit and Freudian suggestion.

"Come and listen to my story 'bout ..." Gather any 40- to 50-something group over a bucket of cheap white wine and it can sing every hillbilly word, along with "The Ballad of Davy Crockett," the classy opening to "Gilligan's Island" and, of course, ... "M-I-C-K-E-Y... M-O-U-S-E...."

And our present "X Generation" believes it's lost.

Maybe my interest in the Beverly Hillbillies was spurred by Elly May, the guileless maiden who always seemed to be wearing a younger cousin's blouse. Maybe it was Granny, the matriarchal moonshiner, or Jed, the gun-totin' philosopher.

Who could forget cousin Jethro Bodine's sensitive portrayal of mesomorphic man; Miss Hathaway's goony, from-the-heart efficiency; or Mr. Drysdale's bubbling, hand-wringing greed?

Whatever the case, "The Beverly Hillbillies" is back as a movie, drawing generally good marks from reviewers placed in the awkward position of having a high time with low-brow humor — the curse of the politically correct '90s.

The movie does have a strong cast, including Lily Tomlin, Cloris Leachman and Dabney Coleman, the latter a much underappreciated man. I've not seen the movie, but I bet the good people win, another triumph for simple country folk over sinister city evil and bad-news bankers.

I'm all for that, even if it only happens in the movies. What's most interesting is that the movie once again pegs hillbillies as the last minority that can be fired at without some organized form of protest. How far do you think a remake of "Amos 'n' Andy" would get? Would "Charlie Chan" fly in 1993, even though he was always successful? In an era when athletic teams named the Indians, Rebels, Braves and Chiefs are drawing flack, the hillbilly icon remains a very marketable commodity.

Kentucky — to its eternal credit — does very little selling of its mountain soul. Travel into the Missouri Ozarks and you'll find people who glory in Hillbillydom, selling their heritage at every

opportunity. You'll find much of the same thing in Eastern
Tennessee, the incredible schlock of Pigeon Forge and Gatlinburg,
at least until you're safe, mercifully safe, in the Great Smoky
Mountains National Park. Cherokee, N.C., is so tourist-ugly it
should be leveled and begun again from scratch.

Perhaps it was only the lack of access roads that spared the
Kentucky mountains the teeming mobs of tourists lining up for
corncob pipes and balsa-wood outhouses. I've spent many happy
days wandering around out there without even finding an antique
shop. People either wore out Aunt Jane's rocker or kept it in the
family where it belongs. Hang tough, Kentucky; once you begin
selling your soul it becomes harder to defend, impossible to get
back.

Loyal Jones, retired director of Berea College's Appalachian
Center, pointed out in a Courier-Journal story earlier this week
that people who live in Appalachia have something that most
other people lack: a strong sense of place, a feeling of belonging.

"I believe everybody in America has a yearning for that," he
said.

He said Appalachia should be judged by its own values — family, land, traditionalism — rather than by the mainstream values of
accumulation, wealth and power. When you dip into the American
mainstream and see its preponderance of glitz, glitter and greed,
the sudden ascendancy of Beavis and Butt-head, it's impossible to
argue with that.

The larger question then becomes: So why did the Beverly
Hillbillies move to California? Weren't family, land and traditional
values enough? Did they have to taste life in the fast lane? Did
Elly May yearn for her own blouses from Rodeo Drive?

Apparently so. All that oil money had to be spent. How many
rocking chairs can your average mountaineer string across a rickety front porch and still leave room for the washing machine?

So stay tuned for the sequel: "The Beverly Hillbillies Go Home."
Miss Hathaway marries Jethro, their twin sons go wacko on drugs
and sleazy sex, they all yearn for a simpler place, the Ozarks is it.

The family returns home, puts its half-dozen BMWs up on cin-
der blocks, puts the microwave on the front porch, tosses radicchio
to the hogs and opens a Betty Ford Clinic for the moonshine-
enhanced.

Coming soon to a cable channel near you.

Oct. 16, 1993

Why is it women can play *and* study?

A few years ago I was at a luncheon given for elongated high school hotshots before the Kentucky Derby Festival Classic basketball game and became a little irritated at the attitude a few brought with them.

The attitude was the practiced insouciance of very talented young men who had been stroked, revered and recruited their whole lives. They expected nothing else. Few seemed to realize that reality was one knee injury away. How could they?

That attitude is often reflected in the grades of these anointed few. There's nothing that says athletes must be poor students; band and drama can take as much time as basketball. Yet it always comes as a pleasant surprise when athletes qualify academically as freshmen. Grade-point averages have become an automatic part of every recruiting story.

Unless the recruit is female.

I first became aware of that while watching my daughter's high school team. It included two valedictorians and a salutatorian; almost all players were on the honor roll. I doubt if a single boys' high school team in Kentucky or Indiana can match that. In my daughter's case, the girls did it while suffering the indignities of second-class basketball citizenship: long trips to games the night before final exams.

My daughter's team was not unique. Of the five new recruits signed by University of Louisville women's basketball coach Bud Childers, two were valedictorians with a perfect 4.0 average; the others were very good students. Of the 32 women players Childers has signed in seven years, 30 qualified right away. The other two were Proposition 48 students who had to sit out a year but did qualify academically the next year.

Childers attributes that, in part, to the fact that men often cling to their dreams of making a living as professional basketball players and don't care enough about grades and careers besides basketball.

"Women in general," he said, "have the feeling that once basketball ends, their educations will kick in.... There's no NBA waiting for them."

Of the four recruits signed by Bellarmine women's basketball coach Charlie Just, three were in the top quarter of their class, the fourth in the top half. Just has seen 100 percent of his women players graduate, but at Bellarmine about 98 percent of the men have graduated too.

Marilyn Staples, Bellarmine's NCAA compliance coordinator, said the female athletes come to school better prepared to deal with academics. "They all know they have to pursue a career when they get out," she said.

Bellarmine Athletic Director Jay Gardiner had a theory that took women's academic success one rung further: The women involved in sports are very disciplined people, better able to focus on all phases of life; athletics is only one part. Male athletes tend to place sports above all else, mostly because our culture does. The bad news: Females' emphasis — and GPA — could change with the tremendous growth in women's sports.

"In five to 10 years we could see the same problems in women's athletics," he said.

That is not yet reflected in the National Collegiate Athletic Association's statistics, which show a declining rate of female athletes being classified as Proposition 48 students — from 27.4 percent of all Division I athletes in 1987 to 19.5 percent in 1994.

Translation: Men are four times as likely as women are to be ineligible as freshmen.

Sorry this has gotten so academic, but it's interesting stuff, worthy of a doctoral dissertation. Women athletes — especially in college — train just as long and hard as men, but have maintained some balance, the right perspective. So far.

So the next time you feel sorry for some guy who complains about trying to balance his grades and sports, just ask him about his sister.

April 25, 1996

Flushed with success

To hear Marvin Maxwell explain it, the idea appeared as suddenly — and as unexpectedly — as a phone call from the Harvard School of Business: *toilet lids.*

Maxwell, the gravel-voiced owner of Mom's Musicians General

Store, has long been a Louisville font of energy and ideas: turning Fourth Avenue into a music mecca; raising money for needy musicians; making the mortgage payments on his log-cabin home. Twenty-five years ago, while just fooling around, he made a guitar from a toilet lid. About a year ago — who knows why — he got the idea to make toilet lids shaped like guitars.

"I just turned the idea around 180 degrees," he said.

Friends laughed at the absurdity of it all. Dave Boone, 45, fellow drummer, went home and made a prototype. He brought it into Mom's last January. "Well, looky here," Maxwell said.

Maxwell is country at heart, MBA in street smarts. He and Boone paired up, nailed down a few trademark names, hired attorneys to run a patent search. Nobody — and how'd this one ever get by Thomas Alva Edison — had the patent on guitar-shaped toilet lids. Nor had anybody ever come up with a product name like Jammin' Johns.

"It got crazy, real crazy," Maxwell said.

"Marvin either put his brain in gear, or took it out, we don't know which," Boone said.

Looking for a manufacturer, Maxwell tucked a red guitar-shaped toilet seat under one arm and drove to Mississippi to visit the world's largest manufacturer of bathroon accouterments.

"He ended up talking to the leaders of the toilet world about this idea," Boone explained.

The people in Mississippi were very kind, which Boon translated to mean, "They didn't call security."

Maxwell was very impressed with the manufacturer's operation: "There were whole trains going in and out of the place with millions and millions of toilet lids." Alas, their enterprises were not fully compatible. "They're doing a $14 million expansion just to keep up with the demand for round toilet lids," Maxwell said.

Maxwell returned home, sought local talent and found it. After matching up a Monticello, Ky., wood-products company with three Louisville-area firms, the Jammin' Johns began flushing through the system. Each is lovingly manufactured from Kentucky oak with deluxe brass fittings. There are six models, each with a name like "Boomer," "Toiletar," or an Archie Bunker favorite, "the Guitarlet." The retail price is $99. The sales brochure says: "You may need to sit down when you see this."

"Buddy," explained Maxwell, "have I gotten to know a lot about toilet parts."

Maxwell and Boone took their lids to a National Association of Music Merchants trade show, where they were afraid they might be laughed out of the building. Instead, they may laugh all the way to the bank. Build a better commode accessory, and the world will beat a path to your door. Who could have guessed humanity's pent-up demand for guitar-shaped toilet lids?

"It could sell millions," Maxwell said.

That's the good news — and the bad news: Production is still on a small scale, and Maxwell is swamped with orders.

Factory representatives from Indonesia, China, Europe and Japan have come calling. A guitar maker is interested in toilet lids. Jammin Johns have been featured on "Today" and may appear on "Late Night With Conan O'Brien." How could David Letterman not yank this handle? Won't these lids open well at Graceland and the Opryland Hotel and in Dollywood and Branson, Mo.?

Every guitar picker in Nashville — and their moms — will want one.

Maxwell is not resting on his assets. He has a whole line of bath products planned. Toilet paper and bath-towel holders made of guitar heads and drumsticks. A plunger with a huge drumstick handle. Music-playing toilet lids containing customized compact discs. A specialized "Studio" toilet lid for $500. Plastic toilet lids to be sold on TV for $29.95. Toilet lids shaped like drumheads. Toilet lids shaped like piano tops — concert and baby grand.

"We're thinking about calling them The Elton," he said.

Feb. 11, 1995

An Elvis Presley pilgrimage

A steady, sullen rain is falling on northeastern Mississippi, gouging new rivulets in the thick, reddish-brown farmlands, misting up around green cedar trees and winter-browned kudzu vines, drumming against the pale concrete of the Elvis Aron Presley Memorial Highway.

The highway eases into Tupelo, population 25,000, the seat of Lee County, the town where Elvis was born to a dirt-poor farmhand and his dark-eyed wife in a two-room shotgun house on Jan. 8, 1935 — 45 years ago Tuesday.

Tupelo, a few miles from the Alabama border, is bigger and

more prosperous looking than the Elvis legend would have it. And save the Elvis Presley Heights Handy-Pak store, the only such listing in the telephone book, it seems to have avoided the commercial Elvis hysteria its native son visited on the outside world.

The tourists are led to Elvis' birthplace by small, almost inadequate signs placed at irregular intervals along the main highways, the last of which fronts a yellow brick building, apparently the home of a reducing salon, which advertises: "Lose Weight Our Weigh."

The house in which Elvis was born is now the frontispiece of the 15-acre Elvis Presley Park. Elvis and his parents lived in the house for three years — and in Tupelo for 13 years — before the search for work pushed his father about 100 miles northwest to Memphis, Tenn.

When Elvis was born in the home's front room — a twin brother, Jesse, died shortly after his birth — the white, clapboard home was one of a clutch of similiar shotgun houses spread along a dirt road in East Tupelo, the poorest section of a town in one of the poorest states in the union.

The other houses have since been bulldozed, and the ground where they stood has been landscaped. The Elvis Presley Youth Center, a red brick and yellow metal building, was built behind the Presley home.

Flanking the youth center is the Elvis Presley Chapel, a strange blend of brick and colored glass, the same mixture of simplicity and wretched excess that marked Elvis' path through life and death, all of it fronted with a $20,000 stained-glass window.

The chapel was built with donations from across the world. Its entrance is marked with an inscription in gold: "With Special Thanks — The Colonel."

Elvis donated the first $20,000 for his park in 1957, proceeds from an appearance at the Mississippi-Alabama Fair and Dairy Show. Original plans called for tennis courts, a picnic area, the youth center and a new, guitar-shaped swimming pool. The dream has not worked out. The old, overcrowded, rectangular pool is still in use, the tennis courts need work, and the youth center has only intermittent use. But there is the Elvis Presley a Man and His Music Nature Trail.

The old house and its grounds have been sanitized, remodeled, sodded and landscaped to the point where little of the early truth is left. A fine brick church has been built across the street. The old dirt road has long since been paved and is anchored with big, new houses.

The small, white Presley house looks conspicuous and well-scrubbed in the clearing. It rests firmly on brick and block, its front porch two feet above the ground. It can be bathed in electric light at night, when once it had no electricity or water. Neat walkways parade around its edges, leading to new front steps. The house has been repainted and its roof repaired. It has a new rough-wood ceiling, new walls and new flower-print wallpaper inside.

None of the furniture now inside the house belonged to the Presley family. One story has it that Jesse Presley was placed in a tiny casket on an old trunk for a period of mourning, but the old trunk has disappeared, or was sold at the courthouse steps at auction.

The poverty and bitter taste of it all has been washed away in the flood of repairs. It is difficult to stand in an asphalt parking lot and conjure up images of a baby Elvis playing outside under the oak and sweetgum trees or crawling onto the hardpan beneath his front porch to chase a kitten.

But the legend began here, and the thousands of pilgrims who visit the home each month want to touch more than an old family dresser.

"It don't even bother me anymore when people come in here and cry," says Essie Clayton, who has worked in the Presley home almost five years. "I'm just used to it by now."

Essie Clayton stands firm as both guard and guide just inside the front door in the room where Elvis was born. A thin rope shepherds the tourists through the front room into the back and then out a rear door toward the youth center, its souvenir stand and the chapel.

The house is owned by the city of Tupelo but is operated with firmness and a certain innocence by the ladies of the East Heights Garden Club. The garden club took over the house in 1971 and furnished it by advertising on the radio for old furniture.

Before Elvis died, the house was open a few hours a day for three summer months. Now it is open every day except Christmas from 10 a.m. to 5 p.m., and more than 100,000 people have been through it since he died Aug. 16, 1977.

The house is roughly 15 by 30 feet. Its two rooms are about 15 feet square — five big steps in each direction. The ceilings are barely eight feet high, and look new. The front room contains an old metal bed covered with a white bedspread, a dresser, three small windows with thin lace curtains and an old radio on a square table. Miss Clayton's rocking chair sits between the bed and the window. Parts of the original pine floor peek out around the edges of a 9-by-12 piece of linoleum on the floor.

The tourists put their money in a small fishbowl on an old treadle sewing machine on the table just to the right of the door: $1 for adults, 50 cents for children under 12.

The back room is a repeat of the one in front. It is dominated by an old, black cook stove, and a battered green kitchen table and chairs. The furniture is mismatched, crude and functional, a perfect if unconscious representation of the way things were.

The two rooms share a common red-brick chimney built into the wall between them. A brown, wooden mantle hugs the top of the black fireplace in the front room. Above the mantle hangs a picture of the baby Elvis flanked by his parents, Vernon and Gladys Presley.

Gladys Presley's hair is pulled back severely behind her ears. Vernon is wearing a dark hat with a wide brim. His lips are pressed tightly together. Elvis is wearing overalls, a shirt with cuffs, and a small soft-looking hat. All three are looking to their left, off camera. There is an uncertainty in their faces, the smoldering, suspicious look of Henry Fonda in "The Grapes of Wrath."

Even at age 3, Elvis had his lip curled in his sneer.

Miss Clayton talks with the flat monotone of someone who must repeat herself 100 times a day, five to seven days a week. Her words are coupled, one barely ahead of the next.

"This is the original location of Elvis' house. His daddy and granddaddy borrowed $180 to build it ... lived here three years and lost it ... they wasn't able to keep up the payments and lost the whole thing ... I don't reckon on how much the payments was ... they was hard times back then."

She will fill in the gaps with some prodding, but does not suffer fools or excessive questions gladly. She explains that Elvis' grandparents lived up the hill when the house was built. When the family lost the home, it was rented to others off and on until about 1958. From 1958 until 1971, it was used to store lumber.

"You can just imagine what kind of shape it was in when the ladies took it over," she says.

Miss Clayton knows the name of the man who foreclosed on the Presleys' $180 note. But the secret is safe with her. This is small-town Mississippi. The man's daughter lives and teaches in Tupelo.

"She thinks a lot of Elvis," Miss Clayton explained. "I'm not going to tell on her daddy."

She says the day Elvis died hundreds of floral arrangements — many in the shape of guitars — were sent to the house. The next day mourners were lined up for 50 to 100 yards outside the front door. They still receive wreaths on the anniversary of his birth, and death, and expect to receive a few Tuesday. More than 130 fans from England toured the home last Aug. 16.

"I had an old man last year, a real old man, and he cried so much we had to walk him through and set him down in a chair," Miss Clayton says. "The people come in here and they like to touch the walls. The big, little, old and young, they cry like a baby.... A lot of people do their crying in here, but they don't know why."

The steady rain slows the tourist business. The few that do arrive don't ask many questions. They are just happy to be in the room where Elvis was born, to absorb its smallness, to come close to him, to be born again.

One is Patsy Griggs. She is small, delicate, well-formed and polite in exaggerated Southern belle fashion. She is an illustrator for a company that makes reclining chairs. She has lived within 30 miles of Tupelo all her life, but has never visited Elvis' house.

"To start so small," she says, "and end up so big."

Wesley and Carolyn Wood and their daughter, Leslie, are from Dallas. They are on their way to Arkansas by way of Tupelo, a 600-mile detour. They played Elvis tapes all the way, shutting out the rain, letting the mood engulf them.

They enter the house slowly, staring at the walls, saying little. Wood unfolds a Polaroid camera. Mother and daughter argue over who will be in the pictures.

"I didn't come this far not to get in a picture," Carolyn Wood says.

She gets in a picture, but her head is cut off, showing more of the chimney than her.

"I don't care," she says.

She says they will also drive past Graceland, the Presley mansion in Memphis.

"I've had tears in my eyes since I got here," she says.

They are followed through by a young couple in matching

checked shirts. They had been there once before, on their honey-moon.

The tourist line includes three elderly couples from Illinois and a man and his wife from Houston, Texas. The man looks prosperous and well-dressed. His wife has the fading good looks of a beauty queen approaching middle age.

"She wanted to see the place," the man says.

A young man walks through alone. He is 22, pale and slim. His brown, effeminate eyes shine with an open and religious innocence. He says he is a singer and a writer, and he is getting ready to tour with Mr. Bob Russell, "who's known all over."

The young man says he is from Johnson City, Tenn. He says he'd sold everything he owned the night before and began hitchhiking to Tupelo to see Elvis' house.

"Me and Elvis have a lot in common," he says. "We each have a lot of love and warmth inside. I just had to start here. It seems funny to be standing in his house."

He says he is on a hot streak. He says a truck driver picked him up in Nashville and happened to be driving to Tupelo. He says the truck driver happened to be a friend of Mr. Bob Russell, and Mr. Bob Russell gave him a job.

"Music is my life," the young man says.

He says the truck driver also gave him a ride to Elvis' house and is waiting for him outside.

"It's funny," the young man says, "I don't even know his last name."

Jan. 8, 1980

The flood's reality hits home from spots along the river's edge

A light frost sparkled on the railing of the Clark Memorial Bridge early yesterday, adding yet another dimension to the sights of Flood Week '97.

From the north end of the bridge, downtown Louisville looked like a well-dressed woman standing in water up to her knees. With the flood running just a few feet below Interstate 64, the familiar reflections of the Galt House lights were compressed, the mirror images almost touching the black Ohio River water.

Yesterday was the day the river finally crested, slowly began pulling back to its rightful dimensions. There was something unfair about the river's prolonged rampage. The weather forecast for yesterday called for clear, sunny-blue skies, temperatures in the 60s. Away from the river, the flash flood had long since receded; clean-up had begun. Yet the Ohio insisted — almost a week after the terrible rains had stopped — on extracting its full pound of flesh.

Sightseers could walk onto the bridge under balmy skies to witness the river delivering its delayed punishment — then walk back to Main Street offices untouched by the spasm of floodwater from a distant rain hurtling beneath them.

The clock in front of the American Life Building on Main Street said 5:57 a.m., the temperature read 28 degrees. A tall, shiny fence surrounded the downtown Belvedere, where a maze of concrete walls signals its renovation. A cold wind blew off the river, bit hard at exposed flesh.

When seen from the Belvedere on most summer afternoons, the Ohio River looks tame, a large lake where towboats and the Belle of Louisville slice and churn the water at work and play. At roaring flood level, backlit by the Colgate clock, the waters are frightening, ugly, laced with eddies and currents that swirl up on its surface like black icing on chocolate cake.

This was not the river we knew, or loved; it was a stranger come to carry us away.

Turning around on the Belvedere, facing the parade of tall buildings in downtown Louisville, the Galt House lights glimmered off the mirrored face of the Kentucky Center for the Arts. A half-dozen men in red jackets were eating breakfast in a lighted office on the Belvedere, standing out as vividly as the restaurant patrons in the famous "Night Hawks" painting by Edward Hopper.

Water was about 3 feet deep in the Riverfront Parking Garage, offering the intriguing possibility that fish were swimming in places often walked by stockbrokers and operagoers. Even in the garage the river's currents were apparent, the backwater swirling upstream against the flow. In its still places, the columned garage looked like a rich man's reflecting pool gone muddy.

The Galt House lobby was calm, dry and pleasant, a breath of warm air before heading out onto Fourth Street. The walkway to the connector between the Belvedere and the Belle of Louisville's wharf was a tunnel of water, the Fourth Street streetlights barely visible above the brown water.

It was here where the enormity of the flood hit home. It is one thing to see it on television or read history-in-the-making in a newspaper. It's another to touch it: *My God, the Belle would be buried; look at all that water.*

A truck was parked diagonally across Third Street, where a pump was noisily trying to suck water from an LG&E building. The blue hose snaked up Washington Street, then down Third Street where its water gushed into the river.

On the Second Street side of the LG&E building, maintenance supervisor John Benz stood with a cigarette dangling in his mouth, watching a larger pump hurl 3,600 gallons of water a minute from a second-story window into the backwaters. LG&E also had other 1,300-gallons-a-minute pumps at work, but the net effect was like trying to empty a swimming pool with a soda straw. The hose attached to the 3,600-gallon pump flopped around like a fish; the water shot out in a mighty cascade; the flood level had dropped only a few inches.

"We had a mess of rain," Benz said.

In the shadows beneath the Clark Memorial Bridge, color-coded floodwall panels of salmon, pink and lime held back 8 feet of water, festive colors for a heavy-duty job. Back up on Main Street, the rising sun flashed blue-pink on the walls of the Humana Building. On Fourth Street, as morning traffic began to stir, a robin sang loudly in a locust tree.

March 8, 1997

In search of the ultimate bouncer

It is the moment of truth, the moment when alcohol intake runs head-on into the unwritten law of nightclub life that says you cannot stand on your table and make rude and obscene gestures at the management.

The blue smoke and noise part. The offender has irritated an

Verna Valentine and Dema Louise   *Photo by Michael Coers*

entire roomful of offendees. A bar bouncer looms like an ice cutter in a swimming pool. His arms snake under the offender's arms and behind his neck. Fingers lock. Muscles knot. The Loud and Drunk One is carried to the front door, feet dangling inches above terra firma, and is rudely mated to a snowdrift. The nightclub door slowly shuts. Peace has once again returned to the valley.

Maybe.

Big Ray is a bouncer. He works at one of the less publicized establishments off Poplar Level Road. Big Ray is 6 feet 6 inches of vertical, and surrounds it with 285 pounds of solid horizontal. He has worked in his bar 18 months. He gets a lot of bikers in his place, but most have the courtesy to park their Harley Hogs outside. Big Ray is happy about this, but says he has little trouble anyway.

Big Ray knows he is talking to the press, so he chooses his words carefully. He overtalks, much in the style of a cop explaining the scene of the apprehension.

"I usually talk to the individual first," Ray says. "What I do next depends on what the situation warrants."

Ray says for the most part the situation warrants that the

offenders merely walk to the door, mount their bikes and weave off to the next bar.

In fact, Big Ray refuses to indulge in any war stories that might thrill the masses of newspaper readers. "I can't think of any examples."

And so it went in downtown Louisville at the Soundstage, where two massive young men stand guard like bookends between quivering masses of post-pubescent if not prepubescent dancers. The pair have adopted a professional basketball referee's attitude toward their work: No harm, no foul and no war stories.

The search for the perfect bouncer continues anew on the Seventh Street Road strip, a two-mile-long section of Louisville dedicated to dancers, alcohol, medium-priced thrills and women who long ago lost their amateur standing.

Few places claim bouncers. And managers of a few of the higher-priced spreads were even reluctant to discuss the matter, citing the potential for lawsuits.

"Wextra, wextra...," the newsboys scream, "Seventh Street has gone Wall Street."

Which brings us to Dema Louise and Verna Valentine, the pride of the Merry-Go-Round Nightclub, 1848 Berry Blvd.

Verna is the little one behind the bar. At 30 she still has a firm hold on her looks, and figures to come in somewhere in the top three in a Debbie Reynolds look-alike contest.

Dema Louise is the bigger one, the Godmother of the place, the woman who keeps the dancers in queue, occasionally holds their hands, claims to operate with all the charm of a Don Rickles in drag, and talks a lot about her small child at home.

Stuff all the macho talk, says Dema Louise, we're your bouncers.

Verna Valentine looks cuddly, but claims the hardness required to handle drunks. In fact, she says 5-foot people can whip the expletive deleted out of a person 6 feet tall.

But she rarely gets the test. In the past year she has asked five people to leave, and they left.

Dema Louise presents a different study. She is 6 feet in heels, and never-you-mind the weight and age. She counts her wigs by the dozen. She has held off Fort Knox hecklers for 18 months. She prefers shimmering basic black, with the neck cut to Tuscaloosa, Ala. She has gone through four husbands but now prefers to live with a guy, saying she loves him too much to subject him to marriage. She has danced in 28 states, not including excitement and confusion.

The lady has been around.

"I got punched in the mouth in Rock Island, Illinois," she says. "When I looked up again two cowboys had got hold of the guy and he is sitting out in the middle of the street with his jaw hanging funny."

Not to worry about Dema Louise taking care of herself with men. She claims she's never lost a bounce when she was able to get in the first verbal punch. She'll talk most drunk men out of the bar. She'll lead them by the neck or nose if necessary.

But when the going gets really rough, the really tough get going.

So Dema Louise says if a man is giving a female bouncer too much trouble, the best method of removal is to grab him somewhere between his knees and his naval and lead him to the door.

She says it never fails.

No sopranos need apply.

Feb. 3, 1979

What's it like to hear your song on the radio? Ask Louise Cox

The words and rhymes — those classic, unpatronizing, unapologetic, country-and-Western words and rhymes — always have lined up in Louise Cox's head, and then pretty much on cue.

Sure, the Muse hands those lines out to people to be used at various levels of sophistication. We all get the same 26 letters to work with, although the finished products might not reflect it.

But Louise Cox can do it. She can flat pound out a country-and-Western refrain in 30 seconds, and every element in its place. There's not a self-conscious word in it. Take her song, "The Postman"...

Please give me the address to heaven.
I'm sending this letter up there.
I'm writin' it to my daddy.
He's in heaven somewhere.

Or this line about a wayward young father, a neglected wife and their child:
.. her bottles were always empty,
and yours were never dry....

Louise Cox was 11 years old when she began writing country songs. She was sitting in school in study hall when the Muse started handing out messages in meter. The first song this grade-school kid wrote had these lines:

Although, my dear, I love you yet,
My wife and two little kids, I can't forget.

She's written hundreds since, most that got no farther than her spiral notebook. In fact, none of them escaped her spiral notebook, save occasional airings in a family band, until a few months ago. That was when Louise Cox went to Nashville to cut a record.

There was nothing special about the method. You and a neighbor could take a three-string ukelele and a washboard to Nashville and cut a record if you had the money. There are studios all over town just waiting to oblige.

But this was different. Louise Cox is now 52. She has been writing her songs for 41 years. She wanted some hot wax of her own. She wanted to hear one of her songs on the radio.

There had been some musicians in the family. One of her daughters, Linda Allbritton, sings in a band in Florida. Another daughter, Terri Jennings, of Bullitt County, sings with a local band called Honky Tonk Heroes.

So Louise Cox selected two songs, picked up her Bullitt County daughter, and headed to Nashville to make a record. It cost about $425, which included studio time, the actual engineering and mixing of the record and 500 copies, with labels.

The studio band included a steel guitar, piano, drums and a lead guitar. The band listened to a tape of the songs about three times, picked up the melody, and was ready to go. Terri Jennings climbed into a recording booth about the size of a shower stall, went through both numbers about three times, and a record was born.

Put yourself in my shoes
And wear them for a while.
You'll find you're getting lonely
Just to see somebody smile.

The finished record arrived a few weeks later. One side was clean, and pretty much true. The flip side included a separate, higher-pitched voice that was mixed into the final product.

"This was my dream of 40 years," said Louise Cox. "I always wanted to do a record, my daughter got to do it, and I wanted to hear it on the radio."

The world's bandstands and radio stations are overrun with frustrated singers and songwriters, so the air time took a little doing, but Louise Cox did it. She had grown up in Shelbyville, still has family there, and had once cut some commercials for its radio station.

Her sister knew some of the present management and took Louise Cox and her record to station WCND, 940 on your AM dial. The station agreed to play — on request — "Put Yourself in My Shoes" and the flip side, "I'm Going Out."

Through some coincidence, there have been several requests for both sides of late.

WCND — on request — played "Put Yourself in My Shoes" about 9:16 a.m. Thursday morning. Louise Cox listened to it sitting in a big recliner in her den, surrounded by pictures of her family, a spiral notebook full of songs in her lap.

She looked off across the room, her eyes focused on whatever it is eyes focus on when one of your songs is being played on the radio.

"If this goes," she said, "if we can get a big push with it, well, you just never know what might happen."

June 2, 1984

Belle's low point evokes a depth of feeling

One of the laws of life says you can't have even a minor episode at sea — OK, fresh water — without having some sort of epic poem or ballad dedicated to it. Thus, with no apologies:

The Raising of the Belle

The news came as a sudden shock,
Our Belle had problems at her dock,
Part sunken there are river's edge,
and tipped a little on a ledge.

Our Grand Ol' Dame was listing sadly,
Chugging along — then leaking badly,
A possible catastrophe,
From paddlewheel to calliope.

"No way" went up the sudden cry,
"We won't allow our Belle to die."
As thousands hustled to be there,
An old, old friend in intensive care.

Get up, get up, you old sleepyhead,
All slouched down in your watery bed,
We love you, need you — you're family,
Proud symbol of community.

You're river, you're city, our ride to the past,
We love your whistle, your wheeze and gasp,
Where else to find such a head of steam?
Who else to challenge the Delta Queen?

You're Derby and antlers and Captain Mike,
You're Thunder and music and Saturday night,
You're magic, the Monarchs, the Louisville Slugger,
You're Pee Wee, Muhammad and all sorts of other.

Photo by Michael Hayman

Get up, get up, you old sleepyhead,
All slouched down in your watery bed.
There's tourists to carry and locals to dance,
A fountain to circle and lovers to trance.

There's places to visit and visions to power,
Jeffboat, the KingFish — the great Water Tower.
Six Mile, Twelve Mile, Eighteen and beyond,
Who's gonna take us if you're gone?

Last Sunday was grim, an unlikely tally,
Water in the engine, carp in the galley,
They sucked out your oil, sent out for some pros
To pump out the river, get you up on your toes.

Around you — *within you* — there came such a ruckus,
Barges and cables and men with lunch buckets,
Reporters, photographers and friends there to gape,
At sick Belle imprisoned by yellow cop tape.

Monday and Tuesday were more of the same,
Concern for your health and not what to blame,
By yesterday morning the big pumps were ready,
Up, up you would come, slow, slow and steady.

Hope was a-rising at dawn's early glow,
Strong men and machines were ready to go,
Old Glory hung proudly for all hands to see,
The only thing missing was Francis Scott Key.

Get up, get up, you old sleepyhead,
All slouched down in your watery bed,
There's honor and pride — and much left undone,
There's children to carry and races to run.

A crescent moon pinned to a steel-gray sky,
Faded to white as the sunlight slid by,
How pink the sunrise, how green the Great Lawn,
It's always the darkest before the dawn.

Get up, get up, you old sleepyhead,
All slouched down in your watery bed,
There's honor and pride and much left undone.
The Belle must rise like the morning sun.

Aug. 28, 1997

It's crushing if Jesse Harris gets his can

BIG CLIFTY, Ky. — So here we have two good men, Jesse Harris, 63, and Russell Witten, 56, sitting under several shade trees, pondering why it is the Laws of Physics have packed their bags and fled Grayson County.

Harris is a man who adds to his retirement income by picking up discarded aluminum cans and selling them. He is paid 17 cents a pound, plus all the cans he can eat.

Witten is a tobacco, corn, cow, chicken, hog and cucumber farmer. With all of the above hoeing and hauling, he earns 17 cents a hour, plus pickles.

The Law of Physics under moderate debate between the two men was: Which weighs more, a pound of crushed aluminum cans, or a pound of uncrushed aluminum cans?

Harris, a serious and reasonable man, said he noticed that if he mashes the cans with his right foot, as he has been doing for years, there are 20 cans to the pound. He says if he doesn't mash the cans, it takes 25 to make a pound.

"I know it doesn't make any sense," Harris said, "but I've weighed them and it makes the cans heavier if you crush them."

You can bet your last case of no-deposit, no-return bottles that
Harris crushes every aluminum can he can get his foot over.

"He don't miss either," says Witten.

Witten, too, shakes his head over the crushed-can findings, but
he has a theory on why it works.

"The only thing I can figure is the air gets trapped inside somehow and makes the crushed cans heavier," he said.

The way in which Jesse Harris gets his can is a story in itself.
When he first started 10 or 12 years ago, he was a pop-bottle man,
but the deposit was only two cents each, and he couldn't find
enough to pay for his shoe leather.

"Now they're up to a nickel, but you still can't get ahold of
them. There's too many other people out looking too."

So a few years ago Harris jumped to the aluminum-can league.

"I've seen him many a time walking along the road with a sack
of cans," Witten says.

Time was, Harris said, he would walk along the road almost
every day picking up cans. Then the competition got stiff again.

"There's a man over to Summit goes out looking for cans in his
car," Harris said. "Him and his wife, and his three boys help too.
Now everybody's picking up cans."

But rather than see Harris abandon the aluminum-can business
too, the good people of Big Clifty have rallied to help him. They
know Harris makes the half-mile walk from his house to town
almost every morning, so many of them leave their aluminum
cans in their front yards. Harris goes by Pence's Grocery, Wade's
Grocery, Witten's Variety Store, and will make a run past the post
office in stoop-shouldered pursuit of aluminum.

The local beer drinkers — be it out of charity or just general
slovenliness — are also a big source of aluminum.

"A few of the boys sit uptown almost every night drinking
beer," Witten said. "They just throw the cans out of the car. They
know Jesse will be by in the morning."

"Once in awhile I find a full one," Harris says, adding he
knows how to empty a beer can as well as crush it.

Though he has quit walking the highways, Harris will still collect 200 pounds of cans a month. He has them stacked in cardboard boxes behind his house. He hires someone to take them to
an aluminum recycler in Elizabethtown every two or three weeks.
In his good years, he could earn $50 a month. He makes less now.

After Harris and Witten finished filling in the history of the business, conversation drifted back to the weight of crushed vs. uncrushed cans.

Harris confesses he will occasionally use his left foot, but his right remains the big hammer. Witten reaffirms that Harris doesn't miss. Harris leads the party to the rear of the house where his cans are stored. He is a little embarrassed about being interviewed on crushing aluminum cans. His cans are stacked about five feet high. Every one is crushed. That makes them 20 to the pound.

"It MUST be something to do with the air," Witten says.

Aug. 28, 1977

Here's to 'check day'! Bottoms up!

Wild Bill has moved with all due speed from a generally inebriated condition to stone drunk, hauling his liver along for the ride. He is a short man with a heavily creased, simian face and wide slits for eyes and a mouth.

He has lost or broken his glasses, so he has found a cheap substitute, a dime-store magnifying glass he wears around his neck on a string. When Wild Bill buys a glass of red wine, he peels the money off a thin roll of dollar bills, examining each bill carefully with his glass, his eye looming Cyclops-like through the lens.

He is drinking in a tavern near downtown Louisville, a dim, friendly, lusterless, rectangular neighborhood bar where many of the customers look as if they have been done over in lumpy wallpaper paste.

The whiskey bottles behind the bar are back-lit with red and blue lights, and the smaller pint bottles near the front window are lined up like headless soldiers. It is a rainy Thursday morning, the first day of November, the day the government checks arrive, the day the stereotypes come due. Every barstool and booth is taken, Elvis is singing "America the Beautiful" on the jukebox, and all's right with the world.

A man and two women sit in a booth going through some diagnosis on the state of each other's alcoholism. One of the women has a wan, vacant face and flat eyes. The second was a pretty blonde, but her face has begun to sag, and pouches up at her cheeks. The man was once handsome, but his looks have begun to erode badly, his face has began to draw in at his cheeks. They are planning a day-long trip to Indiana bars next Tuesday when the Kentucky bars will be closed for election. They have a sense of elation about the trip. It will be a change of scenery. A day in the country.

They say, in no particular order of appearance:

"We went through a fifth and two pints last Saturday."

"If you're drinking every day, if you need a drink every day, then you're an alcoholic."

"I drink every day, but I can quit any time I want. I'm no alcoholic."

"If you drink every day, you're an alcoholic."

"How do you know?"

"I'm an alcoholic."

It is a bar so filled with regulars that strangers cannot hide. Strangers are rocks in the steady stream of intimate jokes and conversation.

Only a few of the customers, including several in business suits, are drunk. The rest are just happy to be there, sitting among friends, comfortable with their self-assigned roles in the show.

"We wanted to walk in the rain on the way over," a woman says. "It's romantic walking in the rain."

Four men are sitting on barstools watching a television quiz game. They make a wonderful still-life picture. Each is hunched over the bar. Their backs are lined up like refrigerator doors. Each has turned his head at the same angle toward the television set. The quiz-show emcee, all teeth and tailored, three-piece good humor, glows brightly in the corner above the pint whiskey bottles.

The men and the bartender are playing along with the emcee. The bartender has the correct answers long before any of the contestants or his customers.

One of the four men is drunk. He has long tattooed arms that look more like thick white cables than flesh and bone. He has stuffed his billfold in a back pocket and thumps on it with one hand as his friends walk past.

"Check day," he announces again and again. "It's check day."

The bartender is doing a brisk, over-the-counter business. Most of the customers are women.

Wild Bill continues to sink ever southward in his booth. His magnifying glass is lost in the folds of his shirt. A woman with a broad, flat face and dingy blonde hair is attempting to rescue him. She is joined by a man whose hair is knotted up with a rubber band behind his head.

It seems that Wild Bill is to pick up his new glasses that day but cannot recall the name of his eye doctor or the location of his office. His immediate future appears bleak.

"Hey," says Wild Bill. "Where am I?"

Every time the front door opens, a bluish-gray light flashes into the room, side lighting the faces at the bar. A half-dozen heads swivel to greet or inspect the new customer.

The latest arrival is a tall, thin man in a powdery blue uniform. It is the mailman making a quick, midday stop from his appointed rounds for a glass of beer.

A waitress complains that the mailman shouldn't be making stops in a tavern when so many people are home waiting for their government checks. A few in the bar who already received their checks that morning applaud and cheer as he walks in.

Nov. 30, 1979

'Gee, honey, you look 6% cuter!'

I have found additional Great Truth in the November issue of Psychology Today magazine. It is an article by one James W. Pennebaker of the University of Virginia on country-Western music. More specifically, the article seeks to lend scientific credence to that widely held theory that has been put to music by Mickey Gilley: "Don't the Girls All Get Prettier at Closing Time?"

Science marches on near the Tidewater.

Pennebaker has a sly wit. He leads into his story by placing psychological labels on several C&W classics, including "one of the all-time behavorial hits, reinforcement theory: 'If You've Got the Money, Honey, I've Got the Time.' "

Alas, he doesn't even mention the latter-day classic: "If I Said You Had a Beautiful Body, Would You Hold It Against Me?"

Gilley's song, written by Baker Knight, refers to that timeless, closing-time practice in many bars where men and women jockey frantically to find someone to help them set their alarm clocks. The

The Closing-Time Phenomenon

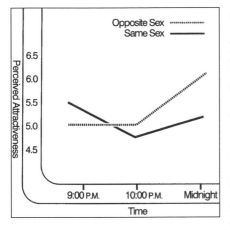

song also implies that normal standards of companionship and taste may change the closer everyone gets to the final gun.

As in, "I just cannot believe how much better looking that blonde/cowboy (pick one) has gotten since midnight."

This is also known as the Six Tequilas School of Romance.

Pennebaker, an assistant professor of psychology and former good ol' boy from Midland, Texas, thought Gilley's hypothesis needed some scientific collaboration. So he corralled six graduate students and herded them out to three student bars near the University of Virginia campus.

Project Looking For Mister Goodbar South was carefully planned. The six students, three male-female teams, talked with 103 men and women. Each team went into a different bar at 9 p.m., 10:30 p.m. and midnight (closing time was 12:30 a.m.). Each team tried to talk only with men or women who were not with the opposite sex — and who were not intoxicated to the point where they could not tell the phone booth from the front door.

Using the rating system as old as the abacus (the system also mentioned in Gilley's song), each test subject was asked to rate the opposite sex in the bar from 1 to 10.

That concluded, each test subject was also asked: "If you were a member of the opposite sex, how would you rate the members of your own sex, using the same 1-to-10 scale?"

And, as the accompanying graph illustrates (see dotted line), the closer it got to closing time, the more attractive the opposite sex became.

Voila!

Also (see solid line), it is interesting to note that the test subjects seemed to have a decreasing regard for themselves early in the evening (no doubt caused by the frequent strikeouts early in the skirmishes), but their self-esteem rose nearer midnight as they began to connect.

This is worth one voila and two eurekas!

Pennebaker offers two long and fairly technical psychological reasons for all of the above. But his motivational theories, in my opinion, can be broken down into two more generally accepted facts of human behavior:

(a) You gotta make hay while the sun shines, and

(b) If you can't be with the one you love, then love the one you're with.

Pennebaker reported by phone from Virginia that his experiment, part lark and partly born of a love for country music, has been accepted by serious scholars. Indeed, it first ran in the Personality and Psychology Bulletin, Vol. 5, which is about as frivolous as your maiden aunt on premarital sex.

Still, dedicated researcher that I am, I sought additional proof of Pennebaker's postulations at The Garage, a Jeffersonville nightspot.

It was a Wednesday night, traditionally very slow and the place was almost empty. So I tried the bouncer.

"Do you know a James W. Pennebaker?"

"No, I guess he ain't been in tonight."

"Well, tell me, do the customers do a lot of hustling in here the last hour before closing time?"

"Yeah, some."

Ain't science grand.   *Dec. 1, 1979*

Many stoop to watch little talent

History flickered briefly across the silver screen at the Vogue Theatre in St. Matthews early this morning. The pint-sized movie classic "The Terror of Tiny Town," the film industry's first and only musical Western featuring an all-midget cast, brushed lightly against a few hundred hearts, then faded away.

Better it had gone down in a burst of small-arms fire.

Critics have consistently ranked "The Terror of Tiny Town" among the worst movies of all time, but they have been too short-sighted. It must be the worst of any size. Smallpox deserves a better reputation.

The movie appeared through the courtesy of Vogue manager Marty Sussman, who is so laid-back he must go to work in a horizontal position. Sussman regularly offers such gentle trash as "Terror" with all the confidence and savoir-faire of a genial college professor whose grandfather donated the 309 acres upon which the university rests.

"Maybe you can link your column with something about Reagan's budget cuts," Sussman said of the midget movie.

Sussman said it took a year to acquire "Tiny Town," a runaway winner in the 1980 New York Worst Films Festival. He said it may be 100 years before he brings it back.

"This ain't New York," he said.

It is hard to know where to begin with "The Terror of Tiny Town." Let us start outside the Vogue Theatre, where a hand-lettered box-office sign posted late last night said: "Sorry —the regular movie is running late. 'Terror' will begin at midnight, hardly worth the wait."

Inside, Randy Newman is singing "Short People" as the customers straggle in. Sussman has already missed his opportunity to charge them half-price.

"Tiny Town" was filmed in 1938.

It starred — according to the film credits — Jed Buell's midgets and included a cast of about 48,000 Shetland ponies. Unfortunately, the credits did not say where Buell found his midgets or where he stored them between engagements.

Happily, many went on to fame as Munchkins in "The Wizard of Oz," where they looked much better in green.

Taking notes in the dark required some cautious shorthand, but the best I could figure it, "Tiny Town" was a brief tale of romance, intrigue and murder in the Old West.

The movie seemed to begin with a bunch of tiny people standing around making small talk. We soon came to learn that one particularly long-sighted midget had plans to take over the county by starting a feud between two short-fused neighbors.

Well, sir, one of these neighbors had a son named Buck and the other had a niece named Nancy. In no time, the two fell in love, short-circuiting the villain's plans.

None of this is to leave out the innumerable scenes in which the midgets walked under the swinging saloon doors to meet with the half-witted sheriff, and no one ever explained what the penguin was doing in the barbershop.

The barbershop scene was a beauty because a midget barbershop quartet kept singing half-notes. Sometime after the singing,

five mounted midget desperados on Shetland ponies held up a
midget stagecoach, killing a midget guard and ending his short
part in the movie. There was also a man in the movie named Dr.
Hy Lowman.

This is not to make small of the funny scene in the bar in which
it took two midgets to play a bass fiddle, or the many times the little banditoes would tie their horses to a hitching post, then walk
underneath it.

Buck and Nancy had some small singing parts, with Buck holding a guitar that reached from his toes to his nose.

Toward the end, Buck was improperly accused of shooting
Nancy's uncle in the small of the back. This so incensed the other
midgets that they bellied and necked their way up the bar, got
loaded on shorty beers, then headed over to the jail to lengthen
Buck's neck.

Buck, of course, had long since escaped jail, and was making big
tracks toward Big Rock Canyon for his showdown with the villain.
The two fought briefly before the villain was blown into a million
little pieces by a big wad of dynamite that had been ignited by his
longtime, but subsequently jilted, girlfriend.

She had a big laugh about the explosion, the lights went on and
everybody went home.

Fast.

July 28, 1981

Chicken Lady story
(in an eggshell)

The Chicken Lady approaches on tired feet, rocking slightly,
leaning forward as if she were dragging the entire world behind
her in a clear plastic bag.

The Chicken Lady has been in the Bank Street restaurant in
Portland before. On her previous stop, she had bought a cup of coffee on credit. That placed her some 30 cents in arrears to management, a debt she manages to erase with a few flicks of a ready
tongue.

She does it with The Ol' Weak Coffee Trick.

"I can pay for my coffee today," the Chicken Lady says. "But that last cup I got the other day was too weak. It wasn't worth nothing. I never had coffee so weak. I gotta have my coffee strong. It wasn't worth paying for."

Management then suggests to the Chicken Lady that if she doesn't like the coffee; she might try looking for credit someplace else.

This line of reasoning makes no impression on the Chicken Lady. She senses correctly that management, however annoyed, will not make a public issue out of a 30-cent cup of coffee.

The debt is cleared without payment.

The Chicken Lady asks for two more cups of coffee, one of them to go. She is holding a dollar bill in her right hand. Its green edge extends out between two fingers like a snake's tongue.

Management reluctantly slips away to a back room to get the coffee. The Chicken Lady settles into her chair like a fat hen on a corner roost. She fixes a steady gaze on one of the customers.

"Can't have no weak coffee," she says.

She is wearing a light green dress and matching porkpie hat. Pale eyes peer out from a smooth, flat, leathery face. She does not know her age. She says her mother knew it, but her mother is dead.

The Chicken Lady says she is primarily concerned with chickens. She lives with her husband, or at least someone she calls her Old Man, and their six chickens, on $132 a month Social Security. "I've got a big fine backyard," she says. "I've got two sheds and a doghouse for my chickens. I paid a man $50 to build me more sheds, but I didn't like them, so I paid another man to haul them off."

The Chicken Lady is one of those people who can be considered a real character provided you don't have to put up with her seven days a week. She said she buys chickens and raises them in Portland. The chickens are her pets.

"I bought a chicken white as naked skin from some boy for $5," she says. "It looked real good. Didn't lay eggs worth a damn."

"Neighbors can do you dirty," she says. "Some people called the police to complain about my chickens. Actually I called them myself 'cause I wanted to know the law. I called the police in Louisville, Jeffersonville and Cleveland, Ohio. They all told me it was all right to raise chickens.

"Now the police holler, 'Hey, Grandma,' when they go by the house," she says. "They don't bother my chickens. The gas man, the water man, they don't bother my chickens neither."

In time, a metamorphosis occurs. The Chicken Lady begins to look a little like a chicken, an old; tired, hunkered-down, porkpie-hatted chicken.

"I have two real cute chickens," she says, cupping her hands and holding one over the other just inches apart. "They are just about this big."

She also has a pair of roosters that keep the neighborhood dogs at bay. "When the dogs get too close, the roosters scare them off," she says, cocking her head with the wary, suspicious look of a worried rooster. "The roosters go, 'Bawke! Bawke!' and the dogs are gone."

"When it gets real cold," she says, "I bring the chickens inside the house to warm them up. I don't leave them there, I just let them get warm. The police said it's all right to have chickens in your house. I wouldn't want nothing to be outside in cold weather. I wouldn't even want a dog outside in cold weather.

"Sometimes me and the old man go sit out back and watch the chickens. They're protected by a fence so they can't go out in the street. I've had my chickens a long time. When they die I don't eat them. You don't want to eat a chicken that just up and dies. I tell the old man to go get a shovel and he buries them for me in the backyard."

Then the Chicken Lady cocks her head and goes back to her cup of coffee.

Oct. 4, 1980

Not quite pari-muletuel
No one was sure how Bullitt premiere of mule racing would go

Mule racing being what it is, no one knew exactly what to expect.

To be sure, the participants were all in order. Five mules — three of them named Kate — were poised at the top of the backstretch chute. Five jockeys, as ramshackle a bunch as ever mounted beasts of burden, were perched in the saddles, dead serious about the proceedings in a silly sort of way.

Ahead loomed 660 yards of mule race. The track, a tight, half-mile oval cut into an overgrown pasture, was defined by an inside rail of white, three-inch water pipe. A hard night's rain had thickened the track's sandy base, making forward progress questionable. A raw wind gusted through nearby oaks, tearing at the leaves. Best estimates of the winning time varied from two minutes to two days.

"To tell you the truth," one of the mule owners said just prior to the call to the post, "I ain't sure what's gonna happen."

He was not alone. When Chett and Heather Myers announced a week ago that mule racing would be held at their Bullitt County track, they were not certain what would follow.

The couple had purchased the track, formerly Bullitt Stables, about a month ago. They named it "Bags-End Stables" in tribute to the hole-in-the-ground domicile of Bilbo Baggins, a jockey-sized character from "The Hobbit."

Three weeks ago the couple revived Sunday afternoon racing with an impromptu card of Thoroughbred and Quarter horse racing — each horse owner putting up $25, winner-take-all.

Mule racing was not far behind.

"Somebody mentioned it," Heather Myers said, "so we said, why not?"

Such is the tone and tenor of Bags-End Stables. It does seem to be operated very much by the collective seats of the Myers' dusty pants. It includes 28 stalls, 18 acres of net ground, a swimming lake to condition horses, and several sets of solid buildings. Many of the horses stabled there are good animals preparing for the fall season at Churchill Downs.

Like anyone a month in a new home, they talk impressively of changes to be made, of fresh paint and a new track rail, of derbies and futurities, of bigger purses ... of mule races.

"If we can get the mules," Heather Myers said. "We'll run 'em."

Yesterday's race drew about 15 people. Each was asked to fork over $1 admission by a dark-haired kid in a blue jacket who guarded the dirt road into the stables.

The spectators were a broad mix of men, women and children, many of whom seemed partial to pickup trucks and coon-hunting caps. They gathered thickly, in clumps, on tailgates, around mules, swapping tales as old as sin itself.

The organization of the preliminary Thoroughbred and Quarter

horse races proceeded easily enough. Heather Myers gathered all
the horse owners around her inside a stable, asked them what
horses they had and what distance they'd like to run.

Like kids in a backyard football game, they quickly worked out
various rules and dimensions, and the race was on. This being
your basic backyard operation, no parimutuel odds were posted,
but some of the throng did gather before each event to conduct a
"Calcutta," a simple wagering system that enables spectators to
bet on a horse without having to hand some stranger behind a
ticket window $2 in exchange for a machine-stamped ticket.

While the Thoroughbreds and Quarter horses ran races of 300
yards, 660 yards and seven furlongs, the mules remained tied to
posts, pickup trucks and barn doors waiting for their moment in
the slop.

For you uninitiated, mules are the sterile offspring of jackasses
and female horses. They are a breed apart, with hammer-shaped
heads and ears like portable television antennas.

Mules are capable of many things, including plowing the back
40, pulling wagons, hauling logs in steep ground and providing
mobile platforms for coon hunters.

But no one has ever accused the mule of being especially graceful, or fast.

Of the five mules entered in yesterday's race, two were owned
by George Houchins of Valley Station, two were owned by Mike
Russell of Garrett, Ky., and the fifth was owned by Johnny Yates of
Bardstown.

None had ever raced before. Two of the mules had been in
training about a week. Russell had worked his pair for an hour the
day before. Yates said his mule had never seen a track.

"No problem," he said. "I ain't riding her anyway."

All parties agreed that the only sensible name for a mare mule
was Kate, which explained why three of the five entrants had the
same name. The other two were John and Annie. Apparently no
one has ever worn himself out naming mules.

The jockeys were selected from the various hangers-on, employees and relatives who were standing around the track. After the
saddling-up and bet-taking was finished inside the barn, the
whole party moved outside to watch the show.

Picture, if you will, a scene in which some 75 grinning people
are scattered across a weedy infield marked by white, plastic
water pipe as five mules line up to run 660 yards in wet sand.

Picture, if you will, five jockeys dressed in everything from red and white riding silks to leather chaps to a coon-hunting cap turned backward.

Please imagine five mules generally headed in the same direction, but jumping, weaving and swerving all the while, the whole scene reminiscent of a wedding couple taking off in their vintage car trailing five bouncing tin cans on strings.

Smile and laugh, if you will, with Mike Russell, whose mules finished one-two, the leader clocked at a blazing 61.25 seconds.

Please pray, if you will, for the slower mules, two of whom may still be somewhere on the far turn headed for home.

Oct. 19, 1981

AIDS memorial garden is the latest chapter in 'spunky' sisters' history

NERINX, Ky. — It took us a while to get from the Motherhouse to the memorial garden. There was a lot to see beforehand, a lot to talk about — and Sister Mary Rhodes Buckler is never too far away from her next sentence. She'd already found a delightful word to describe her order, the Sisters of Loretto.

"We're spunky," she said.

Spunky. Not necessarily a biblical description, but certainly accurate. The Sisters of Loretto — one of the first American religious communities of women — was founded in Central Kentucky in 1812. Buckler is the namesake of Mary Rhodes, who'd come to Kentucky from Maryland, was living with family on Hardin's Creek in what was still raw and dangerous wilderness.

Worried that Kentucky children were not receiving the education she had gotten, Rhodes started a school in an abandoned log cabin. She was joined by two other women, Christina Stuart and Ann Havern. The three pioneers spoke to the Rev. Charles Nerinckx of their desire to live a religious life. Nerinckx, who had been ministering to Kentucky Catholics since 1805, found their cause God-given. A log-cabin complex was built — "Little Loretto," named after the Italian shrine that venerates the Holy

Family of Nazareth.

The Sisters of Loretto opened schools in Perry County, then moved west by riverboat, opening a school for Osage Indians in Kansas in 1847, and another for Spanish-speaking children in New Mexico in 1852.

Meanwhile, in 1824, the Sisters of Loretto had moved their church headquarters a few miles from their original school to a hillside farm at Nerinx, about 50 miles southeast of Louisville in Marion County. They built a church, the Loretto Academy, a convent, residence halls, a guest house and an infirmary for the care of sick and retired sisters.

The complex became known as the Motherhouse: the place that gave them life, the place that brought them home.

The priests lived in a separate house from the sisters and for a time were getting meals served separately. That did not go down well with all the sisters.

"One day they just announced that if the priests were hungry, they should come eat with us," Buckler said.

Buckler and I had talked for months about getting together to visit the Motherhouse and its newest addition — a memorial garden for victims of AIDS. Last week she gave the tour of the venerable buildings, pointing out the banister she had slid down as a child taking music lessons at the school.

She led us into the restored church. It was simple, elegant, beautiful — its stained-glass windows replaced with clear glass.

"That's so people can see in, and we can see out," she said.

She led us along the landscaped grounds, pointing out the lake, the trees, the guests house that can be used for retreats. The sisters volunteer to landscape individual areas, but a sign along one walkway pointed out the benefit of community effort: "If everyone pulled a few weeds they'd all be out."

Words to live by.

The memorial garden, inspired by a sister who had lost a relative to AIDS, was planted this spring, dedicated this summer. It was built into the hillside at one edge of the cemetery where many sisters have been buried. An opening to the garden was cut through the low cemetery fence; the sisters thought it best the two areas be connected.

Huge stones carved by thousands of years of wind and water were hauled to the garden from the creek below the hill. One of the stones, flat and 12 feet across, was made into a bench. Visitors can sit there and see willow trees dip their green limbs into the pond, and the bright yellows and blue bursts of perennial flowers.

The names of four men who died of AIDS are engraved on plaques fixed to the stones. Some ashes from their bodies are mixed with the soil. The garden has room for growth; it's open to all denominations. Buckler was asked if some members of her church had objected.

"We didn't ask them," she said

Sept. 19, 1995

One old goat proves he can still corral a herd

The goat truck was parked along Jefferson Street downtown, always an interesting area anyway. The goats were being guarded by Earl Taylor of Campbellsville, Ky., an old, whiskered man with his hands shoved in his pockets.

The goats — and their babies — peered out through wooden slats, not quite as curious about me as I was about them. Taylor and a buddy, who were on their way home from a goat auction, found a need to visit a friend in a Jefferson Street restaurant. I was on my way to the Merle Haggard concert at Coyote's. It was 10 p.m. Thursday, the night already half-goofy, harshly illuminated by parking lot lights.

A teen-age girl in cutoffs was reaching through the truck slats, petting a baby goat. She ignored the two gobbling turkeys also stuffed in the battered truck.

I asked Taylor about the fate of the turkeys.

"We turn 'em loose on the farm," he said.

This, I am thinking, has to be a setup. There is a song here, something larger than all of us: Merle Haggard, old goats, city lights and loose turkeys. Haggard sings about all of them, which is not to demean his song-writing talents in the areas of praying, drinking, fighting, cheating, lying, dying and Mama. He was recently given some sort of Pioneer Award on one of the now daily country-music-award TV shows. He accepted it graciously, saying something to the effect that he'd showed up in Nashville broke and in 30 short years managed to end up only $5 million in debt.

All I can say is: He earned it.

Coyote's is alive, well and boot-scooting. It was almost sold out, roughly 1,400 cowboy hats supported by an interesting cross-section of old goats, kids and turkeys. Normally a Coyote's crowd can be labeled as "standing room only" because standing is mostly all there is. Thursday night — in deference to Haggard — about 20 rows of chairs were set up near the stage to allow serious worshipers space near the altar.

There was a time when Haggard and his hard-drinking buddies might have had a shot at filling Freedom Hall. He's now come full American Legend circle, back to more of a honky-tonk setting filled with glowing red neon, fans that know the words to all his songs and carcinogenic amounts of aggressively passive cigarette smoke.

There were several moments Thursday night when Haggard's fans seemed more ready than he was. One of them, in fact, periodically held up an aluminum crutch and waved it, a beacon in a sea of uplifted beer bottles.

And that was even before Haggard starting singing: "I'll think I'll just stay here and drink."

That's what I've always loved about this prison-warden, Mama-crying, I-gotta-get-drunk-and-I-sure-do-dread-it kind of music. We have a nation worried to death about crime, but part of the nation is paying $12 to $18 a ticket to hear some grizzled outlaw romanticize it, even lifting beer bottles and crutches in salute.

Considering how many longnecked bottles of beer that places like Coyote's sell, it's some sort of wonder they don't need chicken wire stretched across the stage to protect the entertainers from strong-armed critics.

The guy standing directly in front of me had a better idea; he was hoisting his cellular telephone. His name was Wade Thompson. He'd called his brother, then aimed the phone toward the stage, giving his brother a taste of Haggard.

"I just had to let my brother know I was here," Thompson said. By the time Haggard got around to "Okie From Muskogee," I'd gotten around to a corner of the room where Ronnie Rowe of Louisville was celebrating his 36th birthday with Haggard.

"Merle's all my dad let me listen to growing up," Rowe said.

Rowe, who loved the show, looked fine for 36. Haggard looked a lot older up close than he had from the middle of the room, but don't we all.

He played barely an hour, left without an encore, his departure covered by some guy who said everything but: "Ladies and Gentlemen, Merle has left the building."

I walked out past Merle Haggard American Legend T-shirts selling for $20, caps for $15, handkerchiefs for $6. It was raining on Jefferson Street, and the goat truck was gone.

April 27, 1996

The woman behind the singles ad: Ms. Q-340 did it on a dare

Information   157
Singles

BIG, ugly, fat, white woman seeks a slender and financially secure, good-looking man for a totally serious relationship. I won't cook, won't clean your place, won't babysit any kids, won't hang out at any redneck places. Beware — I'm strong-willed, big and ugly and don't like to be told what to do. I make good money at nursing but have no plans to spend any on you. Send your photo; if you're too ugly I'll throw your picture away. Good luck to one winner of my company and sense of humor. Reply to Box Q-340, c/o CJ, 525 W. Broadway, Louisville 40202.

Let it be said that Ms. Q-340 — the author of the accompanying singles ad that appeared recently in your morning fact sheet — does equivocate a little; she is very big, she is white, she is a nurse, but she is not ugly.

"Attractive." is the word writers often attach to women like Ms. Q-340. It is a kinder and gentler word but does not necessarily imply pretty. She is attractive. She is also very talkative, very opinionated and has a quick sense of humor. She launches protective one-liners like a bazooka. She was sitting at a kitchen table in her small apartment off National Turnpike, a large figure wearing an electric-blue bathrobe edged in trumpeting pink and yellow flowers.

There was not a self-conscious bone in her body. She was picking at a bowl of yellow and orange Fruit Loops, all the while eyeing her interviewer with some suspicion: Why is this man here and what is he really trying to get me to say?

That is simple: "Why did you place an ad like that in the newspaper?"

"I did it," she said, "on a dare. One of the other nurses brought in a magazine like the National Enquirer, and we got to looking at the personals ads. They all said things like 'handsome, attractive, educated man seeks beautiful model.' I said, 'Give me a break.' So I sat down and wrote out the ad."

She says it cost her $68 to place the ad in your morning fact sheet. She exaggerated in her ad, but then again she didn't. Ms. Q-340 truly does not want to mess with rednecks, clean up after children or waste her money on bums. She claims she doesn't have time for any relationships, but that may be the weakest part of her story. Who wants to throw away $68 on a total joke?

"Well," she said, "there was this one letter from a man in Bullitt County."

Her friends told her the ad was read on the morning shows of at least three Louisville radio stations. It had to have been passed around dozens of factories and businesses. So you may be surprised to learn it also brought Ms. Q-340 15 letters the first day, most of them sincere, many of them from would-be suitors desperately trying to read between all the lines.

"Some of them," Ms. Q-340 said, "didn't send a photo. I threw them out right away. If they can't follow simple instructions, they're out."

Yet many of them did. Here was a woman who said she was large, ugly and looking for a skinny man with a thick wallet, and more than a dozen men replied. Almost all the replies were sweet and kind. One inmate from the Kentucky State Reformatory in La Grange wrote to say he was very interested, but would not be available for at least 28 months. You might suspect that some of the men who replied were of the beat-me, whip-me, kick-me variety, but only one of the letters had even a hint of sexual kinkiness, and that was pretty mild.

Most of the men praised her for her honesty, her sense of humor and her willingness to admit physical flaws in this age of Nutrasweet. One man thought she would make a perfect spouse because other men wouldn't always be hitting on her. Another said the singles ad "triggered a Pavlovian desire to correspond with you immediately."

"What this tells me," she said, "is that there are still a lot of nice, generous men out there who don't care about the outer package. They are sincere, they can tell the truth, they care and they can share."

I'm not sure about that either. I've been married much too long to fully understand the loneliness — or shyness — of people who date through post-office boxes. But I liked her explanation, and I think I'm going to believe it, at least until a better one comes along.   *May 5, 1990*

Man returns robbers' loot to bank but can't get loan

What we have here is an O. Henry short story with an ending the Grinch could fully appreciate.

Think of it the next time fate throws $100,000 in cash at your feet.

It began Dec. 20 at the Family Funeral Care funeral home in Louisville's Portland area. Employee Lois Allen had car trouble. Danny Johnson, an old friend, came by the funeral home to fix it. Suddenly, they heard frantic pounding on the funeral home's locked front door followed by breaking glass.

"I freaked out," Allen said. "I didn't know what was going on." Four armed men had robbed the National City Bank branch next door. They ran from the bank, needed a place to hide and tried to smash their way into the funeral home. When they saw Allen and Johnson inside, they ran away, two heading across North 26th Street, the other two rushing for a car in an alley.

Johnson started to run after them. Allen screamed at him to come back, that it wasn't safe; police later found a gun in the alley. Johnson returned to find the robbers had dropped clothing, a knit hat and three bags of money on the porch.

And cash was spilling out of one of them, a plastic grocery bag.

"It was bundles and bundles of cash," Allen said. "The $10,000 wrappers were filled with $50 and $100 bills. There must have been 10 bundles in that bag."

Johnson started to return the money to the bank, then thought better of it, fearing that he might be considered a robber. Instead, he put it just inside the funeral home's door. Allen called 911 to advise police of the robbery.

Soon, 2nd District police were swarming into the area; Johnson motioned them down the street toward the area where the men had fled. Police captured two suspects in a car at 34th and Jefferson streets after a chase.

Police now suspect the other two robbers — playing it cool — walked into the nearby Victor Mathis florist shop, where they bought roses and a teddy bear. They paid cash and made two phone calls — one for a cab — before leaving the store on foot. The men are still at large.

With police chasing the robbers, Allen and Johnson stood guard over the astounding amount of cash at their feet. Nearby residents who had seen the four robbers bang on the door came over to look at the money, but Allen and Johnson asked them to leave. Both confessed to a little temptation — police might never know which robbers fled with how much money — but they never seriously considered taking any.

"Oh sure, it was right at Christmas, my car had just blown up; and Danny was having a tough time financially too," Allen said. "But I would never steal any of their money."

Johnson, who works construction during the summer and drives a tow truck at other times — was having a tough enough time that only days earlier he had applied for a $500 loan at the very bank branch that had been robbed.

"I just wanted to get caught up, pay some bills," he said.

Within a half-hour of the robbery, police returned to the funeral home and learned about the money. An officer guarded the money until the FBI came, followed by a bank examiner. That night Johnson got a call at home from a bank officer.

"When the woman identified herself, I first thought it was about my loan. But she didn't know anything about that," he said. "She told me banks don't normally offer rewards, but in this case it was going to give me $100."

Johnson took out the $35 it cost for the parts to repair Allen's car and gave the rest to Allen.

Two days later, the bank told him his $500 loan had been denied; he'd been too slow making payments on previous loans. Johnson admitted being slow to pay but said he had always paid in full by the time the final payment was due. Having chased robbers and stood guard over the bank's money he thought it might cut him some slack, but it didn't.

So George Villiar, Allen's father, lent Johnson the $500. Villiar has co-signed Johnson's notes before, and Johnson has always paid him back.

Human trust over bottom-line business. That's what's known as going the distance.   *Jan. 4, 1997*

Christmas memories are made this way

If your memories are of a hurly-burly Christmas, a crowded, old-fashioned Christmas with nieces and nephews chasing down a long hallway and grownups laughing in the kitchen, then Leora Paul has the house — and the family — to invite them back.

"Everybody tells me they don't feel it's Christmas until they've been here," she said.

Everybody is right. The Christmas season doesn't begin until Leora Paul throws out the first pitch. She's the Christmas commissioner; 81 years old, stocky, claims to be approximately 5 feet tall — although she may be bragging — and has the general demeanor of Mrs. Santa Claus at a Tupperware party.

She has lived in her Fifth Street home in southern Louisville for 73 years. Her parents and grandparents lived there before her. She recently held her 55th consecutive Paul family Christmas party. The usual 60-plus people showed up, four generations — wall-to-wall Pauls — all crammed into her small, 125-year-old home like Florida oranges in a wicker basket. Leora's full partner in memory-making is her sister-in-law, Mary Louise Fox, also 81. Mary Louise's first husband was Hugh Paul, who died in 1971. Their nine children have provided Mary Louise with 24 grandchildren and 18 great-grandchildren. All nine Paul children were present at this year's Christmas party, along with a seething majority of the succeeding generations, all carrying food. There was one bathroom for the bunch and two television sets — one each for UK and U of L basketball fans.

The smallest guest was Logan Brown, who made his Paul family Christmas debut at the tender age of 17 days. He was borne into the house by his parents, Joni and Rick Brown, a ripple in the deep river of people that continually flowed from the front door toward the kitchen, making a sharp bend through Leora's bedroom along the way.

"You ain't seen nothing yet," said one of the passers-by as coats and jackets began to pile 5 feet high on the bed.

Leora Paul never married; everybody just calls her Aunt Leora to keep life simple. To keep her Christmas shopping simple she buys gifts for everybody, pretty much grouping her purchases by age and/or attention span. She begins her shopping not long after Labor Day. She'll buy a few extra things in every category to be sure everyone is covered. "The younger ones get dolls, paint sets or trucks," she said. "The older ones get blankets. The nieces and nephews get towels."

Everyone, in turn, buys something for Aunt Leora. The mass opening of presents, the noise, excitement and blizzard of paper, is a moment to be remembered, protected and unwrapped the following year. The real wonder: Where does she keep all that stuff?

"The grandchildren won't go to their company Christmas parties until they come here first," she said.

They shouldn't. We're running out of such family traditions — crowded gatherings in old, angular houses; dark and mysterious hallways that little children can always associate with Christmas at Aunt Leora's.

They'll never see another Christmas kitchen like Aunt Leora's. It's something from the 1940s, with a 12-foot ceiling, worn linoleum covering a tilted floor, a sink jutting out from the wall; just about the way it was when Hugh Paul came home from the war on Christmas Day 1945.

They'll never see another livmg room like Aunt Leora's: the cabinets full of ceramic knickknacks; the same tiny Christmas tree perched on the same table for 25 years; Uncle Steve in his silly Christmas hat; Uncle Carl wearing his musical Christmas socks; the big, walnut Ellington piano in the corner.

They'll be hard pressed to hear a family singing Christmas carols in a house that has welcomed them for years, with two generations of family living in the place before that.

Six generations of family. One house. Christmas. For ever and ever, amen.

Dec. 24, 1996

A chilly, sullen day
of salvaging and sorrow

The day after the flood was gray and sullen, with a chill wind that made the brown water even more threatening.

Robert Nix was paddling four people down the center of National Turnpike in his green johnboat. We were on a mission of mercy — to rescue a dog and a cat owned by Kim Curtis, a passenger in our flat-bottom, easily tipped skiff.

On Saturday, Curtis, groping around her back yard in water up to her neck, had gotten her three children out of their home in Fairhaven Mobile Home Village in Jefferson County. To do it she had to carry one child over her head. Yesterday she went back for her pets.

"I was worried about the dog and the cat all night long," she said.

Yesterday was a day for many people like Curtis to save what they could, take stock of what was left, try to make some sense of a natural disaster unequaled in recent local history: more than 10 inches of rain in 24 hours.

People who never expected — never *dreamed* — floodwater would invade their homes, desecrate their most cherished possessions, had spent a night watching it sweep into their lives. They spent yesterday trying to salvage family pictures, wedding albums, fine books, historical documents and baseball-card and comic-book collections.

Many of them had sad, poignant or memorable stories of their own. In Jeffersonville, Marjie Phillips absentmindedly courted disaster driving down Middle Road. She followed a car through a wide wash of deep water, stalled her car in the middle about 100 yards from solid asphalt. She had a cellular phone and was able to get help.

"I had my mind on going to church," she said.

Near Fern Creek Craig Jennings led a tour of his CedarLake Townhomes apartment, where he and his wife had been awakened by somebody walking on their roof, pounding on windows, shouting: "We're flooded, everything's under water, get up."

His apartment smelled like wet newspapers. Workers were hauling off soaked carpet, dragging it like a dead animal across the parking lot, tossing it onto a moldy heap. The couple had moved into the apartment Friday. Most of their possessions had still been in boxes that were covered by water.

"My wife's wedding dress was in there," he said.

Rampaging floodwaters left necklaces of debris on front yards, ripped limestone rocks from walls, scattered cars nose down into ditches and culverts where they littered the road like props in a closed play.

Along Preston Highway, near Okolona, it seemed accident might conspire with disaster to produce a conflagration; a backhoe severed a gas line while repairing flood damage. Jefferson County police blocked off the highway, their red and blue lights flashing frantically. The line was repaired, but the smell of gas lingered a quarter-mile away.

But the most noticeable signs of damage in Jefferson County were near National Turnpike and Outer Loop, where floodwaters had receded a little, but were still dangerous.

Nix, the johnboat owner, had been helping others in the area. He volunteered to take Curtis and her mother, Linda Saylors, as far toward the Fairhaven Mobile Home Village as his boat would go; a rise of high ground would stop him.

The women had planned to walk in the rest of the way, braving water 3 to 4 feet deep to carry out the pets, a walk of perhaps a half-mile.

We rocked a little in the boat as it slid past National Turnpike landmarks: Baird's Auto Parts, Moby Dick, the Dollar General Store. The johnboat skidded to a stop in shallow waters, where County Judge-Executive Dave Armstrong was leading a flood inspection tour. He requested a National Guard Humvee for the rest of our trip. The Humvee growled into the deeper water, casting off spray like a speedboat, water sloshing across our feet inside the cab.

"Saturday night we were driving through water that came up to my chest," said Sgt. James Paynter, the Humvee driver. "It was a night of women and children first.... That's why we're here."

Curtis' mobile home looked like a barge. Buster, her Shar-Pei dog, was peering anxiously out the front window with a *"where-have-you-been"* look on his face. Curtis and her mother waded through the cold, waist-deep water and returned in a few minutes carrying Buster and Petey, an orange cat.

A grateful, excited Buster shivered and shook water all over inside the Humvee as it pushed its way back to high ground. From there a huge orange dump truck took the women and their pets back to their car — the same watery route Nix had to negotiate by johnboat.

Nix was gone. Curtis, Saylors, Buster and Petey went to find someplace warm.

March 3, 1997

Art versus smut: It's Deja Vu all over again in Louisville

The way I see this latest flap over nude dancing in Louisville, it has historically been OK to bare some body parts at the Kentucky Center for the Arts, but you couldn't bare all your body parts in city nightclubs licensed to serve liquor. One is art, the other is... well... not art. Apparently full nudity is better witnessed sober.

So answer me this: If you owned a nightclub and were trying to make a buck, would you rather serve alcohol at $7.50 a drink or Pepsi at $7.50 a drink? Do you really believe all those farm-machine-show guys head out to Seventh Street Road to sample its wine lists?

And now that a judge has ruled what's fair for the bared goose must also be fair for the bared gander, unlicensed, topless-to-nude dancing has been breaking out all over Louisville while everyone goes back to the drawing room to figure out what's proper and what ain't.

And to think the Kentucky Center show that helped produce this mess was the "Will Rogers Follies," a Broadway show with bare-breasted dancers.

It's always interesting when society, judges, lawyers, politicians, nightclub owners and the clergy try to figure out what's illegal, immoral or obscene. Hiding beneath this — and rarely discussed by city fathers — is the fact that Louisville is a major convention town, a place where a little controlled sin is good for business. Seventh Street Road: community asset or necessary evil?

About a year ago the search for truth in these matters brought me eye-to-eye with Bunny Glamazon. She had been classically billed by her proud employer — the Deja Vu nightclub, home of

100's of Beautiful Girls & 3 Ugly Ones — as the Tallest Feature Dancer in North America. I was especially intrigued with Bunny because altitude is not normally the prime selling point with feature dancers.

The Deja Vu lineup card listed Bunny as 6 feet 6, a nice size for small forward or shooting guard. It listed Bunny's horizontal proportions as 63FFF-28-38. She said she reached the 63FFF dimension by adding individual breast circumferences to normal chest measurements. She said she got to do that because she is the Tallest Feature Dancer in North America.

It was all too arcane for me.

By way of comparison, I am about 6 feet 5 and have invented in my dotage a new basketball position: Goalie. Let the other fellas run down to that far basket, I'll just wait here by this net until they get back. My horizontal proportions are none of your business.

Bunny was wearing heels. I was wearing Nike flats. I really don't believe she was up to 6 feet 6, but I'll give her 6 feet 4 and some change. Maybe 6 feet 5 in Air Jordans. A tall woman.

Yet Bunny did not make the column team; it was one of those times when I was all finished with the interview and didn't have a clue what to write. I might have made an obligatory stab at political correctness, but this was not a woman feeling the least bit exploited by a culture that saw her as a sex object.

Sex object was exactly what Bunny had in mind. She was selling it like Fran Tarkington at an infomercial festival. She proudly weaved a tale of corporate financial success. BunnyWear T-shirts, hats, videos and photographs had earned her a small fortune. Her booking fees were high — and getting higher. She spoke of personal growth. No glass ceiling for Bunny.

Then she went out on stage and picked $10 bills off men's noses with her body parts. It was hard to know who was exploiting whom.

I fully realize not all exotic dancers have the business savvy of the Tallest Feature Dancer in North America; it seems to me a lousy way to have to make a living. Yet while greater minds try to figure out how to solve this knotty problem I've got a temporary solution. Send the "Will Rogers Follies" to the Deja Vu and Bunny Glamazon to the Kentucky Center for the Arts.

That way nobody gets any ugly girls.

Sept. 24, 1996

A ring is bestowed with class and care

Bright sunshine spilled across the green grass of Harmony Landing Country Club in Oldham County as Bill and Lois Cromer walked, arm in arm, into 60 years of memories.

Lois, 77, knew nothing of what awaited her, two laughing grandchildren running into her arms gave her a clue it was something special, but her family had kept the secret well. Bill, 73, had almost given it away several times. Now, standing before a smiling group of family and friends, his secret was finally set free.

"Honey," he said, "these people are all here to help you celebrate the 60th anniversary of your high school graduation."

It was more than that — much more. It was a husband honoring his wife, three sons honoring their mother, friends honoring friendship. It was sweet, warm, nostalgic, funny and caring.

It began in 1937 when Lois graduated from Lake Worth High School in Lake Worth, Fla. She had attended commencement ceremonies with her class, but her parents, hurt by the Depression, could not afford to buy her a graduation dress or a class ring.

Bill had never really understood how much a ring meant to Lois until he pulled out his own high school ring last fall to wear to his class reunion in Miami.

"I never considered I would not go to college," Lois would say. "All I wanted was an education.... I studied college catalogs to make sure I was taking the right courses in high school. But there was no money. I never got over wanting a graduation ring."

They married in 1945, having first dated as members of the West Little River Baptist Church in Miami. She played the piano and organ; he sang in the choir. It was a pattern of devotion they have repeated over 52 years of marriage: Lois as pianist and organist at a series of Baptist churches, including three in Louisville; Bill as music director at the same churches and as a professor of Christian education at Southern Baptist Theological Seminary.

Bill began his quest for his wife's graduation ring after returning from his reunion. The Balfour Co. said a 1937 duplicate could be made. He contacted Lake Worth High School and was sent a photograph, a lapel pin and a 1997 yearbook. He wrote to First

Baptist Church in Lake Worth, where Lois was baptized; the minister sent a nice letter and some historical documents.

"I did all this for two reasons," Bill said. "I wanted to have some occasion for presenting this ring to her, and I thought it would be very nice and pleasing if she had some expression of the sweetness of some of the things she remembered from that graduation."

Sweetness is the only word for the graduation luncheon honoring Lois Spencer Cromer at Harmony Landing Country Club at 1 p.m. on May 17, 1997. She was ushered into the luncheon area to the taped strains of Mendelssohn's "War March of the Priests" - the processional of her 1937 class. The program listed the favorite movies and songs from 1937: "Snow White and the Seven Dwarfs," "That Old Feeling," "Thanks for the Memories." Old photographs, certificates and letters were given her in an album.

Bill Cromer knew how often his wife had worked in the background, playing music while others took the stage. He loved her for that, and a thousand other things, so he played a tape of Bette Midler singing "Wind Beneath My Wings" — "Thank you, thank you, thank God for you; the wind beneath my wings."

Then, 60 years after she should have received one, he placed a high school graduation ring on his wife's hand.

"In 1945 I put a ring on your finger," Bill told her, "and I'll put another on your finger now."

One of their sons reminded his parents they had kissed on that occasion in 1945, and they should kiss again. On a perfect afternoon in May, with family and friends moved to tears, Bill and Lois Cromer kissed one another and left the room to the timeless trumpet of "Pomp and Circumstance."

May 20, 1997

A picture-perfect fantasy

The word Jim Jeunesse kept coming back to was "fantasy." The phrase Myra Nethery used was "for the fun of it." The danger is in looking too deeply for reasons in a world much too worried about being politically correct.

Jeunesse, 58, is a longtime Louisville-area photographer, a man whose Yellow Pages ad mentions weddings and reunions but leads off with "boudoir." Nethery, 33, who leads karaoke singing in Louisville-area nightspots, was wearing a filmy white nightgown while posing for boudoir pictures in Jeunesse's home studio.

It is a scene repeated in Jeunesse's studio five times a week — and he knows of several local photographers doing the same thing. There is no need to call in the law, no need to bother the thought police; the women all willingly pose in the barest of lingerie, sometimes less.

The women are mostly the variety Jeunesse labels "the girl next door" — salespeople, real-estate agents, health-club employees, a social worker, a librarian and nurses, especially nurses. Most of them are women between 30 and 40, the oldest being 56. He estimates 75 percent of the women are married, and most of the others have a boyfriend; the boudoir portraits are for the men in their lives, not for public consumption.

In several eases, however — including that of a dentist's wife — the portrait in lingerie does go on the wall in a private office.

"I think the turn-on, so to speak," said Jeunesse, "is that when these women see their pictures they realize how good they can look. I don't think it's an erotic thing. There's just this hidden question mark; many, many women have this hidden desire to look as good as the girls in Playboy and other magazines. That's a recurring theme with my customers: Now their men will have something else to look at besides the magazines.

"I even had the wife of a blue-collar worker tell me that now her husband can put her picture in his toolbox."

Leaf through Jeunesse's thick album of satisfied customers and you can see the truth: The women do look good, some with the help of soft focus and adhesive tape, but many with a natural appeal the camera only magnifies.

"We've tried to get men to pose for portraits, but it just hasn't worked," he said. "The men just don't seem to want to do it."

Jeunesse, who worked in the photo lab at General Electric for 13 years before opening his own studio in 1967, said boudoir photography started in California about eight years ago. He began about five years ago, getting perhaps one customer a week. Now, through an advertising network that includes the Yellow Pages, cable television, a Louisville company that has lingerie parties for women, and even the help of a plastic surgeon who does breast augmentation, he gets about three inquiries a day. A woman can get an album of 12 pictures for about $165.

"I got a lot of business during Operation Desert Storm," he said. "One young couple had just gotten married when the husband was shipped overseas. She had one picture made and sent it to him. He wrote back and said, 'Send more.' She wrote and said they didn't have the money. He told her to get into their savings account."

Another Desert Storm wife posed topless sitting on her husband's motorcycle.

"I just let the women take their own lead," said Jeunesse.

Nethery, a short, pretty, ex-high-school-cheerleader with a radiant smile, knew about Jeunesse's work because her roommate had twice posed for lingerie pictures — and Nethery liked the results.

"I may give one of the pictures to a friend," she said. "I'm keeping the rest."

Jeunesse is a genial, non-threatening man with a white beard and thin white hair. There is a faintly anachronistic air about him; he mostly refers to women as "gals" but quickly puts them at ease with his professional manner.

"No one believes it," he said, "but this is hard work."

As soft music played, and Jeunesse constantly adjusted the lights, Nethery changed her sheer gowns and body stockings. She spread out languidly on a tabletop, crouched on all fours like a cat and leaned against a ladder looking pouty and coy, sometimes with only a gaudy red or white boa — another oddly anachronistic touch — covering bare skin.

Within the hour — as Jeunesse had predicted — Nethery moved from being self-conscious to sometimes taking the lead, but she didn't always look comfortable doing it.

"I'm a little scared and a little excited," she said, "but I'm feeling kind of sexy."

March 3, 1992

Does a law degree come with a literary license?

We highly trained and sensitive journalists are little comforted when such dilettantes as John Grisham — a *lawyer* for crying out loud — makes it so big with a book like "The Firm." It's just not fair. Journalists aren't allowed to stand before some judge begging for another continuance, so who gave Grisham license to write?

Worse, there is growing evidence that Grisham's success is encouraging a whole generation of writer-attorneys. Witness the case of New Albany's Jean Ann Banet, who was driving home recently from Churchill Downs with five people in her car when she was involved in a minor accident in Louisville.

No one in either vehicle was injured. It cost Banet $446.60 to repair her 1989 Pontiac — which probably meant a new hood ornament. What most amazed Banet was that, within a week of this non-injury accident, she had received letters from five Louisville attorneys practicing their writing skills.

Here are examples of their literary efforts — somewhat edited for space reasons. All their letters were carefully labeled as "advertisements." You be the judge. Is there another John Grisham in this bunch?

"Dear Ms. Banet: My name is David Kaplan and I am an attorney at law.... It has come to my attention that you were involved in an automobile accident. Also I understand that the accident appears to be the other side's fault. In cases like yours, you may be entitled to legal rights regarding any injuries you may have sustained.... I will be happy to offer any assistance regarding your accident.... Respectfully, David Kaplan."

"Dear Jean Banet: My office provides legal assistance to people who have been involved in automobile accidents. You may have been injured at the time of your recent accident. Often times, a person doesn't realize he (sic) has been injured until a day or so later. Sometimes the shock or surprise of being in a collision can mask the symptoms of injury at the time the accident report is made. If you find that you did suffer a personal injury, I can help you.... Very truly yours, Thomas H. Watson."

"Dear Ms. Banet: A review of recently filed accident reports at the local police headquarters reflects that you were involved in an auto-

mobile accident. As a result of this accident, you may have certain
legal rights, as well as legal responsibilities. In order to preserve
your rights it may be necessary to take certain actions.... there is
absolutely no charge for our first office consultation. In fact, if you
retain our office to represent you in any claims you may have, you
will owe us absolutely nothing unless we are successful.... Sincerely,
Kenneth W. Wall."

"Dear Ms. Banet: The accident report at the police station reflects
that you were involved in a car wreck. Because of this accident, you
may have legal rights as well as legal responsibilities. For an
absolutely free initial consultation on this matter, please contact
me.... Also please be advised that the new Rules of Professional
Conduct provide that an attorney may advance court costs and
expenses of litigation; the repayment of which may be contingent
upon the outcome of the matter. This is a matter we can discuss during your initial free consultation.... Sincerely yours, Stuart Lyon."

"Dear Jean Banet: Public records indicate you were involved in an
automobile accident.... For over 30 years I have been representing
people like you against insurance companies. I have the knowledge,
the expertise, and most of all, the practical wisdom to guide you....
Do not be misled, misinformed or fall prey to an easy settlement
from the insurance company. KNOW YOUR LEGAL RIGHTS.
Protect yourself. Get information from a lawyer. You have one body
and it has to serve you your whole life. Make sure you receive the
right medical treatment you need.... Very truly yours, Sidney
Hanish."

Quite frankly, my favorite writer of that quintet is Sidney Hanish.
He seemed to have a better sense of plot and inner tension, and I
was particularly impressed with his dramatic use of uppercase. Alas,
Jean Ann Banet wasn't impressed with any of them. She said, in fact:

"After reading these letters I am inclined to think I may never
have to work again. Letters like these promote unnecessary lawsuits.
It is no wonder why our insurance premiums on life and car insur-
ances are so high. In my opinion these laws need to be changed
because it encourages dishonesty."

Actually, Banet also received a sixth letter. It was from a chiroprac-
tor who didn't give a name, but did provide an address and phone
number and warned of potential injuries. That letter opens a whole
new literary field: Great novels by ambulance-chasing chiropractors,
perhaps "The Whiplash."

Sleep lightly, John Grisham, sleep lightly.   *July 17, 1993*

Rowing club's revival offers workout for the body and the senses

It's absurdly easy to wax lyrical about rowing — so focused, balanced and powerful; so beautiful to watch; so nurturing to the mind and body; the rowers alone in their sculls or with a long sweep of teammates.

The sport — the *art* — of rowing is especially nice at 6:30 a.m. on the Ohio River, a silver moon dissolving into the Western sky, the sun a misty, pinkish glow in the East, the needle-like boats flashing upriver toward the dawn.

"It's all I had hoped it would be — and more," said Beth Brown, 39, a Louisville Rowing Club member who converted from swimming about a year ago.

The 50-member rowing club is a nice mix of converts and the long committed. Its early-morning crew includes former Courier-Journal Publisher Barry Bingham Jr., a veteran rower. Louisville attorneys Sandy Taft, Jeff Skora and Joe Burke had all rowed in high school or college. Larry Steinberg, president of A-Bell Electric, began two years ago. Caterer and restaurateur Luckett Davidson began about the time Brown did; the two won the first race they entered.

Tori Murden, who in many ways has led this group up Harrods Creek with its paddles, tells a revealing tale of that victory.

"Luckett's daughter, J.J., called me the next day," Murden said. "She said I'd created a monster. Her mother had always been willing to help her, but now she wouldn't.

"Luckett was in bed wearing her gold medal and her pajamas and she wasn't going to move."

Murden, 31, a Harvard Divinity School graduate and policy analyst for Louisville Mayor Jerry Abramson, has a bittersweet rowing history. A great athlete at Louisville Collegiate, she began rowing at Smith College her sophomore year. Her success pushed her toward the 1992 Olympics, but on the way to the trials — after 18 months of excruciating training — she had an accident, wrecking her car and both her boats.

She borrowed a boat, persuaded friends to drive her to the sin-

gle scull time trials and did fairly well. She didn't do as well in the
actual race, only then learning there was good medical reason:
She'd broken two ribs and chipped a tibia in the wreck. She
returned to Louisville in a post-Olympic funk, found her way out
of it by coaching novice women at the boat club, then ruptured a
disc last summer. Eight weeks after the operation she won a
bronze medal in a race. She sent it to her surgeon.

She and Brown have set even higher goals. "We've decided to
compete in the Masters Nationals," she said.

Murden's revival has coincided with that of the Louisville
Rowing Club, which recently built a new boathouse at Harrods
Creek and 6511 Upper River Road — all the work done by volun-
teers.

The members gather early in the morning, placing their lean
boats in the water to the accompaniment of crickets, or in the
evening hours when many members row the sweep boats.

Morning workouts are often the most pleasing to the senses.
There is less powerboat traffic, fewer waves, a better ambience.
Murden and Brown were out yesterday morning, skimming along
the water beside Sandy Taft and Jeff Skora. The river was high,
and the boaters had to dodge black pieces of driftwood half buried
in the silver water. Several of the boats had neon-like, blinking red
lights, the only way they could be seen. The morning air was a
mix of cool mist and warmer land breezes. The two boats darted
side by side for several miles before the sweating rowers called it
quits.

"Nicely done," shouted Murden, her voice trailing lightly over
the water like a happy thought.

Aug. 23, 1994

TV turned O.J.'s house guest, Kato Kaelin, into a celebrity

I return from vacation refreshed, recharged and with a new goal in life. I want to become a fully ordained house guest when I grow up. I want to hear things that go thump in the night. I want to spend my formative years signing autographs in a shopping mall in Terre Haute, Ind. I want to be like Kato Kaelin.

I have visited with friends on vacation, perhaps overstayed my welcome as mold grew lightly over our worn conversation, but I've never become a full-fledged house guest. That's always seemed a distinction well out of my grasp — an upper-class thing, a money thing, a California thing. Closer to home we just call our house guests unemployed.

House guest. The very sound of it carries a certain mystery. It must be like summer camp without counselors, home alone forever; the shower always warm, the wine rack always full, the check always in the mail; please be close but don't get personal.

I am at some disadvantage here because I've watched little of the O.J. Simpson saga. From what I did see, Kaelin looked like a total frosted flake, the last kid to take a seat in the back row of English class, a Ken and Barbie doll, a shaggy dog story, a beach boy between convertibles, a gigolo between widows; charming, disjointed, suspect, goofy, non-threatening. All in all, the perfect picture of American, television-anointed, murder-trial celebrity.

Newspaper photographs showed Kaelin on the witness stand with one finger bored into a cheek, something you might expect from a certain class of Hollywood figures — like Shirley Temple. His eyes had the vacant look of an empty room. What's a daddy to do if a Kato Kaelin shows up on the doorstep in lustful pursuit of his naive daughter?

Kaelin knows his league. He made his first paid, post-O.J. appearance in Terre Haute signing autographs at a Bottom Half store. Kato Kaelin at a Bottom Half, irony beyond comprehension; what's right with this picture?

His appearance was for charity, but he couldn't even get that worked out. Originally supposed to raise money for the United Way of Wabash Valley, he was rejected by the chapter's executive director, Don Jordan, who said "Mr. Kaelin's status as a celebrity

and public figure stems solely from notorious and tragic circumstances. This United Way chooses not to be a beneficiary in these
circumstances." Instead, Kaelin appeared on behalf of United
Cerebral Palsy of the Wabash Valley.

Guess what? Depending on whose estimate you use, some 2,000
to 10,000 Hoosiers showed up, double-parked their combines outside the mall and went inside to gawk and say howdy to Kato.
Kaelin charged $10 for his autograph, $12 for T-shirts that said
"America's Favorite House Guest," all proceeds — apparently —
go to cerebral palsy. Six women stood in line for hours to be the
first to get Kaelin's autograph. I was surprised he knew cursive.

Kaelin first got plugged in Terre Haute at the request of Bo
Richards, program director of WMGI-FM, a top-40 radio station
with a target audience of females age 18 to 49. Kato actually did a
TV commercial for the station, but Richards — who found Kaelin
more than an airhead — wouldn't give details.

"Why Terre Haute? Because I suspect we were the first to ask,"
Richards said.

He estimated 5,500 people of all ages stuffed the mall when
Kaelin first appeared, another 3,500 outside. Many quivered and
shook when first shaking Kaelin's hand. Almost 20 law-enforce-
ment officers held back what at times became an overheated mob.
Five of them — all teen-age girls — were members of the South
Vermillion Kato Kaelin Fan Club. They had faithfully watched him
on TV after school, thought him polite, sweet and gorgeous. Other
kids from a high school mass-media class brought a McDonald's
box with them for Kaelin to sign because he had eaten there with
O.J. just before the murders. It should look swell in their video
yearbook. I can only hope they got some extra credit for their
efforts.

April 4, 1995

Brief encounter inspires thoughts on Derby, fate, fortune

I was waiting for a bus — the Toonerville trolley connector — to take me to Commonwealth Convention Center to pick up tickets for the Kentucky Derby Festival Parade. The old woman said she was waiting for a regular TARC bus to Southern Indiana to visit her husband in a nursing home.

I've never before bought parade tickets, mostly preferring to get out of Louisville before its downtown streets fill with people carrying aluminum lawn chairs and vendors selling aluminum balloons. I love the Great Balloon Race, endure the forced bravado of The Great Steamboat Race, generally like any Great Parade, worry about the Great Sameness of much of the Derby Week stuff.

So this year — our 20th year in Louisville — my wife and I decided on a new tack; attack Derby Week head-on. We invited family and our best friends from high school to the Great Show. We vowed to take in every Derby sight and sound we could manage, leaving no hoof unturned. Instead of fighting Derby Week ennui, we vowed to go with it. On its terms. With feeling. Just this once. Or twice.

The old woman was short — wearing black shoes and a worn blue dress. Her hair was long, uncombed, with wide streaks of gray. She held three quarters in her hands, constantly pressing them together, rubbing them the way a worried man rubs the tips of his fingers. A regular TARC bus had just left the stop, the woman had spoken with its driver, learned she was an hour early for the bus she needed.

I don't wait well, have always marveled at people who could. The woman accepted her situation with the patience — or the resignation — of someone who has waited before. She walked around a little, as if looking for a place to sit, but there were no benches near the bus stop.

She neatly stacked her quarters in one hand, shifted them around, the coins clinking faintly. It would cost her 75 cents to ride the bus to visit her husband between 8:30 a.m. and 3:30 p.m. The return trip — if made between 3:30 and 5:30 p.m. — would be $1.

It was mid-morning, bright and cheerful. Spring — Derby fever hung in the air like the scent of magnolias. Having gotten into the spirit of the thing, my wife and I had actually begun looking forward to it. She bought new dresses, an official Derby Hat, began polishing the plastic forks. I vowed to polish my shoes.

We mapped out a Great Plan, eager to show off Louisville, share its two minutes in the world spotlight, become as Derbystruck as first-time tourists. I had just purchased tickets to a Derby Week concert before heading to the bus stop, was mentally lining up other events, other purchases.

With little prodding the woman became talkative; her husband had been a security guard in another state, had gotten beaten up in a fight, filed a lawsuit seven years ago, it hadn't yet gotten to court. They had moved to Louisville — her hometown — but her husband's health failed. He was placed in an Indiana nursing home because no places were available in Louisville.

She receives $220 a month in Social Security payments, lives in a subsidized apartment. He receives $540 a month, but all but $30 goes to the nursing home; he had $50,000 in medical bills paid by the government. Twice a week she puts aside $1.75 for round-trip bus fare to see her husband, all she can afford.

Perhaps all this is some level of guilt disguised as slice-of-life, but I don't think so. I didn't feel any urge to hand over my concert tickets, give her money, or even a ride to Indiana. I still don't; our social services net seemed to be doing its job; TARC can handle the rest.

Our lives intersected for about five minutes, but the woman has never quite left my mind. More than anything I guess I wonder how many things must go right — or wrong — to allow some people to be buying Derby Week parade tickets and force others to hoard quarters for bus fare to go see their husbands in nursing homes.

April 11, 1995

A Thoreauly suited scholar's show sets you up for the falls

What more fitting place for a visit from Henry David Thoreau than the Falls of Ohio Interpretive Center in Clarksville, a splendid building perched above its own body of water, a place you should see now — this very spring weekend — to best become acquainted with its craggy, fossilized isolation and the healing powers of nature.

Thoreau appeared at the center Tuesday night with the help of Dr. Kevin Radaker, who wore his Thoreau suit — workman's clothing and suspenders — along with a beard that leapt from his face like magnetized iron filings. Radaker, English Department chairman at Anderson University in Anderson, Ind., has long studied Thoreau, his transcendentalist thoughts, his religious messages.

"My profession is to be always on the alert to find God in nature," said Radaker-as-Thoreau. "To know his lurking places...."

Many of us know the "bumper-sticker" Thoreau, a man more often quoted than read. We toss out the smaller, better-digested nuggets of his often-dense prose. They live because they still resonate truth 150 years later. Thoreau's preachings against conformity, materialism and technological advancement could have been written yesterday. Listen to two of them: "Money is not required to buy one necessary of the soul," and "The mass of men lead lives of quiet desperation."

My favorite — loftily tossed out every time it is suggested that my wardrobe could use an overhaul — is: "Beware of all enterprises that require new clothes."

Thoreau had a receptive audience — the Friends of the Jeffersonville Township Public Library — although some seemed a little long in the tooth to be totally taken with Thoreau's essay on civil disobedience. He thought people — as a matter of conscience — should not obey any government rule considered unjust.

At 29, Thoreau even spent a night in the Concord, Mass., hoosegow after refusing to pay his poll tax to protest his government's condoning of slavery. He was freed by his Aunt Maria, who paid the tax to avoid further family stress. That must have been embarrassing, but what's a poor anarchist to do?

He is most remembered — and quoted — for his book "Walden," an account of the two years, two months and two days he lived in a small cabin he built — with some help — on Walden Pond, a good mile from the nearest McDonald's.

"There is some of the same fitness in a man's building his own house there is in a bird's building its own nest," he wrote.

"Walden" evolved over five years, and seven writings, mostly because previous books had done so poorly that Thoreau had publisher problems. His cabin was roughly 10 by 15 feet and had only three chairs. Four chairs, he explained, would have been "society." Not to mention a tight fit.

He headed into the woods alone not to repudiate civilization, but to intensify his experience, to live "deliberately."

"Be a Columbus to a whole new world and explore the continent within you. Explore thyself," he urged.

Sure. Easy for him to say. The guy was a bachelor with his own tiny pondside home and a large garden. He didn't have car and insurance payments, didn't sweat any day-care or private-school payments. He had the time to walk the woods, wax poetic over bitterns, urge others to enjoy the three prime rules of personal real estate; simplify, simplify, simplify: "I want to drive life into a corner, reduce it to its lowest terms," he said.

The point is *he made time.* He was an idealist, a mythmaker, perhaps a bit of a fraud — he went home on weekends to eat with the relatives — but he endures because the message remains absolutely true: "Men are slowly buried alive under the burdens of their possessions."

Thoreau most feared he would "come to die and discover I had not lived." He died of tuberculosis at 45, a little young in his discovery process. At least he'd found a way to walk meadows and trails, wade in still waters, smell the piney woods. What are you doing this weekend?

April 6, 1995

A lot happens when cups run over with honesty

Many of the 16 men and women were strangers to one another. So it was the white styrofoam cups that made it work. The subject matter was too delicate, too personal to be handled without some sort of crutch, even a styrofoam crutch.

The subject was Sex and the Single Person: The Celibacy Option.

The location was a Human Sexuality Workshop held yesterday at Indiana University Southeast in New Albany.

The Rev. Joe McNally, of Columbus, Ind., a part-time worker at the Louisville Family Relations Center, was the group's spiritual adviser, coach and dispenser of the cups.

The celibate McNally was equal to the task. He set the tone with a joke about the minister who continually complained that half his flock went water skiing on Sunday mornings. For years the minister pledged he would lambast water skiing from the pulpit. But the Sunday he picked to lambast the sport, most of his flock showed up. So the minister spoke on sex instead.

The next day, many parishioners stopped his wife in a store and told her what a wonderful sermon her husband had delivered.

After a half-dozen compliments, the exasperated wife, who didn't attend the service, replied:

"I don't understand it. He knows very little about the subject and he's only tried it twice."

McNally went on to speak of his celibacy as a commitment to a higher calling. But conversation soon drifted beyond his option.

The larger group broke down into smaller groups of four each. McNally gave each group one cup. He asked that each person handle the cup according to his or her views on human sexuality.

The cup, as it passed from hand to hand, became a personal symbol, a means of communication.

There was nothing intimate about the room. The groups were scattered about in theater seats from 15 to 20 feet apart. But the people became bonded by a need to say something, and an even stronger need to have someone who would listen.

"I drew a smile on my cup," said a woman. "I wanted it to

express a totality of all communications. I want others to feel what I feel."

"I took the bottom out of our cup," a man said. "I wanted to put myself in the middle. I want to hold onto the traditional ways, yet be open-ended."

A middle-aged woman held up her cup intact and quietly told a room full of strangers, "I related to the emptiness in the cup. I am a fairly recent widow.... I guess it is a symbol of emptiness in my life."

A priest in the audience said the cup was ripped when it was handed to him, but he put it back together.

"Then I put it next to my head," he said. "I think a lot about my sexuality. I wanted the cup close to me."

"I just held my cup tightly," a woman in a different group said. "I'm trying to find myself. I just had a very bad relationship. I'm afraid of people."

McNally handled the styrofoam cup first in his group. He ripped a half-inch section down one side explaining he felt more people needed to get inside, to understand their own sexuality.

The young man next to him held the cup firmly in his hands, trying to heal the wound.

"I wanted to infuse it with warmth," he said, "I want to close it back up."

The third group member almost crushed the cup in her hands: "Sometimes I have mixed feelings," she said. "What I feel about my sexuality isn't always what some other people want me to feel. I'm being misunderstood."

The fourth group member, a young red-haired woman, gingerly straightened the sides of the cup.

"You have to know your whole self," she said. "You can really get confused. But once you get yourself together, you can really break loose."

She handed the cup back to McNally. The circle had been completed. Each had touched the other. You could feel the closeness. Four lives had merged briefly over a white styrofoam cup.

Jan. 18, 1979

Some journalistic chores leave one with a Grade A guilty conscience

The message came, as they tend to do, in small, inadequate pieces. It said:

Dr. Isabell Masters, running for pres., independent ticket, arriving Greyhound 7.45 a.m. — 7:30 p.m. speech, Church of the Living God, 2401 W. Madison St.

Not many presidential candidates arrive Greyhound at 7:45 a.m., at least not at this stage of the game. By now, most come in with all their flacks blazing, their arrivals well-greased by media co-ordinators, their messages already known, their positions already clear, or professionally obtuse. The only reason the media need go to those press conferences is to be sure some nut doesn't show up waving a loaded pistol.

It was closer to 7:59 a.m. when Masters' big bus with "NORFOLK" written across the front pulled into the station. It, and Masters, had been 17 hours en route from Topeka to Louisville. The St. Louis layover lasted about three hours. She rides the buses because the death of five relatives in a plane crash will forever keep her off airplanes.

The news release, prepared by the church, said:

Dr. Isabell Masters, the 2nd Black (woman) in the history of the United States to run for the U.S. Presidency, brings her campaign to the city.

The former schoolteacher and wife of the first U.S. Black Marine Sgt. Alfred Masters, who returned home from combat duty shellshocked and wounded, which subsequently led to a broken home and later to his death. Sgt. Masters received little attention from the government to help him adjust emotionally, physically and economically.

The 69 yr. old Topekan with a 2 1/2 yr. old Ph.D from the University of Oklahoma will discuss:

• Better benefits and considerations for veterans.
• How to improve: The quality of Education.
• The preservation of health and life on this planet.
• How to reduce High Federal Deficits, Excessive Government

borrowing and wasteful government spending.

• The polluted environmental conditions, the war on Mother Nature and the economy.

Masters, the mother of six college graduates, emerged from the bus looking only a little the worse for the experience. She wore a bright red dress, white shoes and silver earrings. A button pinned to her dress said, "Ms. Who for President in 84."

She explained that her campaign is an extension of her personal evangelism. The decision to run came as a devine revelation in 1981 while riding in a bus from a family visit in Washington, D.C. The revelation occurred about 100 miles out. She announced her presidential bid last Oct. 15 in Topeka.

We talked in the bus-station coffee shop. I kept trying to probe her feelings on the total hopelessness of her situation. She kept saying it didn't matter.

Her campaign gives new meaning to the term "grass roots." Her campaign stops are often in places where she has family or friends, such as Louisville. Once there, she rents a room in a Holiday Inn or Quality Inn and speaks.

She complained a little about the fact that the media discriminate against candidates like her, refusing to cover her talks or take her seriously. I tried to explain why, falling well short. We didn't talk much more about it after that.

From my side of the table, it seemed as though the interview was going badly. She was trying to explain how she would get on the ballots in some states and become a write-in candidate in others. There was no doubting her sincerity, sanity or intelligence.

So I felt a professional obligation to keep asking serious questions, but all the while doubting voices in my head were shouting, "She can't do it! It just ain't gonna work! You're just sitting here playing word games!"

I don't like that feeling. I'm always afraid what I'm really thinking will show on my face. We wrapped the interview up in about 20 minutes, and then she asked if she thought someone from the paper might cover her talk in which she would explain all her positions in more detail.

I told her I thought we should, but I wouldn't be able to make it.

May 28, 1984

Good will, all bottled up and adrift for 10 years, still works its magic

This is a really neat story about caring, coincidence and catching time in a bottle.

It began in October 1985 at Springmyer Elementary School in suburban Cincinnati. A new principal suggested as a school-unity project that each class write a letter, drop it into a plastic two-liter bottle, toss it into the Ohio River and wait for an answer.

Environmental concerns being what they are, we don't do these things now. That's too bad. There's something so marvelously mysterious about notes in a bottle, the whole mystique of having a message bob away to who knows where, to randomly connect with strangers in a distant place. Surely there are biodegradable ways to continue this magic — containers that would harmlessly melt away over time.

One Springmyer teacher, Margie Wright, created a bottle-writing assignment. She asked her 26 second-grade students to write a special greeting, the best one to go in the bottle. The winner was Meghan Gibbs, whose writing style was charming and to the point:

"Hello friends. We are students in Mrs. Wright's second-grade class at Springmyer School in Cincinnati, Ohio. If you find our bottle, will you please write us a note telling us when and where you found it. It's fun to discover new friends in faraway places."

All the students signed the letter, their penmanship classically second-grade: sprawling, enthusiastic, somewhat readable. On Oct. 25, 1985, Meghan — and 40 other class representatives — went to the Ohio River near Anderson Ferry. A handful of small stones was placed in each bottle as ballast, to keep their necks above water. Away the letters sailed.

Time passed. Margie Wright retired from Springmyer in June 1987. In 1990, she and her husband bought a large motorhome and set out on a six-year odyssey across the United States, visiting their three children and eight grandchildren.

Meanwhile, Meghan Gibbs' family moved to Wisconsin. A dozen of her classmates went on to Oak Hills High School in

Cincinnati, where they are now seniors, looking forward to graduation in a few weeks.

The two-liter Pepsi bottle also moved on. It floated past Riverfront Stadium, swung south past Rabbit Hash, Ky., and Rising Sun, Ind., survived passage through the Markland Locks and Dam and finally washed ashore at a riverside settlement called Bushman's Lake in northeast Clark County, Ind. — about 110 miles and 10 years from launch. Jane Younger and a friend, Don White, who own a house near the river, found it last September.

"Don was cleaning up after a flood," Younger said. "He was tossing stuff away when he saw the bottle. He almost threw it away, then he saw something was in it."

The bottle had yellowed. The laminated letter had faded, but it was still easily readable. Younger, fascinated, turned detective. She called Springmyer, learned that Margie Wright had retired. Younger found Wright's address and wrote her a letter, but Wright was traveling and didn't answer.

Younger called the Cincinnati Enquirer, which did a story on the bottle and the dozen Oak Hills seniors who launched it — with a current photo. A PTA group at Springmyer wants the bottle and letter for a display; Younger will provide them with both. None of the other 39 bottles has been found.

A few weeks ago, Margie Wright and her husband — still traveling — were eating breakfast at a Bob Evans in Lexington. She glanced at a Cincinnati paper and saw the story of the letter and the photo of her former students, now grown up and about to graduate. By sheer coincidence she had caught time in a bottle. She quickly wrote Younger a long overdue letter:

"I take pride in informing you that each of those precious children brings back so many warm memories of my years in the classroom.... The greatest reward of teaching is to know you have made a contribution to the lives of so many. I still miss it! Sincere regards, Margie S. Wright."

May 23, 1996

A wanderer's soul,
a salesman's heart?
A life of quiet dependability

Sometimes people's lives just unfold in front of you; rich, complex, poignant, surprising and, ultimately, uplifting. So it went with Rocky and Vera Reichel. So it will go with you.

Rocky, 76, had been advertised as a man who took daily walks in his neighborhood. That he does, walking his way through the sights and sounds of Germantown, the Highlands, Bardstown Road and Cave Hill Cemetery. He has no genda, no regular route, no buddies to meet over coffee.

"I guess I just like to walk," he said. "I like to see what's going on."

Vera Reichel, 70, was born in the Vine Street house where she and Rocky live. They have been married 51 years, had three children. One of them, Gary, was an artist who created fun, interesting, eclectic stuff: busts of Albert Schweitzer and Groucho Marx, a

Vera and Rocky Reichel

huge shoe patterned after the one he had to wear after contracting polio. Gary died in 1980.

Rocky went into World War II working in supply. After the German breakthrough at the Battle of the Bulge he was drafted into the infantry, fighting his way across Germany. He came home in 1945, married Vera, began his career as a salesman. For 30 years he sold a variety of things: bleach, carpet, organs and pianos. He sold Electrolux vacuum cleaners door-to-door. He was a parimutuel clerk at Churchill Downs. He was — and remains — a relentlessly upbeat mam who enjoyed what he did.

Vera met Rocky in 1941. After their marriage she worked as a receptionist. She often wished Rocky wouldn't work quite so many hours as a salesman. But Rocky was a salesman. He had to sell. He always kissed Vera goodbye before leaving the house — even for his daily walks. He still does.

"Every time," said Vera.

Last week Rocky kissed Vera goodbye and headed north on Vine Street, passing a big Lincoln parked at the curb, the only sign of ostentation at a neat, tidy home filled with family heirlooms and memories.

"Vera always wanted a Lincoln," Rocky said. "I got her that about five years ago."

Rocky was wearing a brown shirt, tan slacks and brown wing-tip shoes. He never wears walking shoes. He doesn't trust them; Rocky tries to buy only things made in America.

"I always have," he said.

Rocky is a man of wide tastes. His bookshelves at home are lined with history and biography. He loves the theater and opera, collects old records, taught himself — at age 40 — to play the piano and organ so he could get a job selling them.

"My father could play five instruments," he said.

We walked east on Breckinridge Street, north on Barret and then east on Morton Avenue into the Highlands. Rocky, a short, thick-set, Mickey Rooney-ish man, set the pace. He rested only once.

Vera worries about Rocky when he is gone. His children bought him a cellular phone to carry on his walks, but he won't do it.

"I've never been bothered by anyone," he said.

Rocky has three pianos and organs in his living room. He used to play at nursing homes; now he plays for Vera. Some nights Rocky will play for hours while Vera sits nearby on the couch with her craft work. Rocky always finishes with the same two songs.

He plays Vera's favorite: "Blue Eyes Crying Rain." Then he plays "We'll Meet Again" for their son, Gary.

Every time.

June 6, 1996

Food mart helps put boy back on track

It wasn't any one thing that got so many people at K's Food Mart interested in Jason Easley. There was just something likable about the kid: the unassuming way he hung out and took kidding; his intelligence and street smarts all caught up in his adolescent vulnerabilities; the sense Jason could be — *should be* — doing more than he was doing.

"We all just thought, let's see if we can help him," said Bryan Goranflo, manager of K's.

His store is in Louisville's Highlands neighborhood, at the corner of Bardstown Road and Speed Avenue, a busy, cluttered place with a couple of gasoline pumps and a seven-days-a-week outlook on retail life. Jason Easley, 13, grew up in the neighborhood, rode his bike to K's on errands. The food mart survives on service and banter with regular customers. Jason gave as good as he got.

"Jason and his brother came in here for years," said Goranflo, 28. "I watched them grow up. Then all of a sudden he was grown up and was hanging around here all the time. We began to wonder why isn't he in school?"

Jason had been living at home with his mother, Mari Anne Easley. His parents are divorced. His mother is a cook in a nursing home, doing all she can to care for Jason. She doesn't drive, can't afford a car and often walks the three miles to her job, leaving home at 5:30 a.m.

Jason had perfect attendance from kindergarten up to fourth grade, always an A or B student. As he grew older, as his mother struggled to balance family and work and pay medical insurance and $475-a-month rent, Jason's schoolwork suffered. Last year — his first at Highland Middle School — he missed 63 days.

At best, adolescence is a challenge. Jason's older brother had moved away, leaving him home alone. Jason had difficulty making friends, fell in with the wrong crowd. He would smart off to teachers, got suspended for a fight. His grades fell to all F's. He began hanging out at K's more and more, kidding with clerks Andy Byrd, 22, and Kevin Allen, 23.

"After he caught on that we all wondered why he was in here all the time, he began waiting until 2:20 p.m. to come in," Goranflo said. "But he still wasn't going to school."

Many customers also noticed Jason, including Sheryl Ann Soderberg, a retired teacher. She asked Goranflo, Byrd and Allen about him, then went one step further.

"I'd gone to school with Bob Knight, the principal at Highland," she said. "I asked him about Jason, and he said his only real problem was truancy; Jason did very well when he was in school."

Team K's collectively made a decision: It was going to get Jason Easley up, running and back in school regularly. Beginning last May — as soon as school was over — Goranflo & Staff made Jason show up at K's at 8 a.m. every morning.

Byrd and Allen watched him as they could at night, inviting him over for video games, replacing the brother Jason had lost.

"We talked to him a lot," Goranflo said. "We told him he was at the point in his life where he had to make some decisions. We insisted he come in here on time. Basically, we just wanted to get him up."

Bruce Pierce, a dean at Highland, became involved, worked with Jason and his mother. Jason returned to school this fall with a whole new support group, one that mixed understanding with a dose of tough love.

"We knew he thought it was something of a privilege to be able to come into the store," Goranflo said. "So we told him if he didn't get his homework done, he couldn't come in."

The early news is encouraging, Jason has missed six or seven days this year, but his grades were all A's and B's. Now he wants to be a football player or an accountant; perhaps go to Trinity or St. Xavier. The gang at K's is pleased — with only middle school, high school and college to go.

As the saying goes, sometimes it takes a food mart to raise a child.

Nov. 21, 1996

Teaching can - and should - be a very educational experience

Doss High School teacher Wayne Kolb didn't give me enough rope to hang myself. His was a kinder, gentler approach, the right approach; he allowed me just enough rope to twist slowly, slowly in the wind. It was a very educational experience.

Kolb wrote part of Thursday's column about schools and teaching. That same morning I returned the favor, serving as a substitute teacher for three of his classes in American history and world civilization. Kolb did not tell his students who I was, or why I was there; they had no idea and didn't care. Kolb prepared a lesson outline for me as he would any substitute teacher, then sat in the back of the room to watch.

Have I mentioned it was a very educational experience?

OK, it was also part lark, no true test of what regular teachers — and substitute teachers — go through. I taught three hours and got out. I didn't have to face Kolb's most difficult class, grade papers, prepare the next day's lesson, worry about the six to eight absent students who had fallen further behind. But I got a taste of it, a gut-level sense of the growing stress and frustration in teaching — and a small sliver of the rewards.

"What *do* you do when three of four students keep falling asleep in your class at a time?" I asked another Doss teacher.

"With some of them," he answered, "you let them sleep."

His somewhat facetious answer was a nod toward the reality of teaching a class of about 26 students, at least half of whom have full- or part-time jobs at night. Many of them come from bent or broken families; at least four students already are parents — mothers and fathers. Toss a half-dozen serious discipline cases into that mix and you'll let sleeping problems sleep.

"A constant challenge" is the teachers' mantra. With reason. Of the roughly 75 students I had in three classes, I doubt if three of them had read the assigned text. It wasn't that all were unwilling to learn; every class had its obvious complement of intelligent and curious students. Rather than reaching out to even touch, much less embrace, education, their attitude was more like "OK, teach me." They flat dared you to teach them something. If you got through — and there were times I did — they seemed grateful, but unable to admit it, at least in obvious ways. I could sense those small victories, began to covet them.

Discipline was a constant aggravation, sapped a lot of attention and energy. Many students made it plain — in speech and deed — that they didn't want to be there. These were, in many cases, average and above average, intelligent kids who just didn't connect with school. School was a waste of their time. They had little sense of what they could be, should be — or that they could make a difference. They were just floating through the system like driftwood.

One student, who loudly complained about the newly imposed Doss High School dress code and the school's discipline, will join the military after school. He would welcome the discipline there, he said, because he *wants* to be there.

Many students were at once streetwise — if not world-weary — yet very immature. It's a struggle to get them to connect the past with the present, to see how Supreme Court decisions involving slavery and desegregation affect their lives today, or the modern-day relevance of the Magna Carta.

OK, I remember 16; much of that detail didn't float my boat either. But I've always had a general sense of history, of tying the past with the present, that seems to be missing in our MTV generation.

My first period nemesis was a girl who demanded to hold forth, to test me, to pop off at any and all times on any subject. There was a sharpness to her attitude, a defiance and anger I couldn't deal with in 50 minutes. I confronted her several times, but was not going to let her win, send her to the office or let Kolb referee. Finally, mercifully, she pulled a jacket over her head and pretended to sleep.

To keep things going — and substitute teachers can get away with this — I generally ignored the lesson plan, seized on subjects like capital punishment, abortion, busing of students and racism to get through the hour. My happiness was a girl in second period; she was smart, outspoken and had read the text. She, too, held forth, but more with an honest desire to show what she had learned.

When I think about substitute teaching — and I will do it again — I want to remember her, those brief moments when much of our class was energized — if not awake — when our debate really was an educational experience.

Dec. 14, 1996

Legends like Satchel Paige never really strike out

The newspaper account said Satchel Paige is about to begin work on a television film on his life, "Don't Look Back — The Story of Satchel Paige."

ABC will televise the account of the last of the great baseball legends just before the 1980 World Series.

A newspaper account pegged Paige as being somewhere near 74, give or take a decade, an age which he admits has partially limited his effectiveness.

"The doctors cut out part of my lung two years ago when they found a cloudy spot on it," Paige said, somewhat apologetically, "but I could go an inning against today's hitters. Nothin' wrong with my arm."

Paige got his nickname as a 12-year-old railroad porter in Mobile, Ala., by carrying six suitcases at a time; three each on two sticks he'd prop on his shoulders.

His exact age became shrouded in mystery forever when a goat ate the family Bible containing the pertinent information. Paige had 22 years of barnstorming in the Negro leagues behind him when he got his first shot in the major leagues in 1948 with the Cleveland Indians.

Bill Veeck gave him the chance, calling him up in mid-season. Paige won six, lost one, and had a 2.47 earned-run average, leading the Indians in the World Series.

He made it look easy, but, of course, he was only about 42 at the time.

I saw Paige about 10 years later. He was finished with his taste of big-league champagne by then and was back touring bush towns in a bus straight out of "The Bingo Long Traveling All Star and Motor Kings."

In those days, any self-respecting town with more than 1,500 people had its own baseball team of former local high school heroes, plus a pitcher who was imported from the next county over at $25 a game.

The teams — and I played on two of them — were kept alive by just enough donations from local merchants to buy one uniform per player. The lucky individual would then go to bat carrying the colors of "HARRY'S GULF SERVICE," or the like.

We also always had at least one player who reached AA ball, and who had once been to spring training with a major league club. These individuals were always treated with a special deference no matter how poorly they ran the bases. We even hesitated to borrow their bats.

Just one season of AA ball, coupled with one shot at major league spring training, is generally worth a lifetime of deference in small Midwestern towns.

The "Satchel Paige All Star Team" played against just such a town team one humid evening deep into the summer. The game was only a few miles from where I lived. My old man was as hot to see Paige as I was, so we went together.

The ballpark was a fine one by small-town standards. It had bleacher seats wrapped tightly behind a wood and chicken-wire backstop, and honest dugouts with a ledge where you could prop up one leg while staring across the field at the opposition.

The game was played at night, thus demonstrating that the local club was at least solvent enough to pay its light bill. Several years later, the same club had to cancel the second half of its season at the cold-hearted request of the local utility company.

Its policy was, and remains, I am sure: No pay, no play!

Paige kept us all waiting for at ime, allowing a few youngsters to pitch before making his appearance. He ambled from his darkened bus with all the enthusiasm of a chicken headed toward the chopping block. He was said to be 6-foot-3 and 185 pounds, but the latter was in the vertical creases of his uniform.

Paige took center stage about the fourth inning, his team ahead by a few runs. My old man, long opposed to racial intolerance, was hoping Paige would set the corn-fed locals on their ears. I just wanted to see the man pitch.

He was lean and angular and threw from grooved memory. He was not as fast as the youngsters, but much more crafty. His face rarely showed expression. He threw the ball, and his catcher threw it back, shoulder high, to avoid wasting the old man's energy.

Paige had a good shortstop behind him and two good outfielders, but the locals touched him for two cheap runs to tie the game. He held them off the next two innings, striking out five men in a row, always throwing with exactly the same motion, throwing easily, throwing as he had for almost 35 years, throwing from habit, throwing to ballplayers he would never see again in a town he couldn't remember, throwing, throwing, throwing, throwing.

In his third and final inning, Paige gave up a double to one of the locals who once had his picture in the paper for being one of five shortstop candidates at the Chicago White Sox spring training.

The locals scored twice behind that double, some younger pitcher came in to end the rally, and Paige went back to his bus to wait for his next game.

April 17, 1980

Chapter Three

SORTA SILLY

It didn't take me long to figure out
these Sorta Silly columns were mostly
written on days when nothing else
had appeared to make filling the space
easier. I mostly enjoy attempting
Sorta Silly columns because they
require taking more chances, trying to
skate by on humor, irony, satire or a
strong sense of the absurd rather than a
nice series of adjectives.
The chances of failure are always
greater with the Sorta Silly concept —
and the rewards are not necessarily
higher — but there is some satisfaction
in creating substance from
very, very thin air.

Job applicants work hard at making outrageous statements

Here's an optimistic start for the new year — in Indiana and Kentucky. A friend of mine who spends too much time cruising the Internet came across a survey of vice presidents and personnel directors of the 100 largest American corporations. Each was asked to describe his or her most unusual experience interviewing prospective employees. Read 'em and weep.

• A job applicant challenged the interviewer to arm wrestle.
• Interviewee wore a Walkman explaining that she could listen to the interviewer and the music at the same time.
• Candidate announced she hadn't had lunch and proceeded to eat a hamburger and french fries during interview.
• Candidate said he never finished high school because he was kidnapped and kept in a closet in Mexico.
• Balding candidate excused himself and returned to the office a few minutes later wearing a hairpiece.
• Applicant said that if he was hired, he would demonstrate his loyalty by having the corporate logo tattooed on his forearm.
• Applicant interrupted interview to phone her therapist for advice on how to answer specific interview question.
• Candidate brought large dog to interview.
• Candidate refused to sit down and insisted on being interviewed standing up.
• Candidate dozed off during interview.

OK, we all have bad-hair days. But the employers also were asked to list the "most unusual" questions that had been asked by job candidates.

• "What is it that you people do at this company?"
• "Why aren't you in a more interesting business?"
• "What are the zodiac signs of all the board members?"
• "I know this is off the subject, but will you marry me?"
• "Will the company move my rock collection from California to Maryland?"
• "Would it be a problem if I'm angry most of the time?"
• "Does your company have a policy regarding concealed weapons?"

- "Why do you want references?"
- "Does your health insurance cover pets?"
- "Do you think the company would be willing to lower my pay?"
- "Why am I here?"

Certainly a question we all have asked from time to time, but probably not in mid-interview. If you've not yet been persuaded to spend a little more time studying the Japanese industrial society, here are a few of the more unusual statements made by job candidates during the interview process.

- "I have no difficulty in starting or holding my bowel movement."
- "At times I have the strong urge to do something harmful or shocking."
- "I feel uneasy indoors."
- "Sometimes I feel like smashing things."
- "I think Lincoln was better than Washington."
- "I am fascinated by fire."
- "I like tall women."
- "Whenever a man is with a woman, he is usually thinking about sex."
- "If I get too much change in a store, I always give it back."
- "Women should not be allowed to drink in cocktail bars."
- "Once a week, I usually feel hot all over."
- "People are always watching me."
- "Almost everyone is guilty of bad sexual conduct."
- "I never get hungry."
- "I know who is responsible for most of my troubles."
- "If the pay was right, I'd travel with the carnival."
- "I would have been more successful if nobody would have snitched on me."
- "My legs are really hairy."
- "I think I'm going to throw up."

Jan. 2, 1996

We've been talking up
a storm about the weather —
and Noah

The recent rains — full buckets of almost biblical proportion — sent me in search of history's worst weather report: Genesis 6-10. It's the story of Noah, 40 days and nights of soggy torpor. Talk about your Constant Alert Tone.

Noah was on my mind because I, too, spent time this week nervously gauging the strength of protective wooden beams as ill winds and rain rattled our shelter. Even as I sat in our basement deeply regretting past sins, I couldn't escape the notion that weather forecasts are now so tied to ratings that meteorologists might — on occasion — gild the barometric lily to draw attention.

Their quest is to solve that problem that has baffled us media types for ages: How many ways can you tell people to come in out of the rain?

Not long ago meteorologists knew their place: a few minutes standing in front of silly little maps holding grease pencils. Then station managers figured out what we've known all along: People just can't get enough weather. If all is calm at home, we will endlessly watch repeats of a typhoon slamming ashore on Bora-Bora. Combine that obsession with weather satellites, six-color thunderstorms and professional meteorologists with wit and/or presence — and we're all hooked for 10 hours at a time.

It's fascinating to sit at home — portable radio or television on hand — and eavesdrop on the forces of nature thrashing around outside in the yard — or five states over. Our ancient ancestors could only cower in caves — or perhaps go off and sacrifice a few virgins — while trying to figure out where it all went wrong.

I sat in my basement wondering what the modern meteorologists — or team of reporters and meteorologists — would have done with Noah's flood. Coverage would begin, of course, with a constant alert tone, followed by an emergency weather broadcast from Jarah, the station meteorologist:

"This just in: The National Weather Service has issued a flash-flood warning for the entire world, including Egypt, Mesopotamia and Babylonia. Our radar has indicated a severe line of thunderstorms and possible tornadoes spreading from the North Pole to the South Pole.

"These storms are accompanied by high winds, lightning and camel-sized hail. Please pack up your tents and move to a place of safety, preferably among the wine-cask supports in your local vineyard. Please do not leave your jackasses tied to olive trees. If you must be outdoors, do not seek shelter near trees, but seek low areas away from river banks.

"We will return in a few minutes with a live demonstration of how to use your Turkish towel. But first our live coverage begins with a report from Hebeth, who's with our skycam located near Mount Ararat. Hebeth, what can you tell us?"

"Thanks, Jarah. Hope you've been keeping your pomegranates dry. I've been able to spend the past 15 minutes with a fascinating man named Noah, who seemed to have some advance warning of the storm. Noah has been mighty busy leading animals onto this large, barge-like boat you see behind us, but he has agreed to spend just a little time."

Noah, who looks young for his 500 years, shows up on camera, a dove under each arm. He is glancing nervously up at the sky, jokes a little with Hebeth about not needing his sundial for the next 40 days. Hebeth doesn't understand. He shrugs his shoulders, begins the interview:

"Noah, that's a fine-looking vessel you have there. Could you tell us something about it?"

"Solid gopher wood, every deck and cabin. She's about 300 cubits long, 50 cubits wide and maybe 30 cubits high, counting all three decks. Me and the boys did all the work. Sort of a rush job, but it should be good for 150 days or so."

"You must have been expecting this?"

"Truth is, we were tipped off a little bit. Our original orders were to take two of every living thing, male and female, along for a ride. The order was later amended to seven pairs of clean animals and birds and a pair each of unclean animals which was a whole lot better deal. I was beginning to worry about the feed bill. If you'll excuse me now, I've got some work to do."

Noah walks up the gangplank behind Hebeth, disappears into its side door. Hebeth faces the camera. A driving rain plasters his shirt to his chest. The skycam turns in all directions; the heavens are gray, ominous, forbidding.

"That's it from Mount Ararat, Jarah. Be sure to tell all those

watching at home to go to a place of safety and to please stay
indoors unless they must go outside. I hope all you folks back in
the studio are warm and dry. It's a jungle out here."

May 20, 1995

Now, a timeout from hard sells (*not* brought to you by *Bob's Used Tires*)

I was watching a college basketball game the other night while
becoming increasingly irritated by the gratuitous use of commercials at every break in the action — *this slam-dunk highlight
brought to you by Calvin's Coffee & Doughnut Shop.*

Actually, "irritated" isn't the right word. I find this growing tendency to drop in mini-commercials after every petty analysis,
timeout, score, random statistic or loose ball to be distracting and
infuriating. *These pregame "points to ponder" brought to you by
Danny's Dartboards.*

I expect shameless money-grubbing from professional teams. I
realize these poor college programs need the money to keep the
wolves from their luxury boxes. I know commercial sponsorships
were needed to purchase new scoreboards for Freedom Hall — the
old scoreboard being Mickey Mouse beyond belief.

No doubt television stations mostly call the marketing shots.
But why must we suffer for our basketball allegiances? Must every
break in the action bring a ham-handed attempt to sell something?
*This foul brought to you by Don's Dynamite Shop — More Boom for
Your Buck.*

I fear where this type of advertising is headed. Newspapers
have shown an increasing tendency to cut staffs, reduce news
space, find new and exotic ways to increase revenue, pound the
bottom line into black ink. *This particularly pungent paragraph
brought to you by Irvin's Black Ink & Quill.*

If newspapers begin gratuitously slipping commercials into
news copy, the potential for revenue is enormous. *Looking for high
revenue figures? Call Sal's Stock-Market Salon, 1-800-BIG-BUCKS.* We
journalists are already accused of slipping too much opinion into

the news. Public trust in the media is 25 points below pathetic. Imagine what it would be like fighting your way through commercials just to get to the bottom of a newspaper column. *Kick-boxing, self-taught; call 1-800-NYRFACE.*

We newspaper types tend to place ourselves well above that kind of thing, morally repulsed at even the suggestion of directly mixing news and revenue, unable to imagine doing crass things like live remotes from newly opened car washes. *Carl's Custom Car Care — Your Clean Windshield to the World.*

I realize there is a tendency to overreact to even the possibility of this less-than-subliminal advertising. But look no further than the recent Connie Chung episode with Newt Gingrich's mother to see just how far journalism has fallen. Imagine the possibility of further damage if newspaper advertising was somehow linked to Chung's — and CBS' — unethical, unconscionable behavior. People like Chung make me ashamed to be in the same business. *For sale, female dog in heat; call 1-800-HIL-LARY.*

I take great pride in my work, my profession. Like many journalists — at least journalists of yore — my first two years in the business were spent on the police beat. It was a wonderful training ground where I witnessed the savagery with which human beings can fold, bend and mutilate one another. *Marty's Mortuary — You Stab 'Em, We Slab 'Em.* I was also strengthened while watching incredible acts of human generosity and spirit. *Drink Your Milk at the Cup of Human Kindness Cafe, 1100 Elysian Way.*

Those early years were not without some bizarre moments. I once covered an auto accident where a radio reporter was dangling a microphone over the mouth of the car's driver, who was lying near his crushed car, badly frightened and moaning. When I inquired about this scenario, the reporter said he would use the moans as background for an upcoming public-service message on driver-safety education. *Sam's Sound Studio & Supplies — Your Ear to the Ground.*

It was about then that I wrote the best lead of my newspaper life. It was a story about a man who rode his bicycle through a plate-glass window without being hurt: The rain of pane fell mainly on Bill Smith Tuesday night. The copy desk killed it. *Need Job Counseling? Dial 1-800-RAGE.*

Those were the moments on which to launch a job path, a career. *Marty's Model Shop & Rocket Supplies — As Close As You'll Ever Get to the Moon.* From there, I went on to the education beat, where my first night on the job 1,800 teachers went on strike. I came to Louisville during the anti-busing disturbances. I quickly sought refuge in column writing, an opportunity to open my own window to the world. *Diane's Doors & More: Your Hinge On Life.*

For all of those reasons, I would hate to see my 27 years in the newspaper business sullied in any way by cheap commercialism. *Need a Reality Check? Dial 1-800-BG-MONEY. No credit necessary. Your check is in the mail.*

Jan. 7, 1995

Will faithful woolly-worm watchers fall for tool tales too?

I have never doubted for a second the steady use of woolly worms, brilliant chickens or the thickness of raccoon pelts to predict winter weather. They are all nature's creatures, endowed with her great and mysterious prescience, each at least as intelligent as Willard Scott.

There are woolly-worm skeptics, of course, people who roll their eyes at the thought of grown men and women taking seriously the meteorological prognostications of creatures too stupid to stay out of the middle of a busy highway.

Not me. If the lowly woolly worm knows enough to beef up ahead of time for a tough winter, then who am I — forever buying my winter wear in great haste at discount shops — to argue?

I did worry about the urban folk, the people who live some distance from fatted woolly worms, brilliant chickens and plushly pelted raccoons. If city dwellers missed the media coverage of the woolly worm predictions, they would have no idea what to expect; their winters would be a continuing surprise, a shivering ruin.

Then, while walking through the garage over the weekend, I noticed something very unusual, my leaf rake had grown 2 inches longer.

"Wife," I shouted, "come here. Look at our leaf rake handle. It's grown 2 inches longer, a sure sign of a bad winter."

My wife, who also believes in the abilities of fatted woolly worms, brilliant chickens and plushly pelted raccoons, came out of the house, examined the rake, confirmed my suspicions.

"I'd better check the cedar chest for some extra blankets," she said.

As she left, I walked around the garage, looking for other tell-tale signs of impending doom. Our early December weather had been very warm, practically balmy, but it soon became obvious it would not last; our car had grown another coat of protective wax. "Wife," I shouted, "come back out here. Look at our car. It's grown another coat of protective wax. We are surely in for a white Christmas."

Off on a mission of her own, my wife could not hear me. My neighbor, Curtis, was out in his yard raking leaves. I ran over to him, eager to impart the news.

"Curtis, my rake handle has grown 2 inches, and my car has grown another coat of protective wax. These are certain signs of a terrible winter; constant blizzards and ice storms. Did you know that?" Curtis — holding *his* rake about 2 inches higher up the handle — said he'd already gotten the word.

"My snow shovel's grown a reinforcing bar," he said.

I ran back to my garage, searched the rafters for my snow shovel, remembered I'd left it behind the fertilizer and bug sprays. I hauled it out of its dark and dusty corner, took it out into the sunlight and held it aloft for Curtis to see.

"Look," I shouted. "My shovel's grown a reinforcing bar *and a* fatted blade."

Ice scraper? Where was my ice scraper? It could furnish further proof of a bleak winter. I searched beneath my cluttered workbench, alongside the air compressor, found it. Wow! My ice scraper had grown a leaner blade with a titanium edge. Just bring on Mr. Jack Frost!

I sat down on a yellowing box of 1989 calendars, feeling good about life, its ability to sustain itself. Yes, the country folk had fatted woolly worns, brilliant chickens and plushly pelted raccoons, but urban folk could have winters foretold too.

My wife came rushing back out of the house, eager to tell me something. I stopped her in midsentence: "Don't say a word. I already know. Our wool winter blankets have gone electric."

Dec. 5, 1995

For a writer, this columnist sure has a way with words

Humor columnist Dave Barry — the only guy in America other than Newt Gingrich who gets me laughing out loud — recently described a man as being "a few ice cubes short of a tray."

That, of course, is your well-reasoned insult. It was first made popular — at least in my callow youth — with: "a few bricks shy of a load." I did say callow, not creative.

When I was an adolescent, almost all of our communication was delivered through insult. We would stand around for 45 minutes before school, ripping each other without mercy, but generally with an "understood" edge; putdowns were the social currency of the day.

Maybe that was just a guy thing; we didn't have the slightest idea how to express any real affection. It would have been embarrassing beyond belief had anyone actually tried. We all would have had to transfer to different schools.

The well-reasoned insult was a first cousin to another of our adolescent mutterings: the damning-with-faint-praise phrase. One of my favorites was attributed to former NFL football player and actor Alex Karras, who once told a dancing partner: "Geez, for a big girl, you don't sweat much."

With the current overload of political correctness, stiff-necked politicians and a million special-interest groups ready to pounce on even the suspicion of insult or injury, it's become a lot more of a challenge to properly insult people.

We've lost something there. Too often our insults are crude and rude. Our politicians hurl venom and invective — mostly in desperation or in intellectual poverty — trying to overcome with volume their lack of wit. But with so many people still deserving of scorn, what's the harm in trying a softer, more deftly aimed approach?

Here's a quick list of insults you might want to try out on your neighbors, friends, elected representatives or old school chums. Some well-reasoned insults are obviously variations of an old theme — "He's all hat and no cattle"— but you gotta stick with some standards.

Some of the damning-with-faint-praise efforts do require a little black humor: "Those post office people do a great job of delivering the mail — when they're not shooting each other."

But it was fun to try to invent a few classy, even thoughtful, insults and phases. The list was compiled as simply — and correctly — as possible, primarily for those of you whose conveyor belts don't quite reach the barn. Here goes:

The guy's about two rungs short of a ladder.

She's all harpsichord and no music.

For a Hoosier, you talk pretty good.

We really didn't notice your big feet until the part where you danced with the leprechaun.

As far as I can tell, her disc brakes never quite come to a full stop.

That guy's about two carburetor turns short of a tuneup.

You look like you've lost some weight; you been sick?

I don't care what the mayor says; I thought the parade was a success even if the squad car followed too close behind the horses.

Coach is about three feet short of a yard marker.

You two make such a cute couple, sorta like a woofer and a tweeter.

Coach is about three ticks shy of a 24-second clock.

Her yard light is on, but it's still dark in the gazebo.

Pastor is about three songs short of a hymnal.

She's all fuzz and no tennis ball.

Aren't you too tall to be such a good writer?

He's all buckle and no belt.

That kid's about three pegs short of a pup tent.

I don't believe her floor tile gets all the way to her corners.

For a Baptist, you seem pretty enlightened.

Coach is about two quarts shy of a water bucket.

Listen, for a first-time effort at writing your autobiography, I thought the first two paragraphs went very well.

For a columnist, you seem to be fairly intelligent.

Coach is about two wraps short of an adhesive roll.

Let's look at the bright side of this; until Billy fell over the guardrail, Scout Troop 127 had never looked better

July 22, 1995

$2,000 neckwear is knot a joke; tie it, you'll like it, says salesman

It is a movie. The Armored Car Service bulletproof truck backs into a little niche in a store on the River City Mall. Two armed, uniformed men emerge, each showing great concern for The Task At Hand. One man is carrying a white box. The second man guards the first. They march resolutely into Rodes' downtown store. Their uniform shoulder patches bear their creed: The Life of an Employee — A Sacred Trust.

The guards escort the box to a table covered in black cloth. Three men wait anxiously behind the table. One tears the paper from the box. The television news camera grinds in for a close-up. The white paper and big box fall away. There are four smaller boxes inside. They each contain one necktie. One is priced at $2,000. A second at $1,000. The last two are $250 throwaways.

The ties are full Windsor-knot proof that no one should go broke underestimating the taste of the American public.

The $2,000 number is a bright, gaudy, beach-towel blue. It is an exclusive Countess Mara original studded with nine diamonds (.498 carat) set in 14 karat gold on silk with cut velvet.

The $1,000 tie is a bright, gaudy, canary yellow. It is studded with three diamonds (.16 carat) set in 14 karat gold.

The ties are to good taste what Attila the Hun was to Rome. They are engraved, his-and-her platinum toothpicks in the jewelry box of life. They are made for people who want to cram their money right up your optic nerves.

That, of course, is why almost four dozen of the $1,000 models were sold nationwide last year.

And worse, a special $3,000 model, undoubtedly the Countess Mara Flaming Tacky Special, was sold this year before it could get to Louisville.

"Different strokes," says Countess Mara representative Len Collins, "for different folks."

Collins is a crafty, practical, likable man. Salesman that he is, he is very willing to take your mind in whatever direction you are leaning.

Collins was in felt hats for 10 years before switching to ties. He talks in the clipped Eastern phrases of a man who can tell you five ways to go over, under or through the Hudson River.

He is given to saying 20 syllables in what should be 30-syllable sentences. He tries to talk in roses, but sometimes day lilies come out instead.

"The men wear these ties until it becomes a soil situation," he says, "and then some take the stones and make earrings for their wives."

He tells his tale of Countess Mara.

"The lady has passed now," he says.

He explains the countess was married to some upper New York state royalty. (If Collins can supply the story then he is allowed to supply the upper New York state royalty.)

He says the countess criticized her husband's neckwear one morning at breakfast. Her husband reportedly told her to do better.

"She being a lady of ability to sew," Collins says, "she did. Her ties all used to be made individually by her."

The armored-truck promotion is a good gimmick for Rodes. A small crowd gathers to watch and gape at the expensive ties, along with the regularly priced models. To be fair, some of the ties were attractive. They will be on display at Rodes for several days.

There are a dozen ties in the $125 range, including a monumentally ugly dark blue item embroidered with light green leaves and purple grapes.

"Hey," says Collins, throwing up his hands, "the eye of the beholder."

The beholders crowd in. A white-haired lady says she can't afford to buy too many of the $1,000 bright yellow ties, but says maybe she can swing just one or two.

"I think it's just exquisite," she says.

There are other believers among the beholders, but no immediate buyers. Collins doesn't really expect any immediate buyers. He knows his market.

"You can't talk anybody into a $2,000 tie," he says. "You don't have to say anything."

March 27, 1979

Political oratory preys on convention watchers

I went into the kitchen for breakfast Wednesday morning after one very long evening of watching and listening to the speakers at the Democratic National Convention and learned the entire nation had altered its speech patterns and thinking overnight.

My wife, for instance, said to me: "I have put all my efforts into eggs, not eggshells; into pancake batter, not empty patter; into coffee, not just caffeine; for I have seen and heard the truth, and it is terrific."

"Better," I answered, "to see fresh ideas rise in the pan than to watch old promises rot in the refrigerator."

At that point, our son came into the kitchen and announced that the old-fashioned preaching at the Democratic National Convention had changed his life.

"Was it not the Rev. Jesse Jackson who said he would rather see Franklin Roosevelt in a wheelchair than Ronald Reagan on a horse?" he asked. "Was it not Alice McDonald, the Kentucky superintendent of public instruction, who said President Reagan has put money in bombs, not books, that he has funded guns, but not grades, that he will improve missiles, but not minds?"

"Yes," we answered, "for it is better to light a thousand near-alliterations than to curse the darkness."

"Then what this nation needs," he said, "is new bends, not the same old dead ends; new style, not the same old miles; new skies, not the same old lies; new reach, not the same old speech."

"Better," I replied, "to have one new idea travel on foot than 10,000 foolish notions going Federal Express."

Our daughter, who had watched the convention at a friend's house, came into the kitchen to join the conversation.

"The Smiths were very excited about the convention," she said. "Mr. Smith said right after one of the speeches that he had replaced his despair with care; that he was once uptight, but now had seen the light; that he now found it better to lift a single finger to help the homeless than to shake an angry fist at the Internal Revenue Service."

At that point, my neighbor Bottomly came over to borrow the lawnmower and stuck around to ask a favor.

"My lawn is so great and my time so small," he said. "Yet I think if we join together, if we all hold hands and push toward that same magical goal, if we ask not what we can do for the neighborhood, but what the neighborhood can do for us, we shall not be a selfish place of little people with big problems, but a self-less place of big people with little problems."

I told Bottomly to get lost and go mow his own lawn; we were too busy talking about the convention.

He had barely left when the gas man showed up in his compact car to read the meter.

"I seek not only readings, but writings," he explained. "I do not want to be a faceless part of a big utility company, but rather a well-utilized part of America's industrial face. For it is far, far better to run in peace and union brotherhood with America's gas companies than to allow America to run out of gas."

I told him the check was in the mail.

Later that day, I stopped by for a haircut and found my barber also apparently had been up much of the night watching the convention.

"Please take a seat and wait your turn," he said, "because I have decided to put much of my time in charity, not chumps; into goodness, not idle gossip; into peace, not hair grease."

I quietly took a seat.

"The convention fell upon me like a canvas tent of truth," he explained. "Where once I may have been chaotic and despotic, now I am learned and concerned. Where once I was seedy and greedy, now I am alive and revived."

I asked him how long he thought the feeling might last.

"It is hard to judge," he said, "but I know now that all people, the mean and the green, the old and the bold, the abused and confused, are all the same people under the lather."

I got up and headed for the exit.

"Where are you going, brother?" he asked.

"I have learned," I said, "that it is far, far better to work hard to open the door of hope for all people than it is to just sit idly by hoping the door will open."

July 21, 1984

The happy gas you get with 'service' makes it easy not to get too pumped up

I needed some gas early yesterday morning, so I stopped by one of those mega-service stations soon to be fortified with a 10-foot wall of bagged cypress mulch and pulled up to Pump 16.

"How are you?" the pump asked.

"Gas pumps can't talk," I answered.

"My name is Sheila," said the pump. "I can talk."

I looked around. Most modern gas stations have a speaker system where the attendant inside the store can talk to customers at the pumps. The attendant here was busy with a customer, though. He wasn't even looking my way. I was having a conversation with a gas pump.

"So, do you come here often?" Skeila asked.

Actually, I do. The station is handy, open 24 hours a day. It sells the working journalist's breakfast: sugar-rich apple turnovers and 96-ounce soft drinks. I can buy a Powerball lottery ticket whenever the jackpot crosses into the $60 million, fool's-gold plateau. But I wasn't going to spill my guts to a gas pump.

"Often enough," I told Sheila.

I was annoyed. I longed for the old-fashioned pump, the simple, honest kind where you pulled up, lifted the nozzle, filled the tank, paid the attendant and left.

Now the self-service customer is forced to make decisions. The customer must select "inside pay" or "outside pay." The customer must study octane ratings the way dieting secretaries read "Thirty Days to a Better You." The customer must choose "unleaded," "better-unleaded" or "super-unleaded." The customer must request the car wash, the hot wax. The customer must worry about the environmentally improved nozzles and reformulated gas. The customer must "Push to Start." The customer must pay with cash or credit card, punch the right computer buttons, be sure to "Pull receipt firmly."

I don't want to deal with life's complexities at a gas pump. All I want is gas.

"So Sheila," I said, "what's a nice pump like you doing in a place like this?"

Sheila didn't do coy sarcasm. She was pure business, all the way up to her "Stop Engine-No Smoking" sign. But I did wonder if Pump 16 was programmed to be a "Sam" if a woman pulled up. It was just a thought.

"I am the first in a new line of gas pumps," Sheila said. "Our company surveys have shown the average person spends 37 minutes a month just standing beside a gas pump, squeezing the trigger finger. Our company believes we could offer many other personal services during that time."

Actually, if you can ignore the fumes, I mostly enjoy those 37 minutes of down time. Most of the gas-purchasing decisions have been made by then. You get to just stand there, lost in thought, watch digital numbers race past, even play a little game with yourself: *Geez, those numbers are cookin'. Can I really stop this sucker right on $10?*

All that's left to do after that is to slop some gas on your shoes while replacing the nozzle, then go inside and stand in line another 37 minutes while the guy in front of you buys 9,000 exotic lottery tickets.

But I wanted to play Sheila along, see what else a gas pump might have to offer.

"I understand what you're saying," I told her. "It's the old captive-audience thing, sort of like the advertising on the wall above urinals."

"We prefer to call it marketing the opportunity," Sheila whispered.

"For instance?"

"There's a lot of wasted space on gas pumps. We may sell advertising, add automatic bank tellers, sports scores, motor-voter registration, even give tourist information or stock reports. We could go online, surf the Web, offer airline reservations and 1-900 telephone numbers."

I looked around again. The station was bathed in that peculiar, death-like, all-night-gas-station light. I did not want to be seen arguing with a gasoline pump about 1-900 phone service. I leaned toward the pump:

"Listen, Sheila. We are talking about a major philosophical difference here. All I want to do is buy gas, which already requires an advanced degree in macroeconomics. So stick a nozzle in the rest of that stuff."

Sheila went silent. I went inside to pay my $10 and find a 96-ounce soft drink. When I came back out, Sheila was talking to a good-looking thirtysomething guy in a Camaro about Club Med reservations. I couldn't be sure, but I thought I heard her say something about the Caribbean and free suntan oil.

Feb. 10, 1996

City wants house razed, but one wag is howling at the notice

The truth be known, Lula Mae Clark's little doghouse is taking on water. The thing is held together with rusty staples and old duct tape. Its roofing looks like a kindergarten project done on the last day of school. If its plywood walls were any thinner, you could throw a can of dog food through them. The name over the door must have been done by a giddy barn painter.

But it's home. Not necessarily a castle — not even a stable — but a place to flee to in a world too much with us.

At least it was until Lula Mae Clark — half pit bull, half Jack Russell terrier — received notice by registered mail from the City of Louisville's Department of Inspections, Permits & Licenses "concerning the need for the immediate demolition of the structure and all appurtenances located at 602 Caldwell Street, Louisville, Kentucky."

Oh, boy. At first glance it seemed as if the City of Louisville wanted to take out a doghouse.

But there was one large problem with the demolition notice: the canine Lula Mae Clark lives with her owners, Terry and Larry Clark, at 2809 Jomarie Court, miles away from Caldwell Street.

Still, as the Clarks' mailman told them as he delivered the notice, "I don't know how to tell you this, but I've got a certified letter for your dog."

Larry Clark, a man of considerable humor, read the letter, understood an honest mistake had been made, and did not let that deter him from some honest fun.

"I called the inspections department," he said. "I told a woman there I knew Lula Mae's house needed painting, her roof leaked and I'd had to tear out the carpet, but I couldn't believe the city was going to come out and tear it down."

"Did Lula Mae sign for the letter?" the woman asked.

"No," Clark answered, "I had to sign for her."

"Why?"

"She can't read or write."

"That's a shame."

"Well, what do you expect from a dog?"

The mailing included a card asking that properly owners who shared a common name with the owners of property to be demolished — and who received the notice in error — please sign the card and return it.

First Larry Clark wrote on the notifying letter: "Lula Mae Clark is our 3-year-old dog ... she can't read or write yet." Then he found a red ink pad, slapped Lula Mae Clark's paw print on letter and card and sent them back to the city.

"I don't understand any of it," he said.

The truth is understandable, but not quite as much fun. The canine Lula Mae Clark got her name from the Clarks' daughter, Stacey. The other Lula Mae Clark lived at 602 Caldwell St. in a house the city now finds worthy of demolition — but no trace of her can be found.

To fulfill its legal obligation, the city sent registered letters to anyone whose name was even close to Lula Mae Clark — including people listed in the phone book as "L. Clark." By sheer coincidence, one of those L .Clarks had a dog named Lula Mae.

Clark said Lula Mae is very upset by all this. In fact, protest signs are being hand-pawed in Clark's office: "We're Not Going to Sit for This One!" "They Wouldn't Do This to Lassie!" "Go Fetch, Yourself!" "Dogs are People Too!"

Even worse, Lula Mae may soon be putting the bite on people for protest money. Another fine kennel of fish we've gotten ourselves into.

May 22, 1997

This Wildcat still needs to prove that he's hungry to play

Poor Walter McCarty. Here we are on the eve of the biggest basketball game of the season and the poor kid can't gain weight fast enough to please his boss — University of Kentucky coach Rick Pitino. Many are the players — former UK blimp Melvin Turpin comes to mind — who have eaten themselves out of basketball. McCarty has been ordered to eat himself into basketball — or he'll not start again.

"Yes," said Pitino, the Mad Dietitian, "I'm using this as a motivational tool."

McCarty has tried to do the right thing. When the senior showed up at UK five years ago he was 6 feet 10 inches tall and weighed 184 pounds, roughly the dimensions of a floor lamp. Pitino — believing McCarty to be about 50 pounds short of his guaranteed NBA meal ticket — had only sage coaching advice.

"Walter," he said, "go eat."

Eat? McCarty went at food like a pit bull at a postal workers' convention. Breakfast was three sausage biscuits, three pancakes, 4 ounces of syrup and 20 ounces of fruit juice. Lunch was five pieces of fried chicken and 32 ounces of Gatorade. Dinner was two submarine sandwiches — a 6-ounce and a 12-ounce — washed down with 20 ounces of fruit juice. McCarty's bedtime snack: six slices of pizza and 16 ounces of ginger ale. Counting between-meal snacks, he was packing in 10,461 calories a day. Anyone else would look like the Pillsbury Doughboy. A beached opera singer. The Capitol Rotunda. McCarty could get up to only 222 pounds.

"He's got to be 230 pounds," said Pitino.

Coaches are like that. It's all about willpower — gutting it out, if you will. Coaches are control freaks; they set goals, structure practices, sell multimillion-dollar shoe contracts, do commercials and order endocrine glands to get with the program. Coaches are often in desperate need of reality checks, but you can X this O all the way to the food bank: If McCarty doesn't hit 230 pounds, McCarty's on the pines when the horn sounds.

McCarty — God love him — says he's ingesting all he can for the Cats.

"I'm eating French toast and bacon for breakfast," he said, "and a lot of burgers afterwards."

It hasn't been enough. While some of you may be worrying about the Cholesterol Police, Pitino apparently believes there have been nights when McCarty's food intake has slumped; perhaps only four slices of pepperoni and cheese washed down with 15 ounces of ginger ale.

That's not a pretty picture, coachwise. While there may be nights when McCarty's eating technique is off — a breadstick might fall into his meatball sauce — there's never an excuse for lack of effort. Pitino wants McCarty to make it happen, pay the price, step up to the table, take a cheeseburger for the team.

"It takes extreme dedication," Pitino said. "He's showing dedication, not extreme."

So here we are, the Cats about to host the University of Louisville, the nation's basketball eyes on Lexington and — at last count — McCarty was still eight pounds shy of an authorized load.

"I'm fed up with it," Pitino said.

Easy for him to say.

What to do? We don't want either team with any ready excuses, although with Louisville — Team Yo-Yo — it's hard to know which players will show up hungry. My first thought was a Cheeseburgers for Walter campaign. All fans — Cats or Cards — could mail cheeseburgers to McCarty in Lexington — or just message encouragement via Cheeseburger@catlodge.com. But I'm sure the NCAA Cheeseburger Violations Unit prohibits such — even to the calorie-deprived.

If the game were in Louisville, Cardinal fans could hold up giant cheeseburgers when McCarty went to the free-throw line. In Lexington, Wildcat fans should just hold up pictures of Melvin Turpin.

Dec. 19, 1995

Portfolios are nonsense
up with which he will not put

To: My Kentuckians Fellow.

From: Larry Forgy.

Subject: Reform educational.

Much lately has been made of my criticism of the Kentucky Education Reform Act, the part about writing portfolios especially. Some Kentuckians — mostly Democrats — are complaining that pandering I am to the common denominator lowest while wanting your governor to become. Please clarify let me this.

I believe that writing well important is. As we used to say when I was back growing up in Logan County: "The key of knowledge the door of success unlocks."

Having that said, let me explain my position further. Times these are when the basics of life are fast escaping us while our educational system has become down mired in teacher paper-pushing and little children portfolios writing.

Our teachers need time to more better the alphabet teach. We need to the basic skills return. Proper expression and syntax we can later teach with these building blocks in place fully.

Like my basketball coach used to say back at Lewisburg High School: "Larry, your pants you gotta put on one leg at a time."

Along with the basics of education, discipline to the schools we must restore. When governor I am elected I will personally each school principal a letter write outlining my program for in-class-room calm restoring. Each principal I will direct to write me with the results. Orders — summarily executed — these students and principals will be on behalf of everyone.

Discipline I know. When I was a student undergraduate at George Washington University, my job it was 48 hours a week directing traffic in the nation's capital. Stood there I did, at waving automobiles from 50 states and sometimes drivers Canadian. There I learned all and for once that order from chaos must come. There I learned a structure you cannot build without infrastructure solid first having. There I learned the prime rule of education: Stupid, simple keep it!

Examine let us these fangled-new KERA writing portfolios a lit-

tle closer. Do sentences clean and thoughts clear we really want? Is
there merit any in asking little children to essays write, poems pen,
short stories attempt? Ask — I must — if well expressing oneself
is *that important?*

So subjective this is. Poor teachers overburdened already must
read now the essays, poems and stories of these children little.
Poor teachers overburdened already must into tiny minds peer to
see inside what is at home. Poor teachers overburdened already
must a grade place on a story short, a poem incomplete. Too much
educational envelope-pushing, all that is.

Remind me, it does, of an old saying I first heard while five
years on the state Council on Higher Education serving: Why fool
with a new tractor when the old mule paid for is?

My educational fears and concerns, sincere and genuine they
are. Long-suffered Kentucky has with a school system that worthy
is not of the people of this state fine. Understand your worries, I
do. Writing well and expression thoughtful may appeal to pin-
heads intellectual and editorial writers crazed, but give Larry
Forgy a chance at real educational reform in Kentucky.

Leave you let me with this message. Heard let it be from
Hickman to Hindman, in every school and polling place loudly.
Heard let it be by every parent teacher and school administrator
unwilling to change give a real chance:
Red are roses
Violets be blue.
To become your governor
Anything I'll do.

Oct. 24, 1995

Will garbage workers become big tippers?

Could there be a better, feel-good story in this age of cynicism
and divisiveness than having two sets of Louisville sanitation
workers hit Lotto Kentucky jackpots virtually back-to-back?

Well, yeah, on second thought there could: You or I could cash
in on Lotto Kentucky jackpots virtually back-to-back-to-back.

Feel-good.

Feel-good.

Feel *real* good.

Failing that, however, let's hear it for the men and women who pick up after all of us. It's tough work. There's a certain egalitarian justice in their success; if someone else has to win, let it be the people who have the least immediate hope for breakfast at Tiffany's.

In December — just before Christmas — 17 employees of Waste Management of Kentucky pooled their lottery tickets to claim $9 million in cash. This week 11 employees of Industrial Disposal Co. claimed $1.4 million in cash. The odds of matching all six Lotto Kentucky numbers are one in 5.2 million, or roughly the odds of running through a car wash without getting wet.

"You couldn't sell this as a Hollywood script," said Kentucky Lottery spokesman Rick Redman.

Are you kidding me? This is a Hollywood script. Working titles: "Picking Up"; "Ten Wheels and Flies", "Can Do!", "Stink" and "Bin There, Dumped That."

The cast? Another Dirty Dozen. Danny DeVito — who just sorta looks garbage cannish — has to be a driving force in this one. Robin Williams also drives — and sings opera. The tippers include John Goodman, Joe Pesci and Eddie Murphy. Toss in three "City Slickers" — Billy Crystal, Daniel Stern, Bruno Kirby — as mechanics. Roseanne and Whoopi Goldberg are office workers. William Hurt is the sensitive shop foreman with a philosophical bent. Alex Karras gets to punch out a garbage truck.

The movie is set in Louisville against a backdrop of recycling unrest and aldermanic indecision; some aldermen want twice-a-week garbage pickup; some want once-a-week pickup; two others want to reintroduce pigs to city streets.

The 12 sanitation employees have been pooling their money for years, dispatching DeVito to buy the Lotto Kentucky tickets. DeVito has what he believes is a sure-fire system; he always selects the numbers that correspond to the house numbers at the end of his route.

"For some reason," he tells Hurt at the opening of the movie, "the numbers are always the same."

DeVito gets lucky. Lightning takes out one of the houses. He plays the new numbers, wins, the sanitation team splits $2.4 million in cash — $200,000 each. Eleven of them pay off all their bills and buy new pickups. Seven of them buy farms in Bullitt or Spencer County.

None of the 12 quits work immediately. Their windfall — after taxes — offers a glimpse of the good life, but not the full vision. Three are able to buy new houses, one buys a second home on Nolin Lake, one moves to a condominium in Prospect and begins to worry about the East End bridge.

Tragedy visits Williams; his wife runs off with a solid-waste-management expert from Paducah. Williams sells the house, takes opera lessons, badly fails his Kentucky Opera tryout. Opera officials take pity on him, give him custodial duties, allow him to hum a little "Carmen" backstage.

Goldberg and Murphy become an item, pool their remaining resources, buy a home in Indian Hills. Karras punches out three neighbors at their house-warming party. All other coworkers leave early.

The movie comes full circle when the 12 meet — by chance — at a BP Food Mart in Shively. Each is buying an individual Lotto ticket. Eleven of them are embarrassed by the meeting. Hurt smiles.

Jan. 11, 1995

What don't you know about parking? Apparently, lots!

Give Ron Hasken his way, and the federal government would soon have a new cabinet position: secretary of parking.

While others could dally in the lesser areas of labor, education or defense, the secretary of parking would be responsible for ensuring that every tax-paying American citizen would have a proper place to park the Honda.

The man is onto something. Parking affects each of us almost every day; he has only your best interest at heart.

"Some people are born with great parking ability," Hasken said. "For others, it requires years of study and practice."

Hasken, 52, studies parking. As owner of Ron's Flag City, 203 E. Market St., in New Albany, Ind., he has all too frequently noticed that people parking in the two-hour-limit slots outside his store door have a limited concept of the passage of time. Hasken, in fact, has become a bit of a crank on the subject. Lax New Albany officials now flee in terror when Hasken approaches with parking-overtime-without-penalty on his mind.

"Just because you park in front of the boob tube for hours on end does not mean you are a good parker on the outside," he warned.

Ron's Flag City is a sprawling, interesting, exotic place, crunch-full of hundreds of seasonal flags, garden flags, sports flags, service flags, memorial flags and funny, bogus street signs on the order of "Bobby Knight Way." Hasken has the largest flag featuring KFC's Col. Sanders that you will ever hope to see. He also sells lots of American flags made right here in the good old U.S.A.

"We don't handle foreign-made U.S. flags," he said.

Although irritated about the down-time parking situation in New Albany — some store owners and employees will park on the meterless streets all day taking customer space — Hasken has not lost his considerable sense of humor on the subject. He has ample time to spend — perhaps a little too much time to spend — gazing out his front door at parking lunacy.

"Three or four afternoons a week, somebody will pull into the slot marked "No parking between 4 a.m. to 7 a.m.," he said. "The sign was put in there for the street sweeper.

"So after a few minutes of staring at the sign they'll pull out of that spot and park in the next one over."

Hasken has become such a student of parking that he has decided what the world needs as a prerequisite to getting a driver's license is a parking test.

Not surprisingly, he has already worked one up. Sample question:

In a parking lot divided by lines do you: (A) Straddle the lines. (B) Align driver's-side tires on line. (C) Put front tires on one line, rear tires on another. (D) Try to color within the lines.

His is a full-service parking test; multiple choice, true-false and essay. So answer each one of these questions, true or false:

When entering a parking lot, you accelerate to maximum speed until you see the spot you want.

A parking sign with a diagonal line drawn through it means you can park there as long as you keep your fingers crossed.

If the first attempt at parallel parking fails, it's OK to leave whatever part of the car that didn't fit protruding into the street.

After passing the parker's license test, you must remain parked until you pass the driver's test.

After receiving both licenses, you may then park and drive, but not at the same time.

If you are caught parking on a parkway or driving on a driveway, your licenses will be revoked and you must trade in your car for a tricycle.

Watching someone attempting to parallel park for the first time is called an amusement park.

It is all right to park in a fire zone as long as there is no fire.

If you don't have any change, it's all right to park in front of a meter.

It's all right to park in a loading zone as long as no one is loading or unloading.

A state park is when you park outside the city limits.

If you fail the parker's license test, a stupid license will be issued instead.

Finally, class, your essay question for bonus points: "Explain in detail what part of the 'two-hour parking limit' you don't understand."

Jan. 25, 1997

If spaniel goes pro he'll be a golden retriever

Dennis Sheridan didn't set out to corner the used golf ball market in Louisville. He — and his family — had just very much admired the cut and coloring of a neighbor's dog, a Boykin spaniel.

"It evolved from there," Sheridan said.

His golf story really began in June 1995. After admiring the neighbor's dog, the Sheridans found a Boykin spaniel of their own in Madisonville Ky., with daughter, Tricia, 13, picking it out. They named the puppy "Hershey" because of its distinctive chocolate color.

"Her father is a quail and duck hunter," Sheridan said of Hershey. "They were bred to do that."

Sheridan does not hunt, but he likes to work with dogs. His hunting friends gave him some tips on dog training, and Sheridan began working with Hershey in the back yard every day.

At first it was the usual; Dog Training 101: "sit," "stay," "gim-

Dennis Sheridan and Hershey

mie five." Then, because they were handy, Sheridan began having Hershey return golf balls he would toss into the backyard.

Hershey, already a physical dazzler with shiny chocolate fur and liquid amber eyes, soon proved she had the intelligence and energy to match. The ultimate quick study, she learned that "sit," "stay" and "gimmie five" stuff in a few weeks, graduated to backyard golf ball retrieval in a few months.

"I kinda wanted her to have something else to do," said Sheridan, "so I got to thinking about looking for loose golf balls."

From there it was a short drive to the front nine at Seneca Golf Course, where, about a year ago, Hershey was unleashed on lost golf balls for the first time. Sheridan hasn't even thought about buying a golf ball since.

"At first we were lucky if we got 12 balls at a time," Sheridan said of their weekly visits, "but that changed. By spring we were getting about 50 balls a trip. Our best day was 69 golf balls in 2 1/2 hours."

It's hard to know if that's more a testimony to lousy Seneca Park golfers or Hershey's golf-ball-seeking acumen and persistence.

Either way, the net result is a huge cardboard box filled with hundreds of shiny white golf balls sitting on the floor in Sheridan's den. The painful part is the guy doesn't even golf very often — maybe four of five times a year — and he estimates Hershey has recovered about 1,600 golf balls since last August. What to do with the excess?

"I give them away," Sheridan said.

Yes, fellow duffers, the man gives them away, Titleist, Maxfli, Pinnacle and Pro-Flite alike. They go to family, friends and coworkers.

"We had a graduation party here in June and nobody left without at least a dozen golf balls," said Sheridan. "Nephews, cousins, everybody got them."

Many of the balls are top-shelf, in very good condition. Many have corporate logos. One golfer insists on decorating his balls with a hand-drawn happy face.

"You'd be amazed how many of his balls I have," Sheridan said.

The funniest find was a ball with a political motif, President Clinton's face with the words: "Slick Willie — Guaranteed a Good Lie."

Sheridan, Hershey and I went out to Seneca Golf Course Tuesday night. Sheridan led the way, lifting the thick cover of wild grape and honeysuckle with a long stick. In 90 busy minutes Hershey found 55 golf balls. What she didn't see with her eyes she sniffed with her nose. She dropped each ball at her master's feet, was rewarded with food, water and love — and a bath to follow.

"And I think," said Sheridan, with all due pride, "her best years are yet to come."

Aug. 15, 1996

Amazing Shrinking Disclaimers terrorize would-be car buyers

Having always purchased my Christmas baubles, bangles and beads at Bailey Banks & Biddle, I did blush this week when a man called to ask if I'd seen the firm's latest advertising boost.

"It's bonkers," said the man, an occasionally bombastic bureaucrat. "Practically Byzantine."

The man had a point. The Bailey Banks & Biddle newspaper advertisment was one of those multitiered jobs that began with screaming 20 PERCENT OFF at the top and gradually faded away to an * (asterisk) explaining in teeny-tiny detail the arcane terms & conditions that could apply, including this very interesting closer:

Regular prices reflect offerings which may not have resulted in actual sales.

Quite frankly, dear readers, as bejeweled, beneficent and beloved as Bailey Banks & Biddle can be, I'd much rather seek bargains without needing a barrister to help me barter. Or having to press my proboscis against some ink-stained newspaper bromide to better behold the bottom line.

It's tough enough washing the ink off my fingers.

The very worst offenders in this type of Asterisk Advertising are the automobile manufacturers. Unlike most other TV advertisements — the only real difference these days between most steamy, R-rated movies and blue jeans commercials is that the jeans commercials are better done — the auto industry commercials are relatively predictable.

They will tell you that only beautiful people buy new cars. All ugly customers are rounded up and held hostage on breadsticks and water in the used-hubcap lot. You will be told that life without a $46,000 automobile is no life at all; please check your guilt and/or social conscience at the door. You will see several cheerful idiots jumping up and down like Richard Simmons on a caffeine high. You will see an automatic defroster look sexy. A pickup truck will be shot from a large cannon through a 10-inch steel plate and land intact, its rear-window gun rack still in place.

Then, just as the happy hunter drives his pickup off into the TV sunset, a block of very small, whitish words will suddenly flash onto the very bottom of the screen — disclaimer words that *appear* to say:

Here is small-print, auto-buying help. We take no prisoners. All prices are subject to foreign trade zone specifications, FBI, FOP, MOM, SOS and PDQ. The 1.5 percent annual interest rate is good until 12/31/92. It will be compounded hourly except for all net gain. Taxes, title, dealer prep and kicking the whitewall tires mandatory. National guidelines apply except in Alaska, Hawaii and parts of eastern North Dakota. All legal liability to the purchaser. Other stringent stipulations will apply as we think of them. God bless America. Long live General Motors. In Toyota we trust.

The car commercial you have just watched probably lasted from 30 to 60 seconds. That little block of copy at the end — and I have timed them for years — is on the screen for anywhere from two to four seconds. I have — I promise — even leaped from my chair, sprinted across the living room and pressed my nose against the TV screen — you don't have to wash it afterward — trying to read the stupid thing.

It cannot be done. I don't care if you are wearing track shoes, are carrying a magnifying glass and graduated magna cum laude from the Evelyn Wood School of Speed Reading. I defy you to get over to the TV set and read the disclaimer in the allotted time.

I feel certain that somewhere in Washington there is a Bureau of Disclaimers, Division of the Department of Obfuscation, Ophthalmology Division, that's supposed to enforce federal reading guidelines on those disclaimers. I called Washington to check, but nobody is home until Jan. 20, when Bill Clinton & Co. move in. In desperation I videotaped a car commercial, "froze" it on the screen and finally read one.

This — I promise — is exactly what the disclaimer said:

Help. I am a prisoner in a Japanese automobile foreign trade zone. I have only two seconds to send my SOS. My initials are FOP. Please call my MOM or the FBI. I have been here 15 years and am losing interest in life. All I ever see are four white walls. I must get home to eastern North Dakata. I have no legal rights here. I'm really strung out. God bless America. In Toyota I rust.

Dec. 12, 1992

For 104-year-old Edith Kast, free oysters were a sure bet

Edith Kast was having some fun — you could tell that. Not that she wanted the fun to show too much a 104 year old woman does have her dignity to protect — but her sense of humor will get the best of her on occasion.

"You're not going to put all of this in the paper, are you?" she asked, giggling just a little bit.

Edith Kast and her son Merl   Photo by Larry Spitzer

You'll also have to credit Greg Haner, the manager of Mazzoni's restaurant, 2804 Taylorsville Road, for some of the fun. He's the guy who put up the sign near the restaurant door that said, "Free oysters to anyone 80 years old accompanied by their parent."

Haner did it mostly as a joke, but Mazzoni's is such a Louisville institution — it has been in business for 108 years — that he knew he might have to pay off someday.

"When you get as many generations of Louisvillians as I do," he said, "you know it's in the realm of possibility."

Actually, anything seems possible with Edith Kast. She was born in Iowa on Feb. 16, 1888, one of eight children, four boys and four girls. Her father was a farmer and surveyor, traveling around Illinois, Iowa, Minnesota, Tennessee and Kentucky laying out many of the roads we use today. The entire Kast family — parents and children — traveled from Minnesota to Tennessee in a covered wagon.

"But don't put that in the paper," she said, giggling again.

At 21 she married Joe Kast, another name that has been known in Louisville for almost 100 years, a family of bookbinders practicing a craft nearly as forgotten as the covered wagon.

"We've carried that on a long time," said Edith Kast.

She was married to Joe Kast 61 years. They had two children, Conrad, 77, and Merl, 83. Her health — and she has always eaten anything she wanted when she wanted it — has remained remarkably good. She cares for herself, walks very well but with a cane, and does not need a hearing aid.

She had cataract surgery a few years ago, but she still reads anything she wants, with glasses.

"I'm the wellest person you know," she said. "Everything is still under control.... I drove a car until I got to be 100, but then I thought my eyesight was beginning to get a little bit bad, and I better quit."

She doesn't like television. "All you see are those young girls jumping in and out of bed with men," she said. "I don't like that."

Conrad Kast lives in St. Louis. When he was in town a few weeks ago, he had an urge to make a pilgrimage to Mazzoni's for oysters — and he took his mother with him. It was then that Edith Kast saw the sign about the free meal — and thought it would be fun to come back.

"They asked Conrad if he qualified," she said. "He told them no but he had a brother at home who did."

On Tuesday afternoon Merl and Edith Kast went to vote — she never misses — then headed over to Mazzoni's about 4 p.m. for a very senior citizens' meal. It was, in many ways, a convergence of wonderful Louisville institutions.

"They said they'd come for the free oysters," said Haner. "I knew it had to happen some day."

The Kasts got more than oysters; they each added a bowl of chowder and kale greens, two other Mazzoni specialities.

"We didn't bother to check their identification," said Haner.

"I like good food," said Edith Kast. "I don't like that slipshod stuff . . . but you're not going to put that in the paper, are you?"

Nov. 11, 1992

Another GREAT Bob Hill column!

Let me say from the very first sentence that I have nothing against overheated self-promotion.

Geez, didn't Bob do a great job with that opening sentence?

I honestly think it right and proper that if a local TV station stays on the air during terrible thunderstorms to remind its viewers that 10 inches of rain often equals a flood, the station's general manager should interrupt programming every 15 minutes thereafter to remind its viewers what a wonderful service its Tenacious Tornado Team performed.

Was that a great opening paragraph, or what?

Actually, it's kind of fun to see general managers on the air. Most of the time you consider them to be the sort of people who hide out in some three-acre office where they can better smell all the money, cast a covetous eye on the petty-cash drawer and worry about the cost of the company Christmas party.

No Louisville news organization does a better job with disasters — natural or unnatural — than your Courier-Journal Paragraph Team.

So what if general managers want to continually interrupt the normal gush of programming to gush a little on their own. If they want to pronounce their Tenacious Tornado Team the best dog- gone journalists since Edward R. Murrow and Brenda Starr, well, good, perhaps lifesaving work does deserve a pat on the head.

We run Bob Hill's column every Saturday because we love you and because we care.

It's not that newspapers don't fully understand and appreciate the value of self-promotion. Let some newspaper win a Pulitzer Prize, or have one of its staffers be awarded the highly coveted Mabel B. Ausincloss Award for Distinguished Ontological Reporting, and we'll soon be running three-column by 15-inch house ads pumping up our shoes too.

That Bob, he just spelled Ausincloss and ontological correctly in the same sentence. Only in your Saturday SCENE.

Television stations do have a more difficult struggle. While The Courier-Journal is the only major daily newspaper in this area published in a city that doesn't begin with the letters L-e-x, the TV stations have more immediate competition; they live or die on viewer ratings. You just can't cover any major news events these days without coming across three sat-cams, seven video trucks and 23 news cars, all cleverly labeled "Action News," "Eyewitness News" or "Blow-Dried and Beautiful."

That's another perfect paragraph from your own, alive and alert, Courier-Journal Paragraph Team — not to mention a little smartypants satire.

These continual interruptions for self-promotion can be annoying. But the oddest part of TV self-promotion, as least in my humble opinion — *That Bob; brave, honest AND humble* — is that while the stations will occasionally buy time on other TV stations, or on radio, most of their promoting is done on their own programs; they are mostly preaching to their own choir.

Semicolons, such as the one in the previous sentence, are a regular service of your Courier-Journal Paragraph Team.

There are, of course, people in TV journalism who believe print journalists look down on them, thinking TV work is more shallow, more superficial and more show-business oriented. That is not true. Veteran newspaper types are mostly upset with TV journalism because its big-time talking heads earn three or four times as much money for about the same work, and newspapers have always been too cheap to compete.

Continued brilliant insight into the darker side of journalism available every Saturday morning on Page 3 of your SCENE.

Or perhaps I am overreacting. Perhaps you have become so inured to general managers hyping Tenacious Tornado Teams, or of ratings period stories on teen-age prostitutes and killer bees, that the constant interruptions for self-promotion don't bother you.

A man in continual, desperate search for truth and perspective: Bob Hill, SCENE magazine.

I have a difficult time separating TV "anchor person" self-promotion from political advertising. Watch the professional TV journalists stare into your eyes. Watch them lean into the camera, into your living room, talking to you, confiding in you, always running from place to place, but always in control; calm and professional.

Trust me, they are saying. Trust me.

Watch the professional politicians stare into your eyes, talking to you, confiding in you, always running from place to place, but always in control. Trust me, they are saying. Trust me.

Another Saturday column come and gone, courtesy of your Courier-Journal Paragraph Team. More to come next week. Trust us.

Aug. 15, 1992

From Tonya to Whitewater to Bob Dole, news repetition nearly overshadows basketball

One of the more common criticisms heard of the news media these days is that when we get a story with some legitimate news interest we tend to pound people over the head with it until they are screaming for relief.

Tonya Harding. Nancy Kerrigan. Tonya Harding. Nancy Kerrigan. Tonya Harding. Movie deal. Tonya Harding. Shawn Eckardt. Mickey Mouse. Jeff Gillooly. Nancy Kerrigan. Tonya Harding. U.S. Olympic Committee. Disneyland. U.S. Figure Skating Association. Jeff Gillooly. Special Olympics. Multnomah County. Nancy Kerrigan. Tonya Harding. Tonya Harding. Nancy Kerrigan. Jeff Gillooly. Tonya Harding. Tonya Harding. Tonya Harding. Mickey Mouse.

There are now people so turned off by reading and hearing the same news over and over and over and over and over, they can barely open the newspaper. The repetition is so numbing they find it difficult to read the next word, word, word, word, word:

Tonya Harding. Nancy Kerrigan. Tonya Harding. Special Olympics. Jeff Gillooly. Shawn Eckardt. Nancy Kerrigan. Tonya Harding. Nancy Kerrigan. Tonya Harding. Mickey Mouse. U.S. Figure Skating Association. Multnomah County. Mickey Mouse. Tonya Harding. Tonya Harding. Tonya Harding. Tonya Harding. Mickey Mouse. Mickey Mouse.

Frankly, I don't understand these petty complaints. We in the media have a serious responsibility to hold up a mirror to society, to reflect its own values back on itself. We may look and sound

like a kennel of baying hounds, but we are not embarrassing ourselves; we must explain the nuance, the petty, the mundane to
make you a better-informed citizenry. It couldn't possibly be the
result of mindless, shallow, overkill journalism:

Whitewater. Whitewater. Whitewater. Webster Hubbell. Webster
Hubbell. Rose Law Firm. Whitewater. Hillary Clinton. Vincent
Foster. Washington. Little Rock. Whitewater. Rose Law Firm.
Madison Guaranty Savings & Loan. Newt Gingrich. Vincent
Foster. Arkansas. Rose Law Firm. Little Rock. Hillary Clinton. Bob
Dole. Whitewater. Vincent Foster. Rose Law Firm. Federal Deposit
Insurance Corp. Bob Dole. Bob Dole. Bob Dole. Resolution Trust
Corp.

Whitewater. Whitewater. Whitewater. Mickey Mouse. Mickey
Mouse. Mickey Mouse.

I've been reading every word, watching every TV broadcast,
pulling my pickup truck over to the side of the road when the
radio news comes on so I won't miss a development:

Whitewater. Whitewater. Whitewater. Whitewater. Whitewater.
Whitewater. Whitewater. Whitewater. Whitewater. Whitewater.
Whitewater. Mickey Mouse.

I no longer go to sleep at night counting sheep. I shut my eyes
and visualize a long line of names jumping a fence in front of me.
The words come in great bunches, filling the horizon, storming up
from below ground, falling from the sky, a veritable stampede of
important first names in the news:

Tonya. Tonya. Tonya. Tonya. Tonya. Tonya. Jeff. Jeff. Jeff. Jeff.
Jeff. Shawn. Shawn. Shawn. Shawn. Hillary. Hillary. Hillary.
Hillary. Hillary. Newt. Newt. Newt. Newt. Newt. Newt. Newt.
Newt. Webster. Webster. Webster. Webster. Vincent. Vincent.
Vincent. Vincent. Vincent. Vincent. Bill. Bill. Bill. Bob. Bob. Bob.
Bob. Bob. Bob. Mickey. Mickey. Mickey. Mickey. Mickey.

Certainly the media have an obligation to its readers, watchers
and listeners to keep an eye on government and ice skating, to
patrol the hallways of power to keep you informed of misconduct,
malfeasance, corruption, the triple toe loop.

But there are other stories out there. Perhaps you are part of the
problem; you're just not paying attention. If you would broaden
your interests, perhaps we would broaden our scope. After all,
what could now be more important to us as a nation than random
crime, education, medical care, pollution or losing faith in our
political leaders?

Basketball. Basketball. Basketball. Basketball. Basketball.
Basketball. Hoosiers. NCAA. Final Four. Sweet 16. March
Madness. Freedom Hall. Hoosier Dome. Wildcats. Cardinals.
Hilltoppers. Boilermakers. Rick. Rick. Rick. Rick. Rick. Bobby.
Bobby. Bobby. Bobby. Bobby. Denny. Denny. Denny. Denny. Denny.
Cliff. Cliff. Cliff. Cliff. Cliff. Damon. Damon. Damon. Damon.
Damon. Glenn. Glenn. Glenn. Glenn. Glenn. Glenn. Travis. Travis.
Travis. Travis. Travis. Basketball. Basketball. Basketball. Basketball.
Basketball. Basketball. Basketball. Basketball. Basketball.
Basketball. Basketball. Basketball.

March 19, 1994

For a proper Thanksgiving dinner, don't light the lavender-scented candles

Here — presented strictly as a public service — is news that
could produce some interesting moments over the Thanksgiving
holiday.

The Smell & Taste Treatment and Research Foundation in
Chicago has determined that the aroma of pumpkin pie combined
with lavender can best stimulate an erection. (This according to an
article in the November issue of New Choices: Living Even Better
After 50 magazine.)

OK, sure, I'll be happy to pause a few seconds here to allow
several thousand of you to go out and rummage around the
kitchen. While you're out there, be sure to check out the breadbox
and candy jar because the No. 2 stimulant on the list is doughnuts
and black licorice. No. 3 is doughnuts and pumpkin pie. Is it any
wonder we all like the smell of a bakery?

The man behind the pumpkin-and-lavender plan is Dr. Alan R.
Hirsch, neurological director of the 10-year-old foundation. Its
basic purpose is honorable: the treatment of patients with smell
and taste disorders. It investigates how odors can affect mood,
behavior, learning ability, migraine headaches and exercise
strength.

In the latter category, for instance, its tests determined that the aromas of strawberry and hot buttered popcorn can have the greatest positive impact on strength and endurance. Think that over the next time you sit down to $12 worth of hot-buttered theater popcorn.

"We'd also learned that people who lose their sense of smell due to head trauma often gain 10 to 20 pounds," he said, "so we decided to see if we gave them an extra sense of smell, would they lose weight?"

And that led the foundation folks directly to sex. Their studies had shown that 90 percent of people who suffered loss of smell also became sexually dysfunctional. The initial tests were conducted on male medical students who had blood-pressure cuffs placed on their arms; and smaller, specially designed cuffs on their penises. As they lay on tables, partially clothed, surgical masks coated with various odors were placed over their faces. Brave and selfless as this might seem, please hold your applause until you hear the whole story.

"One student," said Hirsch, mentioning a pioneer thousands of women may relate to, "slept through the whole thing."

Others, including 31 off-the-street males of all ages, did not. They lay there, profoundly plugged into medical science, as dozens of odors were paraded past their nostrils. With each test, the doctors would check readings, take measurements. The masks would be worn for a minute, then the participants would be allowed a three-minute cool-down period before the next odor was brought in.

"The most surprising thing was traditional perfumes had only a 3 percent effect on penile blood flow," Hirsch said. "A cheese pizza had 5 percent, buttered popcorn 9 percent and lavender 40 percent."

Various odors were tried individually, then in combination. Older men were most responsive to vanilla. Medical students were very partial to cinnamon buns.

Allow me to confess here a certain inability to fully picture this event. I shall, however, long regret not being present in this libido laboratory for that magical moment when somebody stood up and announced: "OK, BRING IN THE PUMPKIN PIE AND LAVENDER!"

Actually, Hirsch had to take credit for that bit of bizarre olfactory inspiration.

"I just suggested combining results of the pilot studies," he said.

Hirsch could not fully explain the cause-and-effect relationship between pumpkin pie, lavender and male stirrings. The best guesses are that a certain scent might remind a man of a desirable sexual partner, it could have an anxiety-reducing effect on the brain, or there could be a physiological connection between the smell mechanism and the part of the brain that induces procreative progress. Hirsch said the relationship might date back to when humans first gathered at campfires to eat and ogle — the precursor to our modern singles bars.

The good news for all women feeling left out — again — of this study is that the Smell & Taste Treatment and Research Foundation will soon turn its olfactory attention toward female arousal and food. Still, the larger question remains: What to do with the male results?

Hirsch suggested that Eau de Pumpkin might soon be arriving at a perfume store near you. Given my Thanksgiving tastes, I'm leaning toward lemon meringue pie and sweet potatoes. Then — psychologically linked to millions of other red-blooded males across the nation — I'll turn on the football game and fall asleep.

Nov. 18, 1995

If at first you don't proceed, try, try ...

The epistle came with such a full-bore letterhead — "Mr. Henry W. Mann III" — and went on to detail a story so wonderfully subtle and familiar that it demanded a house call. There I learned that the letter's author — with almost no effort on his part — has procrastination down to a proud science. Maybe you have one of these people living in your house.

"Bob Hill. See what you can make of this — I call it my 'Sink Saga.' It started with a slight drip. (I didn't think washerless faucets did that sort of thing.) I traveled Jefferson County, pothole to pothole, looking for the correct repair kit for a faucet no one stocks any longer. I settled for a 'repair-all' kit that consisted of a quarter-cup of 'O' rings that I tossed into the pile of stuff that keeps me from using my toaster oven.... They're still there."

Mr. Henry W. Mann III lives in a small, brick house on

Peabody Lane. The table where we sat was layered in an avalanche of letters, notices, registration papers, medicine and tissue. Mr. Henry W. Mann III, 54, is retired from Ford with a medical disability, has a lot of time on his hands, although not always enough energy or focus to get things done.

But he does like to think things over. A lot.

"One day I decided to tackle said drip. Upon reflecting I decided that I never liked the faucet anyway. I bought the high-rise faucet I've always wanted but hadn't wanted to fork over the bucks for in the past. When I got around to said project, again upon reflection, I decided that my prized faucet was too nice to install in the now shabby sink. So the high-rise faucet that I coveted for so long now reposes in the pile of stuff that hinders the use of my small freezer."

By now you may think you know where this is going. Domestic Dominoes: You start out mopping a dirty kitchen floor, decide to replace it, end up spending another $22,000 on new appliances, wallpaper, skylights, insulated windows and a burglar alarm to protect it. Actually, Mr. Henry W. Mann III did have such thoughts, but cooler emotions prevailed.

"Since I live in a house as opposed to an apartment, I've always steered clear of the stainless steel sinks that are the stock-in-trade of the rental industry. (Here comes that reflection business again.) Being tired of changing sinks I opted for the run-of-the-mill item that lasts longer and costs half as much. At this point in time I'm feeling quite pleased with all the progress I've made."

Progress, of course, is a relative thing. Mr. Henry W. Mann III admits his life doesn't always proceed in a straight line.

He gets one thing started and something else comes up. He needs to build a birdhouse in the back yard; a friend needs help; the boat in his driveway — which hasn't been in the water since 1993 — needs a few repairs. If it isn't one thing, it's another.

"The day arrived to install my prized faucet and durable, low-cost sink. Reflection again. I couldn't bear to have gleaming metal hardware in a 1950s metal-rimmed counter top. The sink now is in its temporary location in front of the washing machine, still in its red, white and blue box.

Say what you will about Mr. Henry W. Mann III's storage habits — he is a patriot.

"... I now own a nice, mottled-patterned, pale blue counter top that matched the new flooring that replaced the original flooring that had traces of floor-care products that were based on Crazy-Glue. The counter

top now leans against the living room stereo and gets dusted on a regular basis. By the way, the drip has stopped and if I suffer any more reflection, I'll let you know."

As I made my way through the clutter of his living room, pausing briefly to admire the nicely dusted counter top leaning against the stereo, Mr. Henry W. Mann III did offer a parting reflection:

"Taking your time can actually be a shortcut because you might think of a faster way to do something, or you may find out you don't have to do it at all."

Nov. 5, 1996

You put your lawsuit in, you put your lawsuit out . . .

Along with most of you, I have been following The Great Hokey-Pokey Dance Scandal with large interest. Because PokeyGate has now reached Kentucky, it's left me hurt, angry and depressed.

But before we get too deeply into counseling, here's some background for those of you who believe music was invented by Shania Twain, Fugees or L.L. Cool J.

An Associated Press story early this week mentioned that one Roland "Larry" LaPrise had been given credit for writing that dance classic, "Hokey Pokey." LaPrise had to die to get his due — April 4 in Boise, Idaho — but that's often the way it is in the entertainment business.

He had said "Hokey Pokey" was written during the Golden Era of music, when melodies were rich and lush, the lyrics evocative. He's right. Just consider these four memorable lines:

You put your right hand in,
You put your right hand out,
You put your right hand in,
And you shake it all about.

The power of that sweet lyric was so great, so sustaining, that I am certain thousands of you, even while sitting at your breakfast tables, can hear the accompanying music.

Even now you are fighting some terrible urge to stick your right hand out, shake it all about, perhaps spilling coffee all over your

SCENE. Be strong. I need you. This column is barely one-third read.

Although occasionally resuscitated by class reunions, senior-citizen dances and AMVETS polka parties, "Hokey Pokey" is on its last legs. The loss is keen. It was the Wallflower's Anthem; everybody danced the Hokey Pokey. What made it so anatomically fascinating was that the participants, having proceeded to put a right hand in, would then be asked to put a left hand in. This was followed in rapid fashion by the dancers putting a right foot in, a left foot in.

Then, as a wondrous *denouement* to this ballet, a large, giddy, seething circle of wiggling, waving human beings would jump forward simultaneously putting *their whole selves in.*

Do not trust me alone on this one, young readers; go ask Mom and Dad.

With that kind of songwriting legacy, it was no wonder that the relatives of the late, great LaPrise heaped honor upon him, though the original news story contained dark hints that "Hokey Pokey" might predate his 1950 copyright.

That story said American soldiers in English pubs during WWII had danced to an English novelty song called "The Okey Cokey." It had very similar lyrics to "Hokey Pokey," but it seemed "The Okey Cokey" was often danced near the Midnight Hour, when body parts being shaken were not necessarily confined to hands and feet.

Yesterday's newspaper brought shocking news. Bob Degen, 90, of Lexington, Ky., said *he* owns a 1944 copyright for "The Hokey-Pokey Dance." Degen said he wrote the words and music with a friend, the late Joe Brier of Scranton, Pa.

So what about LaPrise?

"He's a faker," Degen said, putting in his two cents.

Degen said he sued LaPrise in California in 1956, with the two parties agreeing to split 40 percent of the royalties. Degen said the rest went to their publishing company, Four-Star Records. Its name being more ambitious than its bottom line, the company went bankrupt. It was bought by another company, making that company part-owners — with Degen and LaPrise — of both versions of the "Hokey Pokey." Degen said he has received about $12,000 in royalty checks, but the Degen-LaPrise feud might scar the great song forever.

One more note. The story also said "Hokey Pokey" actually

might date to an old Shaker song called "The Hinkum-Booby."
The Shakers once had a large presence in Kentucky but died out.
In retrospect, that seemed fairly predictable; the sect had some
great ideas, but their ideas also included strict separation of sexes.
Rampant celibacy has a way of diminishing the flock.

The Shakers — by definition — shook themselves mightily during their religious services. And two of the famed "Hinkum-
Booby" lines went: *"I put my right hand in . . . I put my right hand
out...."*

Damning evidence, indeed. What next? A news story that
Roman gladiators danced the Hokey Pokey on their victims'
chests? How sad that such a great shaking song has come down to
anger, recrimination, even faint shadows being cast across the
Hinkum-Booby.

Millions of Americans have put themselves in to the Hokey
Pokey. It's just terrible the feuding families are so put out.

April 20, 1996

A hairy question
To put their locks on success, will coaches sometimes have to play a little hard bald?

Although we like to believe otherwise,
journalists are just as trendy as real people.
We byte-stained wretches follow social fads,
imitate reportorial strategies, take careful
note of what's going on out there, motiva-
tional-wise.

Hence, I suspected I could be in trouble
when my editor called me into his office.

"Bob," he said, "we've got a problem."

Oh, boy. Raised-eyebrow time. Anytime
your boss tells you we've got a problem
what he or she really means is that you've
got a problem. But I was going to play this

Bold new bald looks for coaches (from left) Rick Pitino, Denny Crum and Bobby Knight.

one with a straight face.

"Yessir."

"Bob, we're coming up on a critical part of our year — salary review time. We need peak performances from everybody. We need to look good for the corporate bean counters. We've all got to pull together, demonstrate some team spirit and unity. We need to become a team.... Bob, we're going to shave our heads."

I stared at my boss waiting for a smile, a hint that he hadn't been drinking too much copy-machine toner. He was as serious as a Catholic wedding.

"Look around," he shouted. "It's mid-March, Big-Dance Time on the hardwood floor. What's the one thing you see so many great basketball players doing to demonstrate their team spirit and unity?"

"Hiring pro agents?"

"Bob. "

I was doomed. There was no wiggle room. I gave him the answer he wanted: "Shave their heads."

He had a point. Unable to give any more than the prerequisite 110 percent, tournament-desperate athletes often step up to the barber's chair.

It makes no historical sense; what did a haircut do for Samson? Yet given the ludicrous look of the modern male haircut — road-kill on a cereal bowl — a shaved head is probably a vast improvement. At the very least, it's a half-vast improvement.

"Bob," my boss said. "We're looking for head-shaving volunteers. And you're going to be first."

I've always been one to pick my moments to fight — and this didn't appear to be one of them. Mother Nature already has me well down the foliage-challenged path. I've even given thought to shaving off my remaining hair, showing up at work one day with a head as slick as a new commode.

But I did have one fighting tooth in my comb.

"Boss man," I said. "It's one thing to ask the hirelings, the occasiorial high school coach, to shave their heads. Heck, most of the time they want to do it, some sort of male-bonding, all-for-one-and-one-for-all, temporarily-gone-stupid thing. I mean if it ain't bald heads these days, it's message tattoos, the guys *and* the girls.

"But what about management? You'll only inspire team unity when the big-time basketball honchos — the Rick Pitinos, Denny Crums and Bob Knights of the world — wince once for the snipper. What would their hairless heads do for team spirit?"

The boss rubbed on that one a few minutes. Meanwhile, I massaged him with all sorts of larger possibilities: Bill Clinton taking a buzz cut for the country; our entire Congress bald as $3 tires; the Supreme Court as bumper hitches; great Americans all.

But the original question hung there like a cheap toupee. How would we look if we joined the players' Shaved Head Society? Would it guarantee unity, a few hairline victories in the NCAA Tournament? A participle less dangled?

Once the question was raised, it had to be turned over to our crack computer-picture crew to work out — or in — the wrinkles. The knobby, approximate results are before you. Some of you may be thinking Dick Vitale or "Saturday Night Live." Others may be thinking: When does baseball season begin?

I, of course, am thinking Mount Rushmore. With ears.

March 14, 1996

What's in a name? If it's a bank, a whole lot of change

The newspaper news from back home — a small town deep in the Illinois cornfields — is that Cliff Danielson, at age 94, is still going to work every day at his National Bank and Trust Co.

The persistent rumor, of course, is that Cliff actually died sometime during the Eisenhower administration. He was subsequently stuffed by a worried banking staff and has been propped up in the lobby every morning since then to maintain community confidence. I never believed that; Cliff thought far too much of the Eisenhower administation to leave it prematurely.

I hope Cliff lasts another 94 years. He personally approved my first bank loan; $1,500 for much-needed new furniture. I was just out of college, married, had established no credit and had no assets. The loan manager was doubtful. Cliff waved me through like a freight train. Cliff had watched me grow up. He knew I'd pay my bills.

I thought of Cliff several times recently as my attempt to refinance a home loan dragged on past six weeks. The banking people were kind. The delay had something to do with a letter of inquiry I never understood. Or maybe it was the bank has just been bought out by a bigger bank and their respective computers didn't like each other. Or maybe my bank was merely merging with a bank in Pittsburgh. Or relocating its home office. Or changing its name. Or something.

That's the problem with banks these days; they're always doing something. I have lost track of their names, numbers and letters. I can no longer tell the players without an alphabet.

I find it odd that banks — wary institutions that depend so much on community confidence and name recognition — would continually go through this orgy of merging and name-changing in such graceless fashion. The one thing I remain certain of is their long-range goals: monopoly situations, charging 18 percent interest on credit cards and paying 3 percent interest on savings accounts and continual high profits.

Sure, some banks have been through some hard times recently, partly because of bad loans, poor management and greed. We're used to that. It's when The First National Bank of Pisgah alphabetizes its name to NBP that we get confused.

Banks spend good money — money that could better be used to raise savings rates to 3.03 percent — to tell us of the name changes. I came into work this morning greeted by a sign on the bus stop that said "First National is now National City Bank — Same people, same services, new name." I would assume all the name changes would require expensive changes in company stationery, computer systems, doormats, outdoor temperature signs and Christmas club checks.

A year from now, when National City Bank is bought out by the emerging Boris Yeltsin First National Bank, we will be faced with another name change, another bus-stop slogan: The National Boris Bank — New people, new faces, same ol' borscht."

To help ease the transition, the advertisements of one of the newly renamed banks has used the face of Arnold Palmer, a man who has not won a golf tournament that mattered since the Van Buren administration. Still, Arnie has a face the public and bankers can trust; tanned, leathery and crinkly as old money.

I suspect most people deal with all this change by just going to the same bank building year in and year out, mostly disregarding whatever name the guys with the 40-foot crane are plastering to its outer wall that week.

If I owned a bank — The First Bob National Bank — I would do things much differently.

For openers the First Bob National Bank would be open from 5 p.m. to midnight on weekdays — and all day on Saturdays and Sundays — to accommodate people who are perpetually irritated that banks are only open while most people are at work.

First Bob would eliminate the three-hour delays on Friday evenings at the drive-through windows by having express lanes for check-cashing only. All drivers found in violation of that rule would get the death penalty.

First Bob would have a child-care area in its lobby where customers' children could play with old money. First Bob would process all loans within two weeks or guarantee an interest-free $500 to any customer. First Bob would offer free tin cans and shovels to any client who felt his or her money was better off buried in the back yard.

Finally, First Bob would never merge, combine, interlock, interface, recomputerize or change its name — so help me Cliff Danielson.   *April 3, 1993*

Chapter Four

PROFILES IN FAST TIME

The best thing about writing
columns is that one size is supposed to
fit all moods, situations and moments;
the Saturday columns are always 64
computer-screen lines long;
the weekday columns are 58 computer-
screen lines long; write it and get out;
next case. The worst thing about
writing columns is that many
situations — and people — are worth
twice as much space. The result is
Profiles in Fast Time; mini-slices of
such as John Updike, Roger Kahn,
Army heroes mixed with Everyday
heroes and lesser-known personages.
But there is something thoroughly
democractic about the fact they all get
the same space.

Kahn captures truth, hope, nostalgia and the child in us all in baseball books

One day last week I was driving home from work and passed a thirtysomething woman and a small girl playing catch in a front yard. I didn't stop, but my assumption was that it was a mother and daughter; my hope was that it was a mother and daughter.

You don't see that much; softball and baseball were not as available to the mother's generation as they are to the daughter's. It was fun to see a rite of spring in such complete bloom.

Because baseball is so intertwined in the American fabric, the sport has always been a good place to keep score of such things — too often in retrospect. The game mirrors our business progress, our labored social evolution; rickety wooden bleachers to domed, sky-boxed palaces; salaries escalating from $7,500 a year to $7.5 million; clubhouses changing from lily-white to white, black and brown.

No one has spent more time observing and writing about these changes than Roger Kahn.

Kahn, 69, writes of the game with expertise, clarity and affection. With one book he added a forever phrase to the game's lexicon: "The Boys of Summer," a look at his life, his father's life — and the beloved Brooklyn Dodgers. Kahn's 50 years of journalism began in 1947, the same year Jackie Robinson came into major-league ball.

"At 69," Kahn said, "I'm old enough to speak the truth."

He's stuck his truth in another baseball book with a July title, "Memories of Summer." Kahn will be at the Hawley-Cooke bookstore at Shelbyville Road Plaza from 2 to 3 p.m. tomorrow to sign the book and talk 50 years of baseball. He will also attend the Monday-night tribute to Jackie Robinson held by the American Civil Liberties Union of Kentucky at the Louisville Slugger Museum.

Part of Kahn's dedication in "Memories of Summer" is to Louisville native Pee Wee Reese: "To Pee Wee, for his friendship." Mark Reese, Pee Wee's son, will also be at Hawley-Cooke and the museum with baseball videos of Pee Wee Reese and the other

Brooklyn Dodgers.

Kahn said when he first began writing about baseball the game was inhabited by players "fleeing the hounds of the Depression." He told a story of Pee Wee Reese being warned by a supervisor that quitting a regular job to go play baseball was really taking a chance.

"I'm young," Reese answered. "I can afford to take a chance."

Kahn worries about the game but doesn't seem to have given up on it. New ballparks and sources of television revenue will keep the game financially alive, almost in spite of the blind, tight-fisted arrogance and stupidity of past commissioners and some present owners, he said.

Building affection for baseball depends on personal experience, touching the game; parents and children playing catch in the front yard. Kahn looked both forward and backward in offering a fix to a declining lack of interest among the young, the next generation of fans.

He said baseball has always basically been a blue-collar sport, that a fascination with high-priced skyboxes and $5 hot dogs is taking the game away from the people it most needs. He remembered cheap seats at Ebbets Field, free entrance for a World War II donation of scrap metal. Kahn would now have a cheap-seat area in every ballpark, free seats for kids after the third inning.

We talked about the movie "Field of Dreams," why men would sit and cry in the final scene as Kevin Costner played catch with his father. Kahn knew the answer; he'd played catch with his father — as the little girl was playing catch with her mother. Baseball and nostalgia are inseparable.

"We're moved to tears by the memory of all those we have loved and lost," he said, "including the child you once were who is no longer there."

April 12, 1997

Diligence pays off for 54-year-old Graduate of the Year

The rosebud was a nice analogy. You have to be careful when applying it in human terms, however; the literary fragrance can get heavy. But with Iva Cox, it made sense.

She grew up on a small Adair County farm, as one of eight children living in a world that stretched only to the nearest hills. She was born partly deaf but didn't know it. How could a young child know what's missing?

She attended a one-room school, flunking two grades before her parents realized her problem. But there wasn't money for a hearing aid — or much of anything else in 1950s rural Kentucky.

"I did fine," she said. "I learned to read lips around the house with Mom and Dad.

"I loved school — math and English were my favorite — but people had to talk loud to me. When the teachers gave me an assignment or something, I didn't always hear that."

She was barely a teen-ager when the family moved to Louisville, where her father found work in a factory. She had been in the city only once. At age 14, already terribly shy and insecure, she was put in sixth grade.

"I was older than the other kids," she said, "but not bigger."

Her teacher — Miss Stinton — helped her get a hearing aid. For the first time, she experienced the world as others heard it.

"It was sorta funny," she said. "It was like everything was too loud."

Her grades quickly improved, and she became a little less intimidated. But at age 17 she had her first epileptic seizure.

"It was at home. Mom and Dad were sitting there on the couch, and I sat down between them. My head went up, then it went back and back and I didn't know what was going on."

She was given medicine that would keep her from having other epileptic seizures, but she didn't have the confidence to go back to school. So at age 17, as an eighth-grader, she quit. A few years later, waiting for a bus to bring her back to Louisville after a weekend trip to Adair County, she met her husband, Norman Cox.

"My sister and I got on the bus, and he just started talking to us," she said.

Norman Cox worked construction, good-paying work, but not winter-steady. They had three children, two sons and a daughter. For more than 30 years, Iva Cox stayed home, raising the children. She no longer had a hearing aid; the old one had long since quit working, and she never replaced it. She just got by. Family and friends knew to talk loudly. Strangers did not.

"That's the ones I would stay back from," she said.

But something inside Iva Cox would not settle for staying back. With her children grown and gone, her husband often at work, she wanted something for herself. Then a doctor told her the state Department of Vocational Rehabilitation would buy her a hearing aid. It did, then sent her to Goodwill Industries for job evaluation. Goodwill provides many services most people don't know about, including education and job counseling. It was able to give her the one thing she wanted — a GED degree, the equivalent of a high school diploma.

"I didn't think I could do it," she said, "but I did."

She went back to school twice a week for a year, rarely missing a class, slowly opening up to the world: "I'd fall asleep at night working on schoolwork. I was determined."

She failed part of her first GED exam, but passed it all the second time. Goodwill found her a cashier's job at Walgreen's, at 970 Baxter Ave. She loves her work, feels good about herself. Her employer loves her; she's reliable and conscientious and gets to use her math.

She's providing income — and medical insurance — for her family. And Goodwill just named her — at age 54 — its Graduate of the Year.

"Watching Iva," said Goodwill job evaluator Susan Clater, "was like watching a rosebud open its petals."

Feb. 17, 1996

What's up, TARC?
Bus bunny rolls with owner

They should be in the movies, Myrtle and T.C. Perhaps a feel good tale from Walt Disney. Or a British comedy, its characters lovably eccentric, marvelously self-aware. Maybe even a cutting-edge

Louisville travelogue directed by, say, David Letterman.

Myrtle is Myrtle Gibson Montgomery, 66, who rolls through life with the exuberant good cheer — and necessary tough edges — of a successful encyclopedia saleswoman. T.C. is her pet dwarf rabbit, good friend and traveling companion. T.C. is short for Tiny Corky. Myrtle had no reasonable explanation for that; Tiny Corky just sounded right. T.C. is her fourth rabbit in 19 years.

"T.C. is the only thing I got that will listen to me," she said.

Not quite. Myrtle, who grew up in foster homes, raised five children after she and her first husband separated. She did it working 33 years at Spalding's Cleaners, standing up eight hours a day pressing clothes. She retired with a plaque, a wish to do more gardening, a need to take typing lessons and a calling to attend Simmons Bible College.

She now tends 12 gardens in her South 40th Street neighborhood and types letters to 30 pen pals, 13 of them inmates in various institutions. She is in her third year of Bible college.

"Me and the Lord," she explained.

Myrtle met her current husband — Franklin Montgomery — in New York last June while on one of her tour-bus excursions around the country. Returning home, she launched a six-month letter and telephone campaign to convince him of the wonders of Kentucky. They married — in Louisville — Jan. 14.

"We were gone for three days after the wedding," she said. "T.C. was beginning to feel neglected."

Myrtle divides her quality pet time among T.C. and four cats, Bully Girl, Sadie, Mutt and Smokey. The menagerie spends much of its time on her back porch curled up in each other's paws. T.C. also has a backyard bunny house with attached leash.

"The cats are my baby sitters," Myrtle said.

Myrtle has never owned a car; she and T.C. do her banking, visit her sick friends and take trips to choir practice, the beauty shop and shopping centers on the seats of $200,000 TARC buses. They travel light, T.C. tucked deep into a cloth shopping bag with his graham crackers and a carrot, his white ears jutting up like ships' masts, his pink eyes occasionally peering out over the edge.

Myrtle loves these trips, lives for that moment when fellow travelers learn they are sharing seat space with a dwarf white rabbit.

"T.C.'s a good little shopper," she said.

Late last week Myrtle and T.C. rode TARC across town to the

Preston Highway Value City; Myrtle had to pay $12.72 on a suit layaway. She stuffed T.C. in his blue-and-white bag, grabbed an umbrella and began walking toward her Broadway bus stop, a long-striding vision in her red jacket, blue pants and white shoes. T.C. — who's been through this before — hunkered down in his cloth hutch.

"I like to stay busy," Myrtle said. "It keeps the devil from talking to you."

Actually, the devil might never get a word in edgewise. Like an actress born, Myrtle lightly held TARC center stage, hands waving, words flowing, happy to be alive, eager to share T.C.

"It takes me awhile to travel," she said. "Everybody stops to talk to bunny."

So they did: on the bus; inside Value City; back on the bus headed home, a nearly two-hour journey of people fussing over a dwarf white rabbit. Myrtle beamed, laughed and talked about a recent trip to Las Vegas. T.C. — a travel veteran — quietly sniffed his nose at the whole thing.

Jan. 24, 1995

Enigmatic artist may have tattooed his message across city

There is no real certainty — and perhaps a shadowing of reasonable doubt — that J. Paschal Brown was the one who penned "Trust Jesus" in blocky white letters across the urban Louisville landscape.

On the other hand, Brown had the faith, ability, motive and paint supplies.

He had the sense of mission — along with playfulness and hope — the good work would require. His artist's apartment was filled with such expressions (directives?) of trust.

And whatever can be made of it, he was born on an Easter Sunday and died — of AIDS — on a Good Friday.

"To me, Paschal was somebody who had the experience of falling in love with Jesus all over again," said Ron Matz, Brown's friend and confidant. "He felt that was an experience he could share."

Matz was the first — and only — person to call following an earlier column in which I'd wondered about the source of the "Trust Jesus" graffiti that adorns Louisville sidewalks, bus shelters, bridge overpasses and traffic-light signal boxes.

It's been out there for many years, and it's been spotted — with the same lettering — in nearby cities, such as Indianapolis.

Matz says he was with Brown one night in Louisville when he spoke of his public works. Matz had given Brown a ride to the Winn-Dixie at Fourth and Oak. On the way out Matz saw the words "PRAYZ HYM" on the wall of a 24-hour diner.

"Whoever did that," Matz said, "sure didn't know how to spell."

"Yes, he did," answered Brown. "It's a play on words. I did it."

Matz said Brown later told him he'd written the "Trust Jesus" messages, working at night, hastily cranking out the lettering. Charlyn Lewis, his Hospice volunteer, said Brown also told her he was the artist. Neither Lewis nor Matz ever saw him at work.

"Paschal felt he had an inner prophecy, a still-small voice inside him that he felt was God," Matz said. "The voice was telling him, 'You now have AIDS. This is your cross.'"

Brown himself was a visual statement, a giant of a man at 6-foot-7, 235 pounds. His beard was full and flowing, his hair shoulder-length, his arms covered with jewelry, a rosary always around his throat.

He had fallen from the Catholic Church, returned to it, embraced it with a vengeance. At a 1991 Gay Pride parade he wore a flowing white robe and carried a large cross, his pet python curled around his neck.

He had credentials as a poet, performer and painter. Courier-Journal art critic Diane Heilenman attended a retrospective of Brown's work after he died April 1, 1994, at age 45.

She said Brown was a remarkably original and little-known talent, his range of works robust, compelling, unnerving, raucous and tender. He used wood, metal, spray paint and fabric to portray anger, humor, charity, hurt, passion and rejection.

Matz called Brown a humanitarian, an enigma, an oft-misunderstood man who attended church service daily, was always willing to help others in their AIDS peer group organization, willing to give up his apartment to strangers in need. He once organized a baptism for a tiny child born with AIDS. He gave generously to AIDS memorial blankets.

"We would go into hospitals or people's homes," Matz said. "Paschal always would do something I was reluctant to do. Before he left he would always ask 'Can we have a word of prayer?' "

Among his many works, Brown painted a portrait of Jesus Christ, fashioned a wood-and-metal crucifix from recycled automobile chrome and vending machines. He used fabric with collage to form "Lost Boys," the storybook gang of boys who left home to join Peter Pan in Never-Never-Land.

Most of his work was sold — some very cheaply — after his death. Some was passed on to family members.

But his most visible art — if he was the artist — graces traffic-light boxes, sidewalks, overpasses and bus shelters. The medium may be somewhat avant-garde, but Brown always was more interested in the message: Trust Jesus.

Nov. 14, 1995

Berg's newest mosaic touches blind and seeing

Our lives are a mosaic, a joining of many different pieces into the whole, a tumble of many-colored experiences that, when fitted together, form the pattern of who we are, where we've been, where we're going.

Dr. Harold Berg has helped form the mosaic of his life by giving pieces of it to others.

His most recent piece is a beauty. Berg volunteered to create a mosaic for the Kentucky School for the Blind. Its purpose was twofold: honor the school's students and staff and memorialize two of Berg's colleagues who worked at the school, Dr. Elliott Podol and Dr. Norman Glazer.

Berg, 76, is a retired surgeon and former president of the Jewish Hospital medical staff. He now has the look and feel of a grandfather-in-residence: bulky sweaters, faintly crotchety around the edges, nice sense of humor, a car license plate that reads "CUT UP," a generous heart.

Berg has been making mosaics for 35 years, work of such treasured quality it's been scattered all over Louisville — in churches, synagogues, schools, Jewish Hospital, the Louisville Zoo, the

Jewish Community Center, the American Red Cross headquarters and the University of Louisville School of Nursing.

In a classy bit of salesmanship he's also seen his work hung in the Israeli embassy in Washington, D.C., and the U.S. Embassy in Israel. There are almost 150 Harold Berg mosaics out there — and counting.

"People joke about that number," said Berg. "I tell them it's very easy to get them around as long as you give them away."

The work for the Kentucky School for the Blind is among his most difficult because it had to be more than symbolic. It had to be hands-on, to be touched and understood by students who couldn't see the yellows, greens and grays of fitted glass.

"We met with the department of psychiatry at the medical school, art therapists, painting therapists," said Berg. "They all agreed it had to be something the students could feel, something with a message."

The literal message came easily. It was derived from a T-shirt worn by the school's Special Olympics team: "Even those who cannot see the heavens . . . can reach for the stars." Translating that into three-dimensional mosaic took some time.

Berg and Ed Carter, an old friend and retired advertising artist, drew many preliminary sketches. Their first thought was to do a pair of hands reaching for the stars, a tough proposition with raised mosaic. They settled for "projections," a series of almost 40 mosaic shafts angled toward clusters of stars, the center dominated by one larger star.

"People are reading a religious message in that," he said. "I didn't intend for it to be that way, but I have no objections.... If that's what they want to feel, that's fine. Feeling something is important."

The men formed the projections with plywood, narrow shafts of wood nailed onto a broad base. That was the starting place on which to glue many thousands of tiny pieces of colored glass.

"Usually I can knock out a mosaic in a few months," he said. "This one took many, many months. The glass is sharp . . . a lot of pieces met at the edges. I had to file every piece. The children will be touching them."

Tedious work. But something that would last, a piece of his life, a place to touch — and be touched.

"People tell me it will last a lot longer than some of my patients," said Berg.

The finished product is now hanging in Houser Hall on the school campus on Frankfort Avenue, where it will be dedicated at 1 p.m. Thursday. It is in a nice location. Warm light pours in through broad windows every afternoon. The ramps leading up and down the various floors give the hall the look of an art gallery.

The mosaic is perhaps 8 feet wide and 5 feet tall. Its colors are yellow, orange, white, gray, blue and a few shades of green. The sighted can enjoy it. Hands feeling along the projections can creep upward toward the stars, tiny pieces of whitish plastic embedded in deep blue and black.

Berg stood well back from his mosaic the day it was first hung, watching the students' reaction. Picture him there, standing on a ramp, a grandfatherly man in a bulky sweater watching children approach his work.

Those with limited sight would approach within a few inches, heads cocked, staring intently at the colors. The blind would let their fingers play over the glass, then move on.

"I had tears in my eyes," said Berg, gently tapping a place on his sweater over his heart.

Oct. 2, 1993

Now, don't make too much of a fuss over Pee Wee Reese

Pee Wee Reese was marching around the lunchroom of the Audubon Country Club imitating the rolling, jingling, leather-heavy gait of a fully equipped South Central Bell telephone-line repairman.

As Reese explained it, his promising Louisville career as an apprentice telephone-line splicer was cut short about 1938 by a professional baseball career that landed him in the Baseball Hall of Fame, placed him in a national TV booth with Dizzy Dean and made him a legend to every little kid who ever picked up a Louisville Slugger.

But here's the thing about Pee Wee: He remains so doggone unassuming you might have thought he remained in telephone-line splicing. At 74, a little gimpy around the knees but still an occasional threat on the golf course, he knows who he is but never lets it get in the way of what he is — a tough, proud, likable home-town boy who never forgot where he came from.

No fussing over him — please.

"I try to avoid things," Reese said. "When I came back from the Hall of Fame, I was asked to be grand marshal of the Pegasus Parade, but I thought ... man ... I don't want to sit up there with all those people watching me.

"When I play in the Foster Brooks golf tournament, a lot of my friends will be out there, and they'll shout at me ... 'Hey, Pee Wee, who's the celebrity in your foursome?' "

With many of our heroes, those words would ring phony. With Reese, they are as genuine as a Don Newcombe fastball.

Reese was one of six children born into a farm family near Ekron, Ky., in Meade County. He was about 7 when his family moved to Louisville's Portland neighborhood. He lived there two years, then grew up around Central Park. During the Depression, his father was often unemployed; Reese's sisters found work; Pee Wee worked for a sandwich company, selling lunches to L&N Railroad workers from 6 to 7 a.m. and bringing home $1.50 a week.

He graduated from duPont Manual High School in the class of 1935 1/2, playing only five baseball games his senior year because of a hand injury. He was 5-foot-5 and weighed about 110 pounds — the physique of a natural born telephone-line splicer, a job he did hold during the 1937 flood.

Except Pee Wee was also back playing baseball.

"We won the city church championship and played the industri-al league champions out at Parkway Field," he said. "We got beat 2 to 1, but I hit one off the outfield wall.

"A guy named Cap Neal came over and asked if I had ever thought about professional baseball.... I said, no, I hadn't — and I really hadn't."

Reese signed for $150 a month — with a $200 signing bonus — to play for the AAA Louisville Colonels. By 1940 he was playing shortstop for the Brooklyn Dodgers. In 1941 — "155 pounds of cold, rolled steel" — he was playing in the World Series against the Yankees.

"I'm four years off a utility pole," Reese said.

"I'm in Yankee Stadium, and I look around and I say, "What the hell am I doing here?"

After World War II — when Reese served in the Navy — he

came back to be captain of the Brooklyn team, playing in every World Series game it later played against the hated Yankees and befriending Jackie Robinson in 1947 during those very difficult days of baseball integration.

Reese always kept his Louisville roots. After retirement, one request he couldn't avoid — "somebody talked me into it" — was lending his name to the Pee Wee Reese Cystic Fibrosis Celebrity Dinner Party. The annual dinner-dance began in the 1960s with about 60 people in Bernie's Back Room, 4023 S. Third St. It now draws about 600 people to the Galt House.

The dinner-dances and auctions of celebrity-donated items have raised more man $1 million for cystic fibrosis. The fun part is that many Louisville personalities — sports figures, politicians, disc jockeys and media types (even your humble correspondent) — serve the food, occasionally toward the floor.

This year's dinner is special because, after 25 years as host, Pee Wee Reese will hang it up; he'll be taking his golf game to Florida next winter. University of Louisville basketball coach Denny Crum will lead the event next year.

Pee Wee will be honored by the home folks about 8:30 p.m.

Don't expect too much of a fuss.

Jan. 16, 1993

Edgar Minor has earned the right to be angry

Edgar Minor's letter came with more than a newspaper clipping. It came with a well-earned sense of outrage, the straight-ahead anger of an honest man, the kind of anger that can build in a guy who's had to learn to live on $3.06 an hour.

The newspaper clipping was about a recent theft in a Louisville Chinese restaurant during which four people created a fuss, then disappeared with a briefcase containing $2,400. The four were arrested a few hours later trying the same scam in another Chinese restaurant; its employees had the good fortune to recognize what was happening and lock the thieves inside.

Minor's letter, printed in sprawling letters on four pages of notebook paper, got right to the point: He said he was "better off by working for $3 an hour than these people (who are) stealing other people's money and things that don't belong to them."

Nor did he let up any on page two:

"I know it's hard as hell to be honest, but it's the only way to go thru life."

Page three:

"I don't have . . . credit cards. I got my money in the bank. I got a beautiful apt. My health is very good and I do have peace of mind. I hope you appreciate what I'm trying to say."

Yes, I did. I found Edgar Minor, 61, at home in his ninth-floor apartment in Avenue Plaza, a fancy name for a Housing Authority of Louisville high-rise on Eighth Street, where he has lived for two years.

He is a small man — about 5 feet 4 and 135 pounds — wearing black work shoes, white socks, blue jeans and a blue shirt over a white T-shirt that shows at the collar. His tiny, $256-a-month apartment is as neat as a display window, its chrome-and-glass kitchen set, his beige couch and ruby-colored Oriental rug, his matching bed and dresser all bought at various sales by him.

Minor's friends call him "Daddy-O." He is well-scrubbed, almost pinkish, flattered and a little flustered by the attention. His hand movements are fluttering, nervous-looking and constant. His speech comes in bursts, then he lapses into silence to see if he is understood.

Minor knows exactly what he is about; the frustration comes in trying to push beyond that and understanding all the while that he may never get there.

"I was born with a mild case of cerebral palsy," he said. "I was born mildly retarded. Not real serious . . . just mildly retarded. And I have a learning disability. That's the three reasons I'm drawing $350 a month Social Security."

To augment that money, Edgar Minor works. He has worked for 40 years. His resume shows jobs at the Naval Ordnance Station, where he made enough money to buy a $10,000 house for himself and his mother, and at Bluegrass Container Co. and Goodwill Industries. From 1984 to 1987 he worked at the Louisville Free Public Library, when its custodial care was contracted out to Louisville Diversified Services, a company that bids on jobs for handicapped people and can pay below minimum wage. It is the company that employs Minor now, a company of which he is very proud.

"I clean bathrooms and tables, and I do a very good job on that," he said. "If you put me on something else I may not do a very good job because I'm not very strong.

"I'm no deadbeat. I pay my bills. That's the only way to go. I've had a checking account for over 20 years, and I've never been overdrawn. I'm a very independent person. I want to do everything by myself.

"If the people in government who wrote all the bad checks had to live on what we have to live on they'd jump out a window."

The theft in the Chinese restaurant bothered Minor because he wants to work. He takes pride in it. He's up at 4:30 a.m. every Monday through Friday to go to a part-time job that pays him $3.06 an hour. He takes home about $37 a week. He walks to Fourth and Oak streets, pushing a grocery cart, to shop. He walks to 22nd and Jefferson streets to find bargains at the DAV store.

He wants more. His goal in life is a job paying $3.85 an hour, but without going over the $300-a-month "ceiling" that could cost him his Social Security.

"I'm frustrated because I can't better myself," he said. "I see people without handicaps who can do all the things I can't, so why do they have to lie and steal?

"I've had to live on $2 and $3 an hour for the last 20 years, and I've done remarkably well. You can tell that. If I can live on $2 or $3 an hour, why can't they live on the money they make?"

Nov. 23, 1991

For duffer/author Updike, the pen isn't always mightier than the sword

John Updike has the laugh of an 18-handicap golfer: delivered easily and well, with full measure of required self-effacement, but hinting at a deeper, more brooding side.

Bogey golf will do that to a man. Or a woman.

Updike, the Jack Nicklaus of fiction, poetry and criticism, will be in Louisville Feb. 25 at the Kentucky Author Forum evening honoring Wilson W. Wyatt Sr. Updike will sign books, be interviewed by National Public Radio's Robert Siegel, perhaps demonstrate the delicate art of smashing a three-wood from a sidehill lie to a terraced green 210 yards away.

Updike first took up golf when he was 25, an age when most golfers have already hurled a half-dozen nine-irons deep into nearby lakes. He's been at the game almost 40 years and still struggles to break 90; a beneficent God ensures that genius does not automatically carry over from the pen to the putter.

Updike has chronicled his golf agony and ecstasy in 30 lyrical essays and stories nicely packaged in one small book, "Golf Dreams" (Alfred A. Knopf, $23). He will discuss that book — among others things — with Siegel.

"I prefer to write in the mornings," he said by phone from his home in Massachusetts. "I do sometimes feel guilty when I'm out on the course instead of writing, but from noon on I can live with that guilt."

Updike won two Pulitzer Prizes writing the life of Harry "Rabbit" Angstrom, basketball star turned car salesman. Reading the preface of "Golf Dreams" leaves the impression that Updike was all but ready to abandon golf for weekends more productively spent selling Volvos.

He came to those feelings when he learned during a routine visit to a doctor that he had shrunk a half-inch in height at the same time he had lost 10 yards distance with his five-irons. This was life — and *death*.

"My image of myself," he wrote, "was that of a 6-foot man who could hit a five-iron 150 yards. In all dimensions, *I was shrinking*.

"My love of golf had been of its generous measurements — its momentary amplification of myself within a realm larger than life. If my golf was to shrink, as I had seen it shrink for others, to a mingy, pokey business of arthritic shoulder-turns and low, hippity-hopping drives that merely nibbled at the yardage, I would rather not tee up."

Yeah, well, golfers revel in whiny worry, self-pity and doubt. They are always either quitting the game or heading out for more lessons, or both. Those moves — and moods — are interchangeable. Updike teed it up last summer, last fall, and will tee it up this winter.

"I was feeling gloomy when I wrote that introduction," he said. "I'm playing a bit better now. I'm looking forward to playing a little in Florida. It's the very nature of the foolish sport that we keep trying."

His 200-page book is thick with observations about golf as life, his most-quoted one providing some sort of a recurring virginity: "When you stand up on the first tee it is there, the possibility of a round without a speck of bad in it."

As a writer, he is always caught between trying to concentrate on his game while observing the humor and angst in the larger surroundings. He offers these brief pronouncements on the latter:

GOLF RELATIONSHIPS: Many men are more faithful to their golf partners than to their wives.

THE GIMMIE GAME: A unique and universally accepted form of cheating.

GOLF CADDIES: The fact is, most Americans are uneasy with servants.

GOLF WISDOM: Golf is life, and life is lessons.

GOLF HOPE: The thought that if we have one good shot in us, we must have thousands more.

Updike recorded "Golf Dreams" on cassette tape. It's the perfect traveling companion for anyone driving to Florida or South Carolina for a few weeks of certain frustration on foreign links. He sees many parallels between golf and writing, each must be polished with patience and practice, practice, practice.

"Both offer spurts of ecstasy," he said. "A really good shot speaks for itself. It comes from somewhere else."

Feb. 15, 1997

Sloth can be overcome. Now chant - Soooooommmmmmm!

My first question wasn't a test. I'm not that organized. I just wanted to know if Jean Banet, organizational specialist, card-carrying member of the National Association of Professional Organizers, could meet me for coffee at 7 yesterday morning. I'd asked her on about 15 hours notice.

"I'll check my schedule," she said. "I'll double-check my schedule."

She arrived at 6:45 a.m., radiating warmth, competence, den motherliness and organizational cheer.

She was born organized, has worked as a dental hygienist for 30 years and is now branching out into professional organizing. She will help organize your life, your business, your garage, your sock drawer.

"Being organized comes naturally to me," she said. "I don't have to think about it."

Easy for her to say. But what about us born sloths. If some people have a genetic predisposition to neatness, can't some people have a genetic predisposition to un-neatness.

"Yes," said Banet, who is professionally sympathetic to sloth, "but the good news is anybody can become organized. There are just several steps you need to take."

She pretty much has it down to an acronym: SOM — simplify, organize, maintain. It's an educational pitch she enjoys giving to business and professional groups. Simplifying begins with reducing clutter. We Americans have so much unneccessary stuff, we now build acres of flat, metallic, commercial storage sheds to house it. We pay big rent to have others watch stuff we'll never look at again. So why not pay somebody to help us get rid of it?

"There are two keys to determining if you really should save something," Banet said. "Is it essential? Is it enjoyable? If it doesn't fit those criteria, it should go."

That may — or may not — apply to spouses.

But Banet said there are too many spouses who become sloth-enablers. They continually pick up after someone in the interest of keeping the house clean but, in doing so, are destroying any real will-to-clean in the process.

"People who are not organized need to make a conscious effort to do it," she said.

She believes mail should always be handled and/or answered the day it's received, a practice I've always reserved only for incoming checks. Don't allow all those stupid, six-new-ones-a-day Christmas catalogs to pile up; get rid of them. Stop saving whole magazines to keep one story; clip out the story, put it in a folder.

Her SOM mantra: throw away, give away, sell or recycle. Soooooommmmmmm.

"The first problem is that people become so overwhelmed with things they don't know where to start," she said. "The second problem is they procrastinate, say they will do it tomorrow."

Well ... there is always tomorrow. If you didn't have to read this column today, I'd rather write it Sunday. Still, one of Banet's clients learned she was wasting about $200 a year in credit-card interest because her desk was so cluttered she couldn't find the bills. A friend of Banet's had a client in North Carolina who found a 9-year-old letter in his "in" basket. My personal best is only about six months.

Lugging photographs of her clean-up projects the way an architect might show off a shiny new home, Banet offered a dazzling photo display of drawers compartmentalized, closets rearranged and shelves hung.

"I had one client so upset about her mess she was hyperventilating," Banet said.

Which brings us directly to behavior modification and maintaining good organizational habits. Once the sloth cycle has been broken, only constant and faithful attention to detail will keep your car, house and work-station neat.

Banet said there is actual empirical evidence that people can and will feel good knowing exactly where to find a screwdriver, a hammer, their reading glasses, sunglasses, gloves, checkbook or car keys. Go figure.

There evidently are also people out there who place soiled socks, underwear and athletic supporters in clothes hampers. I've always thought that's why God invented bedroom floors.

Nov. 23, 1996

The Incredible Honking Lausmans are a fowl-mouthed crew

The printed word alone will not work on this one. You must help. You must summon up that gut-level thrill of watching a flock of geese sweep past against a gray November sky, their loud, insistent cries haunting and evocative. Then cut to Karl Lausman Jr., 14, seated at his kitchen table, filling his house with those same wild calls — the shrill crescendo of a love-sick car horn.

Move on to Travis Lausman, 13, his brother, who also calls geese. Do not leave out Sara Lausman, 11, their precocious sister, who has just discovered her voice. These, then, are the Incredible

The Lausman siblings, Sara, Travis and Karl Jr.

Honking Lausmans of Mount Washington, Ky. — all of whom practice at home, at the table, sometimes 90 minutes a day.

"I'm awfully proud of all of them," said Karl Lausman, 38, father of the clan.

"We do have a neighbor who will love to see us move to Wyoming," said Cindy Lausman, 36, who has learned to live with her children's fowl racket.

Love will do that. In spite of their tendency to be calling geese at odd — and even — hours, the Lausmans are everything you'd want to hear in a family: polite, close-knit, honest, friendly and likable.

Karl Sr., a self-employed carpenter, first sounded the goose call when he began guiding hunters, then began crafting calls for them. In 10 years he's become a master, transforming solid, cylindrical pieces of wood or acrylic into calls with a range of tones impossible to find in the store-bought variety.

"I stand by everything I make," he said.

So do his wife and children. And since Dad had to test the calls, his sons began helping him. Then Karl Jr. went one step further — or actually backward. He reverted to the old-fashioned notion of calling geese with his own, unaided voice.

He became so good he recently won the World Goose Calling

Junior Division Championship in Easton, Md., competing against others using mechanical calls. He was so mesmerizing that had he competed in the adult division he would have finished fourth among 33 professional guides. When Karl Jr. finished his kid-does-goose performance the whole auditorium went nuts — sorta honkers bonkers.

"I was so nervous before the contest started I went into the bathroom and got sick," he said.

There had been some fear that galloping puberty — the curse of adolescent vocals — might cramp his style. It hasn't.

"It helped my voice get deeper and louder," he said.

Travis Lausman is no goose-calling slouch himself. Using one of his father's rosewood calls, he finished third in the junior competition. Last year he finished second in the division.

Sara, 11, a late entry in the goose-calling business, has also proved to be a gamer. She won the 10-and-under division in the Kentucky state contest and shows just as much promise as her brothers. She, too, has dropped the mechanical call, walks around the house calling geese the old-fashioned way.

"You rarely see a woman in goose-calling competition," said her father.

Karl Sr. once competed, had limited success, moved offstage to allow his children to honk their own horns.

"I make 'em, and they blow 'em," he said.

Imagine, if you can, three healthy, active children — and their father — wandering around the house calling geese; practice, practice, practice. The Lausmans also practice outside, accompanied or a capella. Buddies often ask Karl Jr. to cut loose at school, teachers willing, or at ballgames. He's so good he once lured a flock of geese into the yard.

"It is an annoying sound," Karl Sr. said. "We do contain it to inside the house after 10 at night and before 8:30 in the morning." Actually, one of the neighbors did call the police about 11 one night — Karl Sr. had honked one honk too many. And the family is moving to Wyoming in March to live — and serve as guides — on a huge hunting ranch.

"The nearest towns are called Yoder and Chugwater," said Cindy Lausman. "They're 20 miles apart. It should be the perfect place to call geese."

Nov. 30, 1995

The folks who really get the work done aren't always the ones in charge

Sometimes when I watch alleged leaders — or even fellow office workers — circle one another for weeks at a time trying to exercise control or solve some argument or dispute, I think about the work ethic of Raymond Nunn.

Raymond was not born to be a diplomat. He was a construction worker, a man of limited formal education who never would have felt at home in an office, much less at a banquet table. But he had a way of getting his message across.

Raymond was the most naturally muscled man I have ever known. When he lifted things, the cords along the back of his neck would knot up and thick slabs of muscle would gather across his back and shoulders and down across his thighs and calves.

Just watching Raymond walk across a field, his shirt unbuttoned, his arms as thick and taut as ship's rope, you could see the power in the man and sense his presence.

Raymond knew this, of course. There were buttons on his shirt. He could have buttoned them. But that wouldn't have been Raymond.

Raymond had come by this muscle the old-fashioned way; he earned it. He'd been digging trenches and lifting pipes since he was a kid. He had never been in the mainstream of public educational or social concern. To Raymond Nunn, Head Start was something you got on Friday nights to beat the traffic on the way home.

We met during a summertime construction job in Texas. We were laying a waterline across a flat field so some developer could fill it with streets and houses. There were about 15 laborers in our crew, and 14 of them — the black laborers — were being paid $1.25 an hour. I got $1.50 an hour because I was white.

I'm sure that kind of pay structure really bothered Raymond, but we never got close enough to talk about it; that's just the way things were then in Texas.

It was lousy and dangerous work at 10 times the pay. Often the temperature would be in the high 80s when we went to work at 7 a.m. and would be well over 100 when we quit at 5 or 6 p.m.

The technique was simple enough: Some guy on the backhoe would dig a trench 12 to 15 feet deep, we would lay water pipe along its length, and another guy on a small bulldozer would fill it in behind us.

There were almost no safety precautions. One rainy morning a trench caved in, and two terrified men scrambled nearly 10 feet up the sheer face of a dirt wall as tons of thick, wet earth slid in behind them.

The crew took a 10-minute break to clear the trench, added a couple of supports and went back to work.

Raymond was the crew boss. We had crane operators, bulldozer jockeys and even an official foreman — all white, of course — but Raymond was the man, the sergeant, the ramrod.

He just did it naturally. The other people made more money, drove nicer cars and huddled together when things went wrong, but not much moved unless Raymond said it moved.

It wasn't that he talked much or even raised his voice; Raymond came of more heroic proportion than that. Raymond really was the strong silent type. He could give orders without even opening his mouth. A guy could look at Raymond and understand he'd better go pick up a shovel and get in the trench.

I don't know how he did it. But I know I have watched dozens of other people over the years try to give orders, people who were supposed to be in charge but who had no natural leadership ability, and none of them could do it as well as Raymond; it takes a heckuva man to get somebody in the bottom of a wet, 15-foot-deep trench at 7 o'clock on a rainy morning.

Like I said, Raymond knew it, and he took no small pride in that. In a way, that was his extra pay, his other 25 cents an hour. The better-paid people were playing a game; they could all pretend to be in charge, but everybody in the field or down in the trench knew the real score.

Sometimes I think the world is run by the people like Raymond, people who are either denied the chance to be placed in charge or are just more comfortable operating a few notches below the firing line.

It is almost always they — the upper-level city or county employees who stay while elected bosses come and go, the secretaries who run the office for 20 years while bosses are promoted upward — who get the real work accomplished.

And they know it.   *July 22, 1989*

Robert French will tell you it's been a full 100 years

They tried to get NBC's Willard Scott to say something nice about Robert French on his 100th birthday. Willard Scott would say nice things about Death Valley as long as you slapped a silly hat on his head and paid all necessary expenses. But Scott wasn't able to mention Robert French. Scott has a 10-month waiting list of people waiting to turn 100. NBC even provides a special phone number in case the potential honoree dies in the interim.

Not that Robert French's 100th birthday — which occurred last Tuesday — went totally unnoticed. The celebration lasted a week. His family threw him a big party before the big event. On Monday night some good friends took French to Po Folks in Clarksville, a must stop on the centenarian circuit, for a meal of steak, vegetables, cake and ice cream.

In keeping with the tradition of those wild and crazy people at Po Folks, all the waiters, waitresses and kitchen workers lined up and sang "Happy Birthday." There wasn't a dry eye in the non-smoking section.

Tuesday afternoon French had planned to go out to lunch with a few more friends, but then he canceled. He was feeling a little tired. Just how much fun can a 100-year-old guy take?

Instead, it was cake and punch at the Mount Holly Nursing Center, where French has been living for two years. French likes it there, and it wasn't a major decision for him to move. They had taken away the keys to his Cadillac when he was 98, so he figured it was time he slowed down a little bit anyway.

"I couldn't see quite so good anymore," he confessed.

Hey, Robert French played baseball with Pee Wee Reese's father, and Pee Wee will never see 70 again. In fact, French left home before Pee Wee was born.

"I grew up in Ekron in Meade County," French said. "Pee Wee's dad had a farm three or four miles down the road. He played first base and pitched a little. He wasn't too bad a ballplayer."

There were eight people in the senior class of Ekron High School when French graduated. He went to a teacher's college in Bowling Green for two years and returned to Meade County and taught school. That didn't last long. The pay was about $100 a month, and the school term lasted six months.

"I moved to Louisville and went to work in the accounting department for the L&N Railroad," he said.

World War I came along, but it didn't seem to want much to do with Robert French. He tried to do his part, but the Army wasn't interested.

"I was about 5-foot-6 and weighed 112 pounds," he said. "I went to get examined, and this old sergeant picked me up and put me in the back of the room. He said they wanted to win the war, and I was too small to help much. I haven't heard from him since."

In 1923 French married Thelma Cardwell. They were married 60 years and had one son. French's relationship with the L&N Railroad wasn't nearly as permanent. He was the entrepreneurial sort. He went to Tri-City Barber College, then bought a three-chair barbershop at Fifth and Breckinridge. He called it French's. Pretty soon just one barbershop wouldn't do, so French added another. And another. And another. And another. And another.

Count 'em up; six French's barbershops, which he cleverly named French's #1, French's #2, French's #3, etc., etc., etc. He became a regular McClippers — the six of his shops scattered from Fifth and Breckinridge to 18th and Hill to 38th and Broadway. Then French added nine or 10 rental houses, and suddenly he wasn't able to barber quite as much as he had.

"With all that," he said, "I'd get in my car and drive from place to place to place."

For more than 50 years he drove from place to place to place. When his wife became ill, he sold almost everything to care for her. When she died, he lived alone for a few years, then turned in the Cadillac and moved to Mount Holly.

French has since replaced the Cadillac with a stationary exercise bike, your basic, digital Vitamaster 554C, on which he rolls up enough miles almost every day to get to Shively. He pedaled it a little on his 100th birthday, a still-healthy, mostly happy, very dignified man who knows how to deflect the easy compliment:

"Robert, you don't look a day over 96."

"I hope not," he said.

He also knew how to handle the mandatory dumb question:

"So Robert, how does it feel to be 100?"

"I don't know. I haven't been 100 that long."

Aug. 11, 1990

J.C. Flanagan Sr.: Gone from Fourth and Oak, but not forgotten

Toward the end, Joseph C. Flanagan Sr. drank nothing but Wild Irish Rose. He drank it neither wisely, nor too well, and it killed him. He died in his sleep on a Saturday morning two weeks ago in a friend's apartment. His girlfriend of six months was in the bed beside him. He was in his late 50s. The Jefferson County coroner's office said he died of natural causes.

Ora-Mae Mason knows something of the natural causes. She owns the Casa Francesca pizza parlor at 333 W. Oak St., some 10 steps in from the corner of Fourth and Oak.

She has owned the restaurant for seven years. It is a small, cluttered, tired-looking place with a pizza oven, five tables covered with pink-and-white-checked tablecloths and a dozen salmon-colored plastic chairs. A jukebox and cigarette machine are pushed together near the front door.

"Joe's been around this corner for ages," she said, "even since I've been here. When Joe was at himself — and not too much in his cups — he could carry on a very intelligent conversation. He wasn't always a wino. He developed into one."

Joseph C. Flanagan Sr. had family, but none claimed him. He took the reasons for their bitterness to his grave. The funeral arrangements were handled by Ora-Mae Mason.

"Joe'd come in here and sit when the weather was bad," she said. "If I was working in here alone, he'd park on the ledge outside to deter anybody that had any bright ideas. A lot of people thought a lot of Joe around here."

There is a certain toughness among the long-term regulars at Fourth and Oak, and a closeness that comes with it. Ora-Mae Mason checked church and public records for Flanagan's relatives, notified the ones she could reach and learned that none seemed to care.

"It was the first time I ever had something like that dropped into my lap," she said. "I assure you of one thing: It sure made me think."

Flanagan was a veteran and was entitled to a $300 burial

allowance and $150 for the gravesite. Ora-Mae Mason said it was obvious the funeral home did not want to bury Flanagan without receiving a little more money.

"They asked me if I could come up with some more cash from his friends," she said. "I think they delayed the funeral until we got up some more money."

Ora-Mae Mason came up with $25, as did two other friends. The extra $75 seemed to tip the scales, and final arrangements were completed.

"I'm not going to say Joe was perfect," she said. "He had his faults. But I can't see nobody turning their back on a dead friend or relative."

She said Flanagan lived on a veteran's pension and rarely worked, although he was a good mechanic. He was often picked up by the police for public intoxication and made frequent trips to the community treatment (detoxification) center.

"The last couple years he'd try to serve 90 days in jail in the winter so he'd have a warm place to stay," she said. "He dried out for six or eight months about three years ago. He was a sweetheart then, but he fell off the wagon about Christmas."

"He used to be clean all the time," she said. "Always in a suit. If we caught him in dirty clothes, we'd tell him he looked like a wino. He'd go home and shave and put on a clean suit."

When he had money, Flanagan took care of his friends. When he was broke, they took care of him. If he needed a place to sleep, a friend let him sleep in his car. If he needed cigarettes, he could hit somebody for some change. If he got too wild around the restaurant, Flanagan might be thrown out for a night, but he always returned. If he needed a bottle of Wild Irish Rose, a friend might buy it.

"Can't say we did him any favors there," said Ora-Mae Mason.

Flanagan was so sick the night before he died he went to a hospital for treatment. His girlfriend — a drinking companion — went with him. Then they went to a friend's house to spend the night.

"When his girlfrfiend got up the next morning," said Ora-Mae Mason, "Joe didn't."

Ora-Mae Mason will miss him.

"He looked out for people," she said. "He'd walk ladies down the street and help carry their packages. He had feelings."

Flanagan was buried a week ago today in Calvary Cemetery. If any of his close relatives went to the funeral, they didn't sign the guest book. Among the 18 people who did sign were two employees of the community treatment center.

Ora-Mae Mason did not go to the funeral either. She suffered severe chest pains while shoveling snow from her driveway that morning.

"I hit the nitroglycerine tablets and went to bed," she said. "Stayed there the whole weekend."

Feb. 16, 1980

Oh suitable, for tasteful stripes, for one man's storms of brain

Joseph E. Zoeller walked into the newspaper building yesterday with his three-piece dress suit of patriotic and religious significance clinging to one arm and his sweet, shy young daughter clinging to the other.

Zoeller, 33, of 7230 Sky Blue Ave., is a painter by trade and a dreamer by inclination. He said he had been a drinker and a backslider until God suddenly appeared in his life about 6 one dreary, shapeless morning during a poker game in rural Virginia.

The spirit settled in with a vengeance.

Zoeller continually feels the need to preach and proselytize. He is borne by the hurricane winds of religious fervor. They are forever blowing ideas his way.

One is a device that could be used by bricklayers to square corners more easily. Zoeller has invested $2,000 in the device, developing it and attempting to secure a patent. None has been sold to date.

The idea for the three-piece suit of religious and patriotic significance popped into his mind about two years ago. Zoeller believes it popped up because he is a believer in a world ot doubters, a red, white and blue patriot bobbing in a gray sea ot apathy.

His idea was to create a suit that Americans could wear with pride at home and abroad. The suits would be identical in design and color, leaving no doubt as to the politics of anyone wearing one.

"It was just an idea I had," he said. "The suits would be worn everywhere. Rich people would wear them when traveling to Europe and around the world. People could wear them with cranberry shirts, blue shirts or blue ties. The suits would be more popular than Bing Crosby's 'White Christmas.' They would symbolize America everywhere."

Zoeller didn't just sit on this idea of what would become Our National Uniform. He dug out paper and pen and began drawing. Then he dug out $300 and purchased the prototype of what he wanted, a white wool double-breasted suit with a deep-blue lapel, 13 red stripes slanting neatly across its sleeves and pockets and 10 gold buttons, each containing five stars, or one star for each state.

An emblem that includes a wreath of brown wheat and a red cross was attached below one pocket. The white suit trousers have narrow red and blue stripes down each leg. The vest remained a solid white.

For women, Zoeller created a white wool skirt that would match the jacket and would also be lined with red and blue stripes.

"It is a wool suit because Jesus Christ is the lamb ot God," he said. "I wanted a felt collar because felt is closely knit, like a family, and we Americans must learn to be one family. The cross and wheat signify Jesus as the bread of life and the abundance of the United States. It is all coming together now. It must. God gave us His son as a sacrifice. We have lost that spirit of sacrifice. I can't even get my kids to take out the garbage."

Zoeller went beyond designing and purchasing his suit. He found an attorney willing to file a patent design application for the suit, and the paperwork has been sent to Washington. He specifically called his creation a "Suit of Patriotic and Religious Significance."

Normally the fee would have been about $600, he said, but he traded a paint job with the lawyer instead.

"I painted the inside and outside ot his house, basement and doghouse," Zoeller said. "He doesn't have a thing left unpainted."

He also took his suit to a local retailer trying to market it. The retailer said the suits could be purchased from a manufacturer for about $60 each, and sold for $125. But the kicker is a minimum of 500 such suits must be ordered.

"I'm broke," Zoeller said, "and where's a broke house painter going to get $30,000 to order 500 suits. I know they will sell. I just need somebody to help me get them going."   *Jan. 17, 1980*

Mertha Mae Hines has tomatoes in her garden, poetry in her soul

It is the music of spoken language we are dealing with here, the sweet rhythm and poetry of common language made uncommon: The Happy Confessions of a Novice Gardener.

The gardener is Mertha Mae Hines. Her garden is no bigger than the top of your kitchen table. Its fruits may be no larger than the ones you grow.

But we want to talk about quality of life here, not quantity of tomatoes.

She calls it her "proud garden."

A thousand poets with all their subtle shadings of thought and imagery couldn't improve on that.

Mertha Mae Hines lives in a big, solid brick house at 4319 Hale Ave. She lives there with Perry Hines, her husband of 67 years. He is 89. He is a big, though aging man, with big hands, hands that swallow others' in a handshake, hands that spread out like meaty shovels across his knees.

Mertha Mae Hines is past 80 and holding. She is a tiny woman, the daughter of a midwife and a Civil War soldier and preacher named Jacob. She is the last survivor of a family of 12 brothers and sisters. Her voice is a musical instrument, rising and falling in accompaniment to her words.

She grew her first garden this year. She had wanted it to be a tiny square, but her husband made it a small oval instead. Then he went back inside to let his wife tend it. A niece brought her four tomato slips, and she bought five more wilted plants at a sale for $1.

But listen. Let her tell about it.

" . . . So I took the five plants and put 'em under my arm and brought them home. I knew nothing about a garden. Never had a garden in my life . . . and me past 80....

"I brought 'em home and I didn't feel too good but I went around and stuck holes and put them in the ground. I took a box and sat on it and just dragged it around. That's how I planted it.

"I put tomatoes, I put onion sets down in the ground I didn't know how to dig, and I put potato eyes in the ground....

"A neighbor gave me some beans — white beans, navy beans — and I planted them. I never knew a navy bean would grow 'cause I never knew nothing about a garden. Then the tomatoes come up and I got hold and measured them and they is just as high as I am tall.

"A few weeks ago my nephew looked and saw this great big tomato at the end of the garden. I went and plucked it because it was so close to the gate and I was afraid somebody would pass along and pick it up.

"It was so heavy, I said 'I believe I'll measure this tomato.'

"I got a string and put it around it. And I measured the string and it was 15 1/2 inches around the tomato. I said that was a mighty lot of inches."

Later on, "I went to the senior citizens (center) and they marveled at it. And then I went and got on the bus and went to town. The storekeeper come up and said it's too heavy to weigh on his scales. He looked right at me and said it was too heavy. I left the tomato there and come straight home and kept tying up, tying up (tomatoes) 'cause they getting so heavy."

She's past 80, and holding, and her voice sings.

"I was born first day of May, my mother loved flowers and I do love flowers today. She was in the flower garden when that time came, least that's what they claim, and they nicknamed me Mae, born first day of May.

"My husband brought the soil here. He enriched the land . . . married 67 years . . . I read the Bible in my kitchen right over my table . . . I read the Bible every day . . . I start the day with the Lord.

"We never had any children for our own, but I helped to raise my sisters' and brothers' children . . . more than 100 still living . . . no end to the generations.

"Had one nephew from here in this house and left here and gone to Racine, Wisconsin. He helps make cars in Wisconsin. His own mother is still living, but he gets here to see me before he sees his mother . . . I'd taken care of him so you know he must love me."

And her being past 80. And there's her proud garden.

"See these tomatoes . . . I've tied and tied and tied them . . . and I have lots of small ones coming up. I was marveled. I didn't think those things was any good . . . they was wilted . . . five for a dollar.

"Just look . . . just look at the tomatoes . . . and beans . . . I had beans all around the tomatoes and given away beans.

"Oh my goodness, my goodness, my goodness, I'm proud of my garden. I never saw nothing like it."

Sept. 18, 1979

The rambler: No holdin' or foldin'

Lord, how he does ramble.

Sentences pour out of his mouth at 300 to 500 words a minute with gusts of up to 800.

His feet and thumb have worked in conjunction to rack up some 291,000 miles of intercontinental hitchhiking, a feat duly noted as the world's record on pages 464-465 of your 1979 paperback edition of the Guinness Book of World Records.

DeVon Smith. A man for all reasons. The pride of Wampum, Pa. Tracer of lost causes. Superthumb.

Smith, picket-fence thin at 53, rambled through Louisville this week. He's put his thumb in semi-retirement now, preferring instead to ride in the big belly of a gray and silver bus.

He began rambling in 1945, says he went professional in 1957 when he began keeping records of every ride (6,613 and counting) and hasn't glanced in the rear-view mirror since.

Smith has embraced more causes than a radical priest. This is a man who honored Napoleon on his 200th birthday by collecting post cards and signatures from every town in the United States named Napoleon and shipping them off to France.

He has made two "space trips," riding his thumb to such meccas as Jupiter, Fla.; Sun, La.; Pluto, W. Va., and Neptune, N. J., to collect signatures.

He hammered out the world's biggest handmade brass key, stamped in the states of the 22 American towns named Elizabeth and presented it to a representative of Queen Elizabeth.

Alas, the several thousand signatures he collected to honor Premier Chou En-lai didn't get him a trip to China.

Back home in Wampum in the off-season, Smith makes his living chopping up junk cars with an ax and selling the scrap.

DeVon Smith   *Photo by Cort Best*

"Actually, the cars aren't so bad," he says. "I have a much more difficult time chopping up the washers and dryers and refrigerators and things like that."

There have been few years when his one-man salvage business has grossed more than $3,000, less hubcaps.

He travels literally by the seat of his Salvation Army pants, his thin shoulders draped in a red blazer littered with souvenir pins and patches of his various odysseys.

"I don't use hotels," he said. "I sleep on the bus."

Still, there have been some real milestones in his career. He did travel to the geographic center of 13 states, gathering 4,000 signatures on a 168-foot birthday card for Johnny Carson.

The card got on Carson's show, but Smith didn't.

And there was that 6,000-mile jaunt on the trans-Siberian railroad. And the free airplane trip home after he was stranded in Brazil.

And, of course, the autograph salute to Richard Nixon. And the 10,000 signatures and 21 post-card albums he gathered to honor Bob Hope. And the post cards he gathered in England to honor the 350th anniversary of the Mayflower landing.

And night owls may still be able to catch Smith on the old Groucho Marx show "You Bet Your Life," a show that may be the only item around more well-traveled than Smith.

"I just called Groucho's manager and said I wanted to be on," Smith said. "They want to be sure they're not dealing with a lunatic or something."

But his finest effort was the Bicentennial birthday card he gave to the Bicentennial Commission.

Starting in a $50 car in California, Smith drove 10,000 miles and collected 21,000 names on a 676-foot pleated birthday card.

Plus a special 20-foot celebrities section.

"I was on the road 41 days," he said, "and I slept in the car 35 nights."

Smith lives with a brother and their 79-year-old mother in Wampum. He slips through the country so quickly he asks that all copies of newspaper stories, post cards and letters be sent to his Wampum home, ZIP Code 16157.

"That way Momma reads the mail," he says, "and she knows where I've been, and to that point that I'm all right."

Somewhere in here, of course, we should deal with why Smith does all this. But he can't really explain it. That's the way it is with rambling men.

Smith was in Louisville on his latest cross-country venture, which is to honor the 100th anniversary of Tom Edison's light bulb. He started, of course, in Sparks, Nev., and went through Edison, Calif.

And he did want to get to Frankfort, Ky., the only state capital in the United States that he hasn't visited.

Edison lived in Louisville for a time. So Smith wanted to come here. And he's asked all Louisvillians to mail a souvenir post card (along with a letter, Edison memorabilia or newspaper clipping) back home to Wampum to verify his stop, to thank Edison and to tell his Momma he's all right.

Mrs. Smith, the last time Louisville saw your son, he was doing fine.

April 19, 1979

A salute to old soldiers — and a salute to devotion

The letter, written more than 50 years ago, was folded like a tiny map, creased, ragged at its edges, probably unreadable. It was folded like that because Roger Spaulding — who on Aug. 30, 1945, became the first U.S. Marine to land on Japan at the end of the war — has kept it in his billfold as a reminder: mail from home, mail from the woman who would become his wife.

"She doesn't even know I have it," he said, carefully refolding the letter, sliding it back into his billfold. "But I saved this one."

Roger Spaulding

There has been so much to save — and savor. Unfold those World War II memories and remember and honor those still with us. Already the veteran ranks have been badly thinned, their trumpets muted.

"I don't have that hatred," said Spaulding, 74. "I lost my hostility for the Japanese people before I got off Japan."

His emotions were more raw when the Marines pulled him to active duty in 1942. The high school sports star from Sheridan, Ind., was at Purdue University, hoping to become a veterinarian, when the Marines called. He had eight weeks of boot camp in San Diego, then set his sights higher: the 4th Marine Raider Battalion.

"I heard it was a commando outfit," he said. "It was the elite part of the Marine Corps. I was itching to fight."

After five months of more training, his battalion — 986 enlisted men and 37 officers — headed for the South Pacific. He was soon part of a mission to scout islands for enemy radio stations. Five-man squads were dropped off submarines in rubber boats and told to return at a set time.

"If we were even 15 minutes late, the submarines would leave without us," he said. "The subs couldn't stay. There was always the danger one of us might be taken prisoner, give away the sub's location, and it would be sunk. We lost five Raiders one time and later found out the Japanese had beheaded them."

The 4th Marine Raider Battalion would make stops in places where such savagery became commonplace: Guadalcanal, New Georgia, Emirau, Guam and Okinawa. He was on Guam 37 days. Eighty-six of the 200 men in his company were killed, and all but two were wounded. Spaulding was nearly beheaded by a charging Japanese soldier; a nearby buddy saved him. During his 98 days on Okinawa, he lost every man in his 12-man squad five times. He never met some replacements; they would be sent up at night, be gone by morning. A hand grenade blew fine pieces of metal into his face. Until a few years ago, the tiny bits of shrapnel were still working free from his cheek.

Spaulding was offered a 30-day leave — a chance to go home —

before the invasion of Japan. Only about nine of his original battalion of 1,000 men were left; the rest were dead or wounded. He turned down the leave; he didn't want to go home, then have to come back. Then the atomic bombs ended the fighting.

Because it had done so much to bring about the end of the war, his squad was picked to secure Tokyo Bay for the Sept. 2, 1945, peace signing aboard the battleship Missouri. Before going ashore on Aug. 30, Spaulding was told that the mission was to silence four 16-inch guns guarding the harbor. No one expected any trouble. Spaulding was told not to start any shooting.

"Sir," he replied, "we're disciplined."

He was told to have his men keep their rifle safeties on.

"No, sir, I can't tell my men that. But we are disciplined."

Spaulding and his squad went in before daybreak. He was the first to step off the landing craft onto Japanese soil. He found 37 Japanese soldiers in a nearby building, eating breakfast. There was no trouble.

Spaulding spent 18 days in Japan. As he traveled the villages, he saw hungry children, desperate mothers. Three years of anger drained from him; the killing was over. "They didn't want this any more than I did," he said.

He came home in autumn 1945. In 1948 he married Helen Stephenson, the woman who had written to him for three years during his Pacific duty. Before he went to war, they had not met; he had gotten her name through the girlfriend of a Marine buddy. They bought a 460-acre farm in Jennings County, raised three children, have given their years to the Peace Corps and as Methodist missionaries in Liberia, Costa Rica, Russia and on a Navajo Indian reservation.

Until recently he spoke little of all this. He has always honored his Marine buddies and recently was honored by his hometown. Now it's our old soldiers' last hurrah, their final bow, their moments together as precious as a letter saved 50 years . . . *Semper fidelis* . . . always faithful.

Aug. 26, 1995

Linkletter produced good TV by avoiding teachers' best kids

Art Linkletter was talking about interviewing children, and the joys and pitfalls lurking within the process. He was doing so while eating breakfast in Louisville's Seelbach Hotel: half a grapefruit, two poached eggs and — here was a surprise — some hash browns to add a little kick to dietary sainthood.

At 84, Linkletter looked good, sounded good, must be good. He wore a knit shirt, gray jacket and the casual air of a man who has launched 10,000 interviews. He was in Louisville to help Humana launch a nationwide program called Active Outlook for its 375,000 chronologically enhanced members.

He travels 200,000 miles a year lecturing on getting old well, staying optimistic and finding reasons to get up in the morning.

"The slogan we have is, 'Living better longer,'" he said, "with longer in second place. Nobody gives a damn about living longer if longer is not better."

In his lifetime, he said, average life expectancy has increased 29 years, and 70 percent of our national wealth now belongs to people at least 50 years old.

"For the last 10 years," Linkletter said, jokingly, "I've been watching this whole thing of the acquisition of the world by seniors. It's a big plot. But up until this time, nobody's made much of a concerted effort to figure out what we should be doing with our extra time."

From 1944 to 1969 — on both the radio and television versions of "Art Linkletter's House Party" — he made a fine living coaxing funny thoughts from schoolchildren perched on hard chairs. Linkletter confessed the secret of their humor in mid-poached egg:

"Their teachers were under instructions to pick anyone they wanted, but I told them I didn't want the good kids. I would prefer they choose the kids they wanted out of class for a few blessed hours."

He leaned back and laughed. Everyone else at the table laughed too.

The reality is, the world has changed so much, radio and television have changed so much, that even the thought that an adult could make a syndicated living these days getting kids to say the darnedest things seems impossible. Somebody would sue for psychological damage or child abuse.

"Kids from 4 to 10 haven't changed much." Linkletter said. "Kids 12 and over sure have. Plenty."

Linkletter is a human line of demarcation in our television society; locals 40 and over can remember his show the way they remember Louisville's "T-Bar-V Ranch" with Cactus Tom Brooks and Randy Atcher; people younger than that can barely remember black-and-white television.

Linkletter began his own life as an orphan, abandoned in a small hospital in Moose Jaw, Saskatchewan, in 1912. An old couple named Linkletter adopted him. His new father was a shoemaker who preached on Sundays. They were very poor; Art Linkletter began his work before the public handling church collections; his family ate from those collections.

"I never did look for my birth parents," he said. "I always had the feeling the people who adopted me were my real parents because they earned it, while the other people were my parents because they had a whim behind a billboard somewhere."

He wanted to be an English teacher but got sidetracked into radio in 1933 by a surprise call from a station manager wanting an announcer: "I didn't ask salary, or hours. That was the Depression. If he had asked me if I was interested in coming down to his station and being a brain surgeon, I would have said, "Yes.'"

Linkletter has not held to his sense of humor easily; a daughter killed herself on an LSD trip and a son died in an auto accident. He managed to learn from his losses and used that knowledge to work with others who also had lost children.

About a month ago, CBS-TV broadcast a special with Bill Cosby and Linkletter. Linkletter showed clips of his old show, the interviews with kids. Unbeknownst to him, the studio audience consisted of adults who had been on his show as children.

After the show, the adults affectionately mobbed him, many wearing pins or carrying dolls he'd given them 40 years ago. CBS has promised Linkletter three more shows. He's looking forward to doing them.

June 17, 1997

Chapter Five

ENDINGS

For reasons known only to my
psychoanalyst, I often write about
funerals, the ends of things, the sense
of loss surrounding people and places
dearly departed. The funeral of
Muhammad Ali's mother — who was
called "Mama Bird" — the death
of U of L basketball player Derek
Smith, the calculated, illegal
destruction of Highland Park by
economic greed and politicians
supposedly elected to help people each
created powerful — and tragic —
moments. Death is a part of life, but
I'm sure glad this is one of the shorter
sections in this book.

'Blight' ideas add insult to injury

The residents of Highland Park, Prestonia and Standiford have begun making bitter little jokes about their situation now, constantly reminding one another that they live in a "blighted" area, with every little crack in the sidewalk or flaking piece of paint a reminder of their pitiful condition.

They talk like that because it's always easier to joke about a hurt than to talk seriously about it, especially to strangers. The words don't come easily anyway. The pain, frustration and anger run too deep.

Earlier this week three urban-renewal plans necessary for the eventual destruction of Highland Park, Prestonia and Standiford labeled all three neighborhoods as suffering from economic blight.

The roughly 3,500 people who live there are to be moved out, about 1,400 dwellings will be leveled and most of the land will be used for commercial development around an expanded Standiford Field, not for the airport expansion itself. A painful irony is that money realized from the sale of the land might be used to pay the relocation costs of its former owners.

Some of the neighborhoods do have obvious pockets of economic blight, mostly because previous forms of progress — expansions of highways and the airport — made the area more unattractive, and some people gave up and left.

But to label all of it blighted, particularly the Standiford neighborhood, is a travesty — and the worst form of governmental arrogance. Even more frightening is the thought that, if the Standiford neighborhood is found to be economically blighted, then your neighborhood could be next.

Don't take my word for it. Get in your car and drive through Standiford. You'll find exactly what I did. Almost all its houses are brick. They are well-kept, with shutters on most front windows and wrought-iron railings around the front porches. Dormers have been added to the fronts of many of the houses, skylights to the roofs and garages to the back yards.

It's too early to see the flowers, but you'll see lawn after lawn that's obviously been well-tended. You'll see neatly trimmed shrubbery, azalea bushes getting ready to bloom and spreading dogwood trees. You'll find pin oaks rising 150 feet into the air and huge hackberry and ash trees.

There's very little crime in Standiford. It's convenient to all parts of Louisville. There's not much turnover in houses. Only about a quarter of its residents are over 65, so it has an excellent mix of young and old. The mean household income is $31,600, not bad for an economically depressed area. The average market value of a house in Standiford is $43,683.

Does that sound blighted to you?

Yes, Interstate 65 slices past one end of the neighborhood. Yes, the airport slices past the other. Yes, you can hear some traffic and the noise of the planes, but it is not overpowering. The residents are used to it. They accept it as a tradeoff for the benefits of being there. They believe it's something they can live with, even with an expanded Standiford Field.

The noise, dust and pollution are certainly no worse than living in an apartment or condominium in downtown Louisville, an area the city is trying to promote at the same time it has suddenly become worried about the eardrums of the residents in Standiford.

I'd bet there's more blight in the Old Louisville neighborhood near County Judge-Executive Harvey Sloane's home than there is in Standiford, so maybe he should take another one of his walks out there.

Beyond all that, what hurts the residents of Highland Park, Prestonia and Standiford the most is what the urban-renewal reports have done to their pride. Many of the people are elderly. Many stayed there because it was home. Many invested a lot of money in their houses. They took pride in their homes, their neighbors, their neatly trimmed hedges and their pin oak trees.

Then their government, because it had to be done to justify the airport expansion, labeled their neighborhoods economically blighted. Not only were the residents being forced to move; they were insulted.

"I just can't tell you how much that hurt me," said Cleo Henry, 70, who with his wife, Marie, has lived in a neat, trim, well-land-scaped home in Standiford for more than 30 years. "It's a disgrace for them to think like that, to have people read the story in the paper and come up and say, 'I didn't know you lived in a blighted neighborhood.'

"I love this neighborhood. It made me so hurt and angry I can't begin to explain how I feel. I just can't.

"They've been telling us all through this thing to 'trust us, trust us, we'll take care of you' — but now look at what they've done."

March 11, 1989

Merger musings: It is the end of an era...

Although you will not notice much immediate change in the product, the news from the more corporate end of this business is that — effective tomorrow, Sunday, Dec. 1 — all news staffs of The Courier-Journal and The Louisville Times will be merged.

There still will be two newspapers, but after competing journal-istically with each other for 101 years, nearly half as long as this country is old, the two staffs are going to join up in the interest of better papers and economic necessity. The bottom line says you can't have one without the other.

Very few reporters, photographers or even mid-level editors are bottom-line people. Many of us are even uncomfortable with the notion that newspapers are a business; we would just prefer to wander around in unfettered pursuit of truth, justice and man-bites-dog epics while people working one or two floors below us go through that awful process of having to sell advertising to pay the bills.

I think what I dislike the most about this merger is that it is such a reminder that we are a business, that the sanctity of the First Amendment isn't worth much unless we can come up with about $70 million for new color printing presses to remain eco-nomically competitive.

What's most odd about the merger is that so many people seem to think we've had only one staff all along, anyway. If I had a dime for every time I've had to explain to people that I worked for The Louisville Times and not The Courier-Journal, I could buy out Sallie Bingham and purchase the new printing press.

But it's true, folks.

For all those years, reporters from The Louisville Times and The Courier-Journal have been in separate pursuit of news to fill the white space around the grocery ads.

For all those years, and that would include thousands of

reporters and editors, one paper has been looking over the other's shoulder, although not always willing to admit it.

There always has been that little "high" attached to not only getting a good story, but getting it first.

But after today, symbolically if not officially, it won't be that way anymore.

I've had a sense of loss about this all week, but partly because there will still be two newspapers and partly because the changes will come gradually, I find it hard to put into words.

Maybe it's because the very first paper I worked for — a biweekly in the town where I grew up — tried to expand too quickly into a daily. The move — abrupt, poorly planned and underfinanced — was a disaster. The newspaper eventually folded.

The second newspaper I worked for was purchased by the Gannett newspaper chain. It cut the staff by about 40 percent, folded the afternoon paper and bled all the money it could from the news operation.

Some fun company, that Gannett.

After those experiences, the Bingham companies seemed about 72 percent heaven, a place that seemed removed from all those ugly business decisions, a paper that for all its faults has always been a good place to work. Now — not quite suddenly — all those bottom-line considerations are popping up again.

All this, of course, clashes directly with my rather archaic view that the whole function of newspapers is to print the news and raise hell, not advertising rates.

I have been thinking all week that today is the last Louisville Times in 101 years that will be put out exactly in this manner, and something profound need be said about that.

Or at least readable.

And nothing will kill a columnist quicker than trying to be profound.

My first thought upon learning of the merger was that the staffs of both papers had shrunk so much that something had to be done — and the merger, if done right, could be a very good thing. I still feel that way.

But I've also been thinking of all the people who have worked for the Times, who enjoyed the competition, who feel a closeness for each other and the paper we put out, who sense the same loss I feel without being able to put just the right typewriter key on it.

This is a unique business in many ways, not the least of which is being able to handle several emotions at the same time. After months of rumors — both good and bad — we got the news of the merger on a Friday morning.

There were about 15 people gathered around the copy machine passing out copies of the official word. We read it. We gathered in small groups to discuss it. Eventually we drank a few beers over it. But we put out the next edition of the newspaper first.

Nov. 30, 1985

Ring's return seals memory of airman's love

The circle is complete now. Lawrence Dundon's wedding ring is back home in Louisville; a journey of 52 years is over.

It ended about 2:30 p.m. yesterday at a warm reception at Baptist Tabernacle when Alfred Montgomery of Belfast, Northern Ireland, placed it in the waiting hands of Ruth Gillespie. Her face, as usual, was strong and impassive, but who knows what was gomg on in her heart?

"It's been a very moving experience," Gillespie said.

She married Lawrence Dundon on Oct. 21, 1939, in the old Baptist Tabernacle, now located at 2854 W. Market St. They had dated six years. In 1941 the couple moved into a small house at 219 N. 33rd St., the same house where Ruth Gillespie lives today.

Lawrence Dundon was drafted into the service, became a radio operator on a B-17 Flying Fortress and died with his nine crew members when their plane smashed into a hill in fog near Belfast on June 1,1944. His body was buried in Ireland, then moved to a U.S. military cemetery near Cambridge, England.

Ruth Gillespie was never able to visit the grave, or learn many details of the crash and the funeral. All she had were his dogtags, a group shot of his crew and photographs of their time together.

In time she met a printer named Woody Gillespie, began dating him and married him in 1946. They would have four children and were happily married almost 50.years before he died last December. Lawrence Dundon was always remembered and revered in the Gillespie house. But the memories and mementos of their time together stayed in the background, in Ruth Gillespie's personal thoughts and scrapbooks.

Until Alfred Montgomery found their wedding ring. As a boy, he had climbed the Belfast hill where Dundon's plane had crashed.

Montgomery's father, a museum director, had often taken him there. Montgomery, 31, shared his father's reverence for military artifacts. One day in 1994 — 50 years after the crash — Montgomery was picking through the soft dirt in the wooded hillside when he found what he thought was a steel washer. When he cleaned it up he could read an inscription in the dirty twisted metal: "Ruth-Larry 10/21/39."

With only that slim evidence, Montgomery spent two years searching through 8th U.S. Air Force records trying to find information on Larry. By telephone, fax, cassette tape and mail he sought the Dundon family, finally contacting someone in Louisville — and then Ruth Gillespie.

"Yes," she said, "I would very much like to have that ring."

With the help of an Irish newspaper — the Belfast News Letter — Montgomery brought the ring to Louisville on a 20-hour airplane trip Saturday night, then to her Baptist Tabernacle Sunday afternoon.

Ruth Gillespie has been a valued stalwart in the church all her life. About 75 friends and church members gathered for the informal ceremony, along with all four of the Gillespie children who knew what the ring — the whole afternoon — meant to their mother.

"What's amazing," said Bill Gillespie, one of her sons, "is that the ring was found by perhaps the only person who might respect it, would want to find its owners. Anybody else might have just stuck it in their pocket."

Many people in the room remembered Lawrence Dundon, the war years, the long separations and the moments of grief. The reception not only brought family together, it reunited old friends. One niece was wearing Dundon's military wings; a friend remembered double-dating with Ruth and Larry; two women remembered their wedding.

"At least I think I do," said one. "It was a long time ago."

Montgomery, a tour-bus driver, will be in town all week, his trip becoming a Full Louisville; hospitality aided by the Galt House, Actors Theatre, the Kentucky Center for the Arts, the Louisville

Science Center, Churchill Downs and Lynn's Paradise Cafe.

Mayor Jerry Abramson named him an honorary Louisville citizen.

Warm applause greeted Montgomery as he moved toward the front of the room, passing flower baskets decorated with American and British flags. He spoke a few words, then handed the ring to Ruth Gillespie. The room was silent, expectant, as she held it in her hands.

"Words cannot express how I feel," she said.

Pastor Eugene Enlow spoke of a ring of love, a circle of grief, a happy and sad occasion. He asked that everyone remember Lawrence Dundon. As Ruth Gillespie held the ring, all heads in the room bowed in prayer.

Sept. 23, 1996

She shall be like a tree planted by the rivers of water

The Lord is my shepherd; I shall not want.

It had snowed the day of Elmer Mattson's funeral, a thick, wet, sloppy snow that made the sloping paths of Mount Moriah Cemetery treacherous to walk but painted the low hills surrounding the country church near Henryville, Ind., into a pastoral landscape — stark, silent and peaceful.

And as Helen Mattson turned to leave her husband of 55 years for the last time on that January day in 1985, she picked a single red rose from the bouquet on top of his casket.

He maketh me to lie down in green pastures:

He leadeth me beside the still waters.

He restoreth my soul: He leadeth me in the paths of righteousness for His name's sake.

Helen Mattson's garden had been full of such flowers: purple violas growing in a black metal pot; a blue clematis that climbed the trellis outside her back porch; the nodding heads of the yellow, white and lavender irises beyond her kitchen window; the fat clumps of day lilies, daisies, sedum and roses that grew behind the house where she walked at night, making her rounds.

Yea, though I walk through the valley of the shadow of death,

I will fear no evil: for thou art with me;
Thy rod, and Thy staff they comfort me.

Helen Mattson was always generous with the things she grew
— as was Elmer, who proudly raised a broad hillside of vegetables
behind their small house in Shively. They gave their three married
sons all the vegetables anyone could want, and gave perennial
flowers to nieces and nephews by the box full — flowers that
would become living reminders of the people who raised them.

They had always lived simple, honest lives; Elmer as a longtime employee in a Louisville distillery, Helen as a nanny in other
people's houses, and, for a time during World War II, as a seam-
stress making cloth bags in a Charlestown, Ind., ammunition factory.

If Helen had a genius beyond raising flowers, it was her ability
to do things with her hands — embroidery, crochet, tatting or
plain needle and thread. The bounty poured from her fingers for
60 years. Patchwork quilts, Raggedy Ann and Andy dolls, lifelike
stuffed animals she called her "toys," wonderful tablecloths, lacy
pillow cases, delicate doilies; each made with pride and perfection,
all of them family treasures — much of it blue-ribbon stuff at the
Kentucky State Fair.

She was old-fashioned, strong-willed and occasionally fussy. A
favorite family tale involved the time a few years ago when Helen
felt so short of breath she feared a heart attack. She called a daughter-in-law, who quickly called her husband, Helen's son. An ambulance was sent to the house, then the daughter-in-law and son
rushed over. They found Helen standing at the kitchen sink doing
dishes. She had sent the ambulance back; she said she hadn't been
properly dressed and wasn't about to go to the hospital in that
condition.

Thou preparest a table before me in the presence of mine enemies;
Thou anointest my head with oil; my cup runneth over.

Helen Dieterlen Mattson died last week in the arms of a daughter-in-law after a long bout with cancer. She was 87, and was
buried alongside Elmer in that sloping piece of land in Mount
Moriah Cemetery — not too far from the old Indiana farmhouse in
which she had been born.

The minister spoke of her generosity, kindness and love of flowers. A sweet-voiced woman sang of Helen walking in the Lord's
garden, a grandson gave a lovely tribute, and many people wept
at their loss   rejoicing all the while that Helen, no longer in pain,

had gone to a better place.

The graveside service was brief. Family and friends stood silently on the hill while the minister intoned the familiar "ashes to ashes, dust to dust." As the mourners turned to leave, many of them — young and old — picked flowers from the bouquet on Helen's casket; a pink carnation, a white carnation, a single red rose.

Surely goodness and mercy shall follow me all the days of my life:
And I will dwell in the house of the Lord forever.

Sept. 28, 1991

Some things a bulldozer can't destroy

It says something when a man will come back to his barbershop to clean it before the bulldozer comes through. It says something about pride, honesty and work ethic. It says something about the way things used to be in Highland Park.

Not that Bill Polston's barbershop is anything special — at least not now. Its white, pressed-tin ceiling has flaked badly.

The silvered mirrors have yellowed. The layers of flowered wallpaper have long since blighted, and one barber chair has a raggedy hole where Polston's thumb poked through while giving 35 years' worth of customers a better look in the mirror.

The whole shop — inside and out — has the sad, beaten-down, boarded-up look you find all over Highland Park these days as airport expansion grinds relentlessly forward.

But last Saturday — on his final day of business — Bill Polston was determined to clean it up one more time.

Think about it: 35 years of barbering at 404 Hiawatha St. — much of it 10 hours a day, six days a week, 30 to 45 customers a day, no time for lunch. If you remember that Lucien Karnes ran the same barbershop for 30 years before Polston bought it in 1957, then you have 65 years of barbering in one place.

Think about spending your entire working life in one very public room; the friendships, the arguments, the sense of neighborhood, the sense of belonging, the hassles of having a door that opened to anyone who wanted in, the stress of being on your feet

10 hours a day, the tedium of always being so available.

Then, suddenly, it was all over, the time had come to give it up. Somehow Polston had turned 66. The airport had come. Most of his friends were dead or had moved away, and that one room, so full of memories — good and bad — didn't belong to him anymore.

"I don't really blame the airport people," said Polston. "They've been fair to me. There has to be progress.... But it's just amazing how fast the time goes. It's all gone before you know it."

The fates had long ago decreed that Bill Polston would be a barber. His father, Chester Polston Sr., operated the five-chair barbershop in the old Greyhound bus station on Broadway for 42 years — a legendary place for Fort Knox soldiers. Three of Chester Polston's eight sons became barbers. One of Bill Polston's four sons became a barber.

The fates had briefly offered Bill Polston one shining option: professional baseball. He played five years in the Chicago Cubs' organization in the 1940s, never reaching the majors, but coming home with a wife, Mary Adkins Polston, 62, whom he married at home plate in a Class D baseball park in Kingsport, Tenn., in 1947.

Then came a family. Then came the barbering business. Then, in 1957, came the barbershop in Highland Park — a shop Polston jokingly calls "The Curse."

"This was always a hard place," said Polston, talking about the blue-collar clientele of Highland Park.

"I started out charging 75 cents for children and $1 for men. Then I went up to $1.25.

"The long hair of the 1960s really hurt me. I was up to $2.80, but business got so bad I cut back to $1.15. I was afraid to raise it after that. I needed the business. I had a family to raise."

When Bill Polston cut his final head last week he was charging only $3, $2.50 for senior citizens. "These people just don't have the money," he said.

Somehow Bill and Mary Polston, now married 44 years, put their sons — the ones who wanted to go — through college. Somehow — with Mary helping as a factory worker and cafeteria cook — they took care of all their obligations. Somehow enough old friends and customers showed up to make Bill Polston's last day more of an Irish wake than a funeral.

A son, Tom, 42, showed up with a gift from all the sons: golf clubs. Virgil Baumgardner, 86, showed up, singing a few old ditties. Marvin Priddy, 66, showed up to claim he was Polston's first customer. Clayton Riggs, 73, showed up to argue that point.

Polston, a kind, genial man, fought off any tears with his quick sense of humor, but his sense of loss was apparent, and very deep.

"You run a place for 35 years," he said, "and you feel it. This place is mine. It may not be much, but it doesn't belong to anybody else; it belongs to me. There's nothing else like it in the whole country."

He shoved his hands into his pockets, staring out the window at a small pickup truck being used to haul away one of his barber chairs and an old mirror.

He said his shop was a little dirty now, but he'd come back Monday to clean it up.

Jan. 25, 1992

108 years of simple life was her legacy

The obituary said Lillie Love Vinegar lived a simple life, a life dedicated to family, home and garden, a life given to kind acts and sweet thoughts. There is no evidence to the contrary, but Lillie Vinegar lived for 108 years, more than a century of repression, tumult and change, and the tides of history could not have made it easy.

She was born on Aug. 22, 1885, the daughter of former slaves, one of a cabin full of children who grew up on a Georgia farm. They lived closely with the land, raising their own food, butchering chickens and curing hams. She married James Swanson, a Methodist minister, and they had six children, two sons and four daughters. At age 40 she and the minister separated; she moved to Louisville with one daughter, Marberine Swanson. In later years she married a man named Eli Vinegar.

"She was a member of New Coke Methodist Church for many, many years," her obituary said. "She loved to garden, plant flowers, save seeds and quilt blankets for her grandchildren. She was known for her gentle, loving, cheerful way at home."

Cecelia Conley Jones was one of those grandchildren, a beneficiary of many of those quilts, two for every bed in her new house.

The quilts are gone now, all used up keeping great-grandchildren warm, perhaps the best use of all.

"Granny wanted us to use them," said Jones. "She said they were better used than treasured."

Jones lived with her grandmother many years, memories she cherishes like the warmth of an old quilt. In the hard times — her mother had to go to work at age 12 to help support the family — the family slept four to a bed; Lillie Vinegar and three grandchildren. The family survived on domestic work, cleaning other people's houses.

In the better times Lillie Vinegar was Jones' teacher and friend, showing her how to collect flower seeds, identifying all the edible plants that grew in the wild. You could not walk into Lillie Vinegar's house without being invited to eat; you could never leave without taking home some homemade bread or cookies.

"She was plain and simple, loving and nurturing," said Jones. "She'd wear what we used to call cotton house dresses, always ironed and starched.

"When you think back on it she must have lived with a lot of stress, but complaining was never a part of her life. She was always busy sewing, cooking, whatever."

The Rev. Alvin Goodwin stood behind Lillie Vinegar's casket at the W. P. Porter Mortuary, 2611 Virginia Ave., searching for the words to explain that, marveling in 108 years of her life, certain of where she was bound.

"This is a home-going celebration," said Goodwin, his voice rising, melodic, striking a natural cadence. "We are thankful for the life of Sister Vinegar, we are here to pay our last goodbyes, but knowing on the other side there are many hellos...."

Lillie Vinegar lay in a blue dress edged in green flowers. Her face, kind and peaceful, was partially shrouded beneath a white veil. A basket of blue carnations rested lightly on her bluish-gray casket, the words "Family" spread across them on a blue ribbon.

The mourners sat in folding chairs facing Goodwin, a generous mix of four generations, including one son, two daughters, 11 grandchildren, 28 great-grandchildren and one great-great-grandchild. Lillie Vinegar had been ill the past several years, not always able to communicate with family, her death a release from mortal worries.

The Rev. Jerry Williams of the Christ Temple Apostolic Church, his voice deep and booming, spoke of the celebration of one "who has lived so long before God on the face of the Earth." Anthony Conley Jr., a great-grandson, spoke of Lillie Vinegar's endless enthusiasm.

"I would say, 'Grandmother, slow down before you fall down.' But she never did. If she fell down, we had to pick her up, but it never stopped her."

Their words, heart-felt and poignant as they were, could not capture 108 years of life. Lillie Vinegar, a simple woman, had out-lived eulogy. Her legacy, Goodwin said, would be a broad remembrance of a long life lived well; her death the sweet victory of eternal reward.

Goodwin, leading a procession toward a side door, ended the service with the 23rd Psalm, "The Lord is my shepherd, I shall not want...." As he spoke, voice rising with emotion, six of Lillie Vinegar's great-grandsons picked up her casket and lovingly carried it down the steps toward a long, gray hearse.

A pianist, partially hidden around a corner, played the joyful, upbeat sounds of "I'll Fly Away."

Oct. 30, 1993

Two Louisville men shared the same name, but not the same fate

What makes the story more intriguing is that Dallas Embry knows it could have been his decaying body that was found on Ohio Street beneath a highway overpass.

The victim — also named Dallas Embry — had been dead five days or more, apparently of natural causes. He was a longtime Louisville street person who'd been on a first-name basis with police, EMS workers and emergency-room doctors.

The surviving Dallas Embry knows a lot of people too. He grew up in Louisville, was married and divorced, and now lives in the same small house in the Portland area where his parents lived. He's been hanging out in the Louisville music scene for 15 years: free-lance writer and critic for the Louisville Music News; talent coordinator and booking agent for Homefront; employee at

Phoenix Hill, Uncle Pleasant's and the Rudyard Kipling. He was one of those often-unnoticed people who keep things moving.

The jobs never paid a lot; much of the work was volunteer. Most recently Embry, 47, worked for the Census Bureau in Jeffersonville, Ind., but he's been laid off since November, living on the edge.

"Not too long ago I was working at the Waterside Festival and I told a lot of people I was about this far from being homeless," said Embry, two of his fingers held about a half-inch apart. "I don't know, maybe a lot of people took that to heart."

The short Courier-Journal obituary said a Dallas Embry was found beneath the Interstate 71 overpass. He was 54, survived by a son, three sisters and a grandchild, and would be buried in a pauper's grave at River Valley Cemetery.

The musician friends of the other Dallas Embry read that, didn't think it quite fit the man they knew — he didn't seem that old — but they couldn't be certain. Embry's friends found themselves in a very awkward position — having to call him up to ask if he were dead.

Some friends did call the musicians union or Louisville Music News. Others — Kenny Pyle of the Rudyard Kipling; Mark Smalley, who owned Uncle Pleasant's; Betty Hansel of the Louisville Dulcimer Society — called Embry's house.

"The first call I got was from Betty," Embry said. "Basically, she told me she didn't think I was dead but she wanted to call to make sure.

"She delivered a little eulogy about how much I was loved and how much I'd be missed. It kinda gave me that Tom Sawyer, Huckleberry Finn thing where they got to go to their own funeral. It was kinda nice getting all those eulogies while I was still alive."

Not one of the callers seemed disappointed when Embry answered. "I was apparently well-loved," he said.

After almost a dozen calls, Embry turned over the chore to his answering machine, his message an opportunity few could resist: "This is Dallas. I'm unavailable to talk to you right now, but rumors of my demise have been greatly exaggerated."

Embry called The Courier-Journal soon after the obituary appeared, hoping some sort of clarification could be made: "I left a message saying I wasn't dead and I'd like to talk to somebody about it."

Beneath the comic relief, however, Embry felt a few cold chills.

Although they had never met, he had long been aware of the existence of the other Dallas Embry; the dead man often hung out in the Phoenix Hill area. One time when the younger Embry had gone to an emergency room to be treated for pneumonia, the doctor greeted him with a surprise:

"You're not Dallas Embry."

"I beg your pardon."

"You're not the Dallas Embry I know."

The experience has left Embry grateful, a little uneasy and somewhat introspective; he had connected with a dead man at a very basic level. "I can see it possibly being me," he said. "I'm unemployed and I know it can happen.... It's kind of scary.

"Like everyone else, I've thought at times about how many people would come to my funeral. This kind of gave me an idea of what it would be like."

Aug. 18, 1994

Through tears of joy and sorrow, the common denominator is love

Jim and Laurie both liked country music and the boot-scootin' kind of dancing that came with it. He was tall, blond, good-looking and quiet, an ex-professional football player with a wonderful grin. She was tall, very pretty and outgoing.

They were always a handsome couple, two-stepping their way around the outer lanes of country music.

Their wedding was to be a family affair, a big, rolling, much-anticipated event done with style, planning, food and drink, country music and The Lord's Prayer — in somewhat equal measures. That was on Saturday night.

Gary and Sally are old friends. We went to high school in a time and place where our friendship became cemented in common memories. We could be apart for years and be comfortable again in seconds. My wife and I — and our children — were going to stay at their home for the wedding, attend it together. But when we arrived Friday night, we learned Gary's father had died

Thursday night. The funeral would be Sunday. A soloist would sing The Lord's Prayer.

The wedding was in a big Presbyterian church with stained-glass windows. Jim stood at the altar in his tuxedo, grinning. Laurie looked beautiful in a white dress that hinted of country music. Her brother played "The Wedding March" on his fiddle. The minister, a man with a gift for being able to say exactly the right thing, stood at the altar, grinning along with Jim. After Scriptures were read and rings exchanged, the soloist sang a joyous Lord's Prayer, her voice filling the church, tears running down the cheeks of the families.

Gary's father, George Scott, had been a farmer, living in the same house for 72 of his 75 years. He had been married to Gary's mother 55 years. His funeral was in the same Methodist church where Gary and Sally had been married, where their daughter had been married, where my wife and I had been married.

The casket was placed in a long hallway near the sanctuary, the funeral flowers crowded close around it: red roses, pink carnations, white lilies. George Scott had died at home, peacefully, surrounded by those he loved, those who loved him. A granddaughter placed a gift in his casket: a jar of dry-roasted peanuts. The family linked arms, smiled at the peanuts — and cried.

The wedding reception was held at a museum-restaurant where tables surrounded a big, oak dance floor. The happy couple were toasted with champagne, then gracefully danced around the floor. The guests watched, smiled, applauded and shared in their happiness.

The minister at the funeral had a gift for being able to bring smiles, even laughter, as the family shared stories of George Scott. He had been a small man; hard-working, tough, very proud of his strength. One mourner cried and laughed at the same time as he remembered how George would always shake your hand until it hurt. A granddaughter tearfully remembered how her grandfather would pick her up, hold her. A daughter-in-law remembered how, as a joke, she had given him long underwear with an electric cord so he could stay warm at night.

"I don't think he ever used them," she said, and everyone laughed.

Jim and Laurie laughed, danced, linked arms and posed for pictures until well after midnight. They had been certain to thank their parents "who have shown us what true commitment and love are all about," and "God, who brought us together and made this love possible."

The soloist at George Scott's funeral sang "Amazing Grace," and then, near the benediction, sang The Lord's Prayer — tears welling up in the eyes of his family. The service ended with an upbeat, hand-clapping rendition of "Soon and Very Soon."

George Scott's casket was taken to Ohio Grove Cemetery, a country spot near the old home place. One of the mourners held a great-granddaughter in his strong arms, an answered prayer, a continuation, a glory forever, amen.

Aug. 30, 1994

'Everybody thinks their mother is the greatest'

It fell to the Rev. Kevin Cosby, pastor of St. Stephen Baptist Church, to bring together all the tender emotions evoked by the death of Odessa Lee Grady Clay, the woman whose family called her "Mama Bird."

Cosby — a slim, elegant, passionate man — spoke of towering trees, and before him sat Muhammad Ali, whose fame has spread around the world, and his brother, Rahaman Ali, who found his own way in Muhammad's shadow. Speaking of the unseen roots that anchor and nourish great trees, Cosby spread his arms wide over Odessa Clay's gilt-edged casket:

"If the tree stood tall," he said, "it must be because of the roots."

Odessa Clay's roots go back to Carlisle County at the western tip of Kentucky. She was born there near Arlington in 1917. She moved to Louisville when she was 5, graduated from Central High School, worked for a time at the old Philip Morris factory.

Along the way she met Cassius Marcellus Clay, a gregarious, fun-loving sign painter. They dated three years before marrying, then lived on Grand Avenue, where their eldest son, Cassius Marcellus Clay Jr. — who would have a lot of his daddy in him — made friends with a tall, lanky neighborhood kid named Ned Arter.

"Miss Clay was a very warm person," Arter said. "When you

Photo by Michael Hayman
Jamillah Ali embraces her father, Muhammad Ali

think of a mother, you think of her."

In time Cassius Clay Jr. took up boxing, won an Olympic gold medal, became heavyweight champion of the world. He declared his Muslim faith and changed his name, and he was stripped of his title because of his religious beliefs. Ali was dead center in a national firestorm of controversy — a black man refusing to back down. Through it all he could always go home, the source of his strength.

"Nothing ever changed Odessa," said Henry Sadlo, a Louisville attorney who's known the family for 30 years. "She was one of the nicest people you'd ever want to meet, but she would stand up and fight for her boys."

Those are the recurring themes among those who best knew her: kind, thoughtful, loving, unpretentious, tough as she had to be. Odessa Clay was mother of one of the most remarkable men in sports history, yet she mowed her own grass, cooked her own meals, delighted in her own jam cake and settled for a comfortable, middle-class home when she could have had a mansion.

"She was her own person," said Alecea Ali, 27, the oldest of her 13 grandchildren. "Yet she admired and respected both her sons. She loved them. She lived for them. Nothing could come between them."

Hundreds of people went to her visitation at A. D. Porter & Sons Funeral Home on Tuesday night, a teeming mix of men in dark suits, women in fine dresses and youths in basketball jerseys. Her death Sunday at 77, almost six months after a stroke had left her unable to speak, was almost a relief.

"We would tell her, 'Grandmother, we love you,'" Alecea Ali said. "She could only nod her head in reply."

Her family, Rahaman and Muhammad among them, had been with her continually at the Hurstbourne Care Centre.

"Everybody thinks their mother is the greatest," Muhammad Ali said Tuesday night.

In yesterday morning's funeral, Cosby made quick reference to "Mama Bird" — gentle, fierce, protective. Older church women who would have loved Odessa Clay if she had never had *any* sons gathered in front of her casket, praised the serene smile on her face and the soft pink dress and matching pearl jewelry the family had chosen for her final rest.

The service was a thoughtful, judicious and ultimately uplifting mix of Baptist and Muslim. The mourners gathered in a long, flowing line down the center of the church; Rahaman and Muhammad slowly bent over the casket to kiss their mother good-bye. David Cosby Jr. sang "Amazing Grace," and Carol Kirby brought joyful tears from the assembly with a soaring, soulful offering of "His Eye Is On the Sparrow."

"Without the mother, the tree could not have stood so tall," the Rev. Cosby said, his arms reaching out to the family. "It's only appropriate that we say thank you to the roots of greatness."

Aug. 25, 1994

In a shop right out of the '50s, meet the barbers of civility

It has been a partnership with a view, a sense of place, a good living with the fringe benefit of friendship — an arrangement so deceptively simple that Eddie Ward and Harold Brooks made it last a lifetime.

"I needed somebody," said Ward, 67, whose name comes first on the "Ward & Brooks" sign above their Crescent Hill barber-shop.

"I stayed 40 years," said Brooks, 69, who did take two days to make the decision.

It was just that easy. But Ward and Brooks can make easy look so, well, easy. They are so nicely molded into their chairs — cups of instant coffee perched at their sides — that they have become part of their own decor. They relax so well, laugh so quickly, are so

Photo by Pat McDonogh
Harold Brooks, seated, and Eddie Ward are partners in friendship as well as in business.

genuinely pleasant that a good haircut is almost a bonus.

Truth is, they do work at it. Their two-chair shop at 2640 Frankfort Ave. is a monument to equanimity; University of Kentucky *and* University of Louisville statuary and posters. Faded golf balls — middle-of-the road brands like Fairway and Precept — are on sale in a cardboard box, four for $1. The obligatory fishing poster, beach-scene postcard from Florida and Louisville Redbirds baseball flier are tacked at customer height.

Ward and Brooks will happily talk sports, weather and neighborhood news. They endure politics, but only briefly. Their shop offers escape, civility, Readers Digest humor along with $6 haircuts — $5 for senior citizens. They are the way we were. Norman Rockwell could have painted "First Haircut" here: crying child, concerned mother, bemused barber. The Ward & Brooks radio plays music, not the angry rush of political discourse.

"I have to pay taxes and cut hair no matter who's in office," Ward explained.

He is from Lawrenceburg, Ky. He drove a bus, worked as a railroad telegrapher and came to Louisville to attend Tri-City Barber College. In 1955 — three years into cutting hair — he wanted his own shop. Crescent Hill was the place.

"I liked the neighborhood," he said.

Brooks is from Kirksville, Mo. A vending business brought him to Louisville, a customer bought him out. A friend soon talked Brooks into a new career.

"When I told my wife I had enrolled in barber college, she broke down and started crying," he said.

Laughter rolled through the shop. Ward went to make more coffee. Both men use the same jar of Folgers instant, but Ward had a surprise confession; he'll try a little cappuccino.

"I have to lock the door first," he said.

They have never tired of the view out their window, the vibrating thunder of countless trains along Frankfort Avenue, the long row of angular, two-story houses along North Hite Avenue. They judge the seasons by the flowers planted along the roadway across Frankfort Avenue, the bursting clump of ornamental grass — emerald green in late spring, straw yellow in fall.

Their stories are funny, sad, polite, easy-listening, middle-American; the sore-footed man who came into the shop with his shoes on backward; the train wrecks; the kids from St. Joseph Children's Home who came in a station wagon — six at a time — until all 60 heads of hair were cut.

It has been a long, fun, marvelous journey now almost over because Brooks has become ill, works only part-time, and the shop may soon be up for sale.

But you'd never know it to talk to them, to hunker down in a barbershop chair and listen to old buddies laugh and remember as Crescent Hill rolls past outside their window. It's still safe in their shop. It's still somewhere in the 1950s. It feels good and warm, like the very best memories of school, family and friends. Outside, across Frankfort Avenue, the ornamental grasses stir gently in the wind.

March 7, 1995

A GI's last mission for honor, duty, country and his captain

Then the first man squatted down . . . and took the dead hand, and he sat there for a full five minutes . .. looking intently into a dead face, and he never uttered a sound.... And finally he put the hand down, and then reached up and gently straightened the points of the captain's shirt collar, and then he sort of rearranged the tattered edges of his uniform around the wound. And then he got up and walked away down the road in the moonlight, all alone.
Ernie Pyle
The Death of Captain Waskow

Of all the marvelous moments in the heartfelt tribute of Dana, Ind., to native son Ernie Pyle this week, none was sweeter than when Riley Mack Tidwell — the grieving soldier in Pyle's World War II column — stood awkwardly in the spotlight holding the hand of the sister of Capt. Henry T. Waskow.

The Waskow column — Pyle's most famous — was written in the frozen Italian mountains in January 1944. Tidwell was 19 at the time, a tall, raw-boned farm kid from Texas. He had known the gentle, conscientious Waskow — another Texan — for 18 months, served him as a radio operator and runner, loved him as a son loves his father. Waskow died next to Tidwell, a shrapnel wound in his chest, shoving Tidwell out of harm's way as he went down.

On orders, Tidwell came down off the mountain seeking a replacement officer. It was so cold the soldiers melted ice from the trees to make coffee. For three days Tidwell waited for someone to bring Waskow's body down from the mountain, but winter weather and enemy fire made it impossible. On the third night Tidwell found a mule, went up the mountain and brought back the body of the man he still refers to as "my captain."

"I knew where the captain's body was," he would explain.

The return trip took four hours, Waskow's body strapped to the mule as it picked its way down the dark, treacherous trail, no one else moving up or down the mountain. Tidwell had trenchfoot so badly he could walk only on his heels, his feet bundled in thick gauze, his thoughts on the night and the dead man with him. An enemy shell burst nearby, hurling shrapnel into Tidwell's back, the side of his face and his left wrist — the latter an injury that would require seven operations.

As Tidwell came off the mountain with his captain, a group of men moved toward him. One of them was Ernie Pyle, his country's most famous war correspondent, a small, shy man who wrote of the war by living with it. Tidwell knew nothing of Pyle or his column-writing. The soldier just told his story and went on with the war, his sense of country and duty so strong he later would go AWOL from a recuperation area in North Africa, crawl onto a cargo plane and fly to rejoin his Texas unit for the Anzio invasion.

Tidwell only learned about Pyle's fame — he was syndicated in hundreds of newspapers — after returning to the states. Although Tidwell was never named in the Waskow column, someone had linked the incident to him, and used his public-relations value in a movie about Pyle called "The Story of G.I. Joe." Tidwell briefly toured with Robert Mitchum and Burgess Meredith — actors in the movie — but he had other plans. "I wanted to go home," he said.

He went to Gallatin, Texas, becoming a truck driver, visiting family, including Esther Grable, a sister in Louisville, and George Tidwell, a brother in Caneyville, Ky. Riley Tidwell has been called often about the Waskow column, but this week's celebration in Dana — the 50th anniversary of Pyle's death by a Japanese sniper — was special.

It was special because the Ernie Pyle museum — his boyhood house — was expanded by two Quonset huts. The two-day event had speeches, a military band, hundreds of home folks proudly gathered in a big tent waving small American flags. It had a new book — "On a Wing and a Prayer" — a collection of Pyle's aviation columns. It had the sad notes of "Taps" blown across the west-central Indiana farm fields by an unyielding wind.

It was joyous, poignant, unpolished, small-town America — made more so because Mary Lee Waskow Barr-Cox, 72, the sister of Capt. Henry T. Waskow, was there to hold the hand of Riley Tidwell, 71 — the same hand that had rearranged her dead brother's uniform more than 50 years ago. They stood side by side, lips pursed, faces taut and determined, blinking back tears.

The moment — the passing of an age — was made more special because Tidwell is ill with cancer. He has been given less than six months to live, but he was able to complete one more trip for honor, duty, his country and his captain.   *April 20, 1995*

At Cave Hill, he's at home
with ghosts of Louisville's past

Frank Williams has walked the green hills of Cave Hill Cemetery so many times he has become a part of its charm and mystique. He calls Cave Hill his paradise on Earth, and he cannot be far wrong.

Certainly the 300-acre cemetery is the most beautiful spot in Louisville. A walk through Cave Hill is a history lesson with a side trip into economics. Men and women who helped shape Louisville, Kentucky and our nation are buried there, from military heroes to robber barons.

Huge family fortunes and even larger egos are marked with towering obelisks, sculpted marble figures and massive granite mausoleums. Most were built in that wonderful era when people believed if you couldn't take it with you, you should at least well mark the spot where the struggle ended.

Yet, thousands of others are buried there too. They are buried in simple soldiers' graves marked with even stones that march steadily across a grassy plain. And they are buried beneath thick hardwood trees, or delicate dogwoods or above a quiet lagoon where white ducks slide scross the flat water.

Williams, of 4222 Norbourne Blvd., walks through all this two or three times a week the year around. He is not so much fascinated by death as he is curious about its trappings. He is a small, dapper, articulate man at total peace with himself and his cemetery. He visits Cave Hill often because his wife of 40 years is buried there. He stays to walk among its beauty and to ponder the meaning of the place.

"Every death is unique in itself," he said. "Each grave contains a story of a struggle, an illness, a heartbreak or a tragic accident. So few of us are prepared to deal with these things."

But let us not portray here a picture of a morose man given to relentless stalking of the Grim Reaper. Williams is a sensitive, intelligent man who, if anything, is an optimist. He can find subtle humor in his work, such as when he quotes Woody Allen on the matter of death:

"'I don't mind dying,'" he reports Allen once said, " 'if I'm not there when it happens.'"

Williams is a retired design artist and fashion coordinator in his 70s. But rather than slowing down, he is pursuing an art degree at Jefferson Community College and has been on several world tours, the most recent to the Holy Land and the Egyptian pyramids and tombs.

"I even rode a camel," he said, laughing. "I did it all."

He walks Cave Hill with measured step, a tourist on familiar turf, pointing out the local landmarks. He is a familiar sight to the guards, whom he greatly admires, and has been known to help them arrange flowers.

Many of his friends are buried there, and he has learned the histories of hundreds of other people who have joined them. He will often pause at a discreet distance when people he does not know are being buried in new graves, adding his prayers to the others.

He cannot fully explain his attraction to Cave Hill, but he is comfortable with it. He is mystified with his ability to help people find gravesites there, even when he has not visited them before.

"I wonder about a lot of things like that," he said.

Williams had always planned that he and his wife would be buried in Calvary Cemetery. But one day in 1967 while driving home alone he said he felt an unexplainable urge to drive to Cave Hill to look at gravesites. A salesman showed him a site, but Williams thought it too expensive, and said he would go home and think it over.

"The next day I gave the man a check," he said.

Williams said his wife had undergone a series of operations in the 1960s for a brain tumor and complications. He said near her death she requested that her gravesite have a tree over it. One Sunday just before his wife died, Williams said he went back to Cave Hill and noticed that a small dogwood tree was growing over the site.

"Of course, there's a lot of trees at Cave Hill," he said. "But I had never noticed that tree before."

His wife died Jan. 8, 1974, and Williams began his regular trips to the cemetery. He wrote of one visit on a page of a book he has on life after death.

"A visit to Edith's grave," the notation says, "there isn't much to see, but there is a lot to feel."

He said he believes the human spirit is quickly moved to another, better world after death. And knowing that, he said, has given him peace.

"I will join her," he said. "We all will."

He said his wife's dogwood tree grew straight for a time, and then began leaning toward his wife's headstone. It is another fact he likes to ponder.

"Sure, I talk with her when I'm in the cemetery," he said. "And I talk to her at home too. But I try not to let people hear me. They wouldn't understand."

Aug. 30, 1979

Hundreds mourn loss of Derek Smith by celebrating his life

Of all the words and tributes offered at Derek Smith's funeral yesterday afternoon, perhaps nothing said more about the love and respect accorded him than his funeral procession — a line of mourners stretching almost across Louisville, from 15th Street to Cave Hill Cemetery.

In symbol — and in fact — Derek Smith, former University of Louisville basketball great, had again united us. His tragic death, at just 34, was a shock that affected the whole community. His hundreds of mourners included family, community leaders, U of L teammates and professional coaches and players. They were black, white, old, young and, in some cases, chance acquaintances beguiled by his small-town honesty and directness.

"I can be a mean old woman," said Neda Triplett, who met Smith in a continuing education class when he returned to U of L to complete his degree, "and Derek Smith was, without a doubt, the sweetest human being I have ever known in my life."

Smith died last Friday while on a cruise. The cause of death has not been determined.

So great was the sense of loss that Smith's funeral service had to be moved to the large auditorium at St. Stephen Baptist Church, 1008 S. 15th St. Even that was barely able to contain the mourners and couldn't contain their emotions.

Dozens of funeral wreaths cascaded across the altar above his casket: red roses, yellow mums, white daisies. The mourners

Photo by Keith Williams
Among Derek Smith's 1980 Cardinals teammates serving as pallbearers with Jerry Eaves, at left front, and Darrell Griffith, right.

moved carefully to the casket, bit at their lips and wiped tears from their eyes.

Several of Smith's former teammates rested hands on the casket, then reached out, gently touching one arm. U of L coach Denny Crum walked up with the funeral program rolled up in his hands, an unconscious gesture he made with game programs so often while coaching Smith in the championship years at Freedom Hall. For a split second, time stood still. Then Crum bowed his head and walked away.

The service began with the 23rd Psalm. Sydney Smith, Derek's young daughter, moved to the pulpit, an angelic figure in a white dress, with long, black braids. In a strong, clear voice she read "A Tribute to Daddy," finishing it with "God loves you, and so do we." A vocalist followed with a powerful song: "I Won't Complain." It was warm in the church. A few mourners waved their programs like fans and fought back tears.

Tributes followed from Smith's coaches and former teammates. They centered on Smith's intensity, his integrity, his loyalty and his love for his wife, Monica, his son, Nolan, and Sydney.

Assistant U of L coach Scooter McCray, a Smith teammate, helped fill the church with needed laughter as he described a 16-year-old Smith, fresh out of Hogansville, Ga., "still sucking on his thumb."

McCray went on to praise the Louisville community for "helping to raise Derek and the rest of us." He finished by talking about Smith's love of a challenge, his work with children, his personal growth and ability to bring out the best in people.

"Derek touched all of us," said McCray. "That's why we're all here. We need to carry that love and touch somebody else."

Former teammate and new assistant U of L coach Jerry Eaves, a close friend of Smith's, said he hadn't cried over the loss. Rather, he said, he wanted the community to "celebrate a great man." Eaves went on to speak passionately of Smith and Smith's wish to become more than a basketball player — and came perilously close to breaking his vow not to cry.

The Rev. Kevin Cosby of St. Stephen Baptist Church reminded the mourners that Jesus, too, died young: "It's not how long you live, but how well you live."

The Rev. James Pitts ended the service with a rousing, booming reminder that Derek Smith had run a good race, had reached his goal, had met his maker. "Amen!" shouted back the mourners. "Amen. Amen."

Afterward, the funeral procession stretched along Broadway to Cave Hill Cemetery. A light rain began to fall as the casket was placed under a green tent. A minister removed lilies from atop the casket and handed one each to Monica, Sydney and Nolan Smith as keepsakes of a good husband and father, each flower a powerful presence with a golden heart.

Aug. 16, 1996

Jimmy welcomed our waves

Your cards and letters to Jimmy Myers covered a 12-foot section of wall at the Neurath & Underwood Funeral Home on Thursday. They were the "thank yous" that had given him joy and satisfaction as he lay dying and will be a source of pride and comfort to his family for as long as he is remembered.

For years Myers, unable to work, had sat in a lawn chair in a shaded place along River Road and waved at passing drivers. He did it because he liked to wave. Last November, stricken with emphysema, then cancer, he had to stop.

The news of his imminent death in a previous column brought him more than 175 cards and letters. They came from Indianapolis and Paoli in Indiana, Hopkinsville and Murray in Western Kentucky, the mountain communities of Eastern Kentucky and people who drive along River Road.

Pam Holzknecht of Louisville was thoughtful enough to include a Polaroid photo of herself sitting in her van waving, just so Myers would recognize her:

"Dear Mr. Myers . . . I want you to know that your wave started my day out with such positiveness and contemplation.... I also thought you were smiling because you weren't fighting the Rat Race anymore....

"I lost my mother to cancer two years ago. I cared for her the last six weeks. I then realized how important it is to tell people how they have influenced lives. I want to thank you for all those waves and smiles. Many of my friends appreciated your waves as well. You made a difference. Truly."

Holzknecht was one of the regular wavers, a diverse group of people who had a common bond in an everyday man:

"Mr. Myers. I just wanted you to know God and I are thinking of you today. I miss you on River Road. The White Cadillac Man." . . . "Jimmy, I drive a gold Mercedes and met you at Christmas 1995, when I stopped and gave you a box of candy. My best to you and your wife. Allen Corbin." . . . "Jimmy, I would wave at you on River Road going to and coming from Nugent Sand. I drive a '92 Ford dump truck, number 104. I enjoyed waving at you. I wish you good health and happiness. Ray Moore."

One of Myers' favorite letters came from two brothers, ages 9 and 10, who live in Pleasure Ridge Park, but would travel down River Road about once a month: "We are so sorry to hear of your illness and want you to know we love you and miss you and will pray for your strength and also for your family. You are our hero.... God bless you.... Brandon Wyatt-Farris and Garrett Farris."

Myers' wife, Juanita, said family members would take turns reading letters to Jimmy until the day he died. They were thankful for the mail, the many prayers. The letters were spread around his room at Hospice of Louisville, then taken to the funeral home where Jimmy's sister, Hallie Calvert, lovingly placed them on flat boards, the wall, the carpeted floor.

Many cards had a waving hand drawn on them. Employees at Kentucky Connection, a carpet-binding company, went one step further, sending an elaborate, home-made pop-out card: "Jimmy, A friendly wave makes a person feel special at any time of the day. We at the Kentucky Connection send back to you a wave today."

Melody Knopf of Eastwood said she was a "fellow-waver," but traveled her neighborhood on foot. Her letter was friendly, chatty, as if from an old friend, with a little bit of waving travails included: "I've been training people how to respond to a wave. When I first began walking and waving, a lot of people were perplexed and didn't know how to respond. Now some of them wave first. What progress."

Paoli (Ind.) Police Chief Ronald Shrout wrote, "We need more people like you. Wishing you well." John and Fay Ray of Murray, Ky., said their Sinking Spring Baptist Church had placed Myers on its prayer list and wanted to share its love.

An entire second-grade class at Jacob Elementary School sent Myers letters: "I try to instill in my students the value of small kindnesses," wrote teacher Debbie Powell, "and I used your story as a legacy to them, and others."

Jimmy Myers was buried in Evergreen Cemetery yesterday. He wasn't looking to leave a legacy, but he did: Be kind, be thoughtful, wave. He was faithful to himself right to the end, waving to other patients from his hospital bed as they passed his door.

He couldn't help it. He just liked to wave.

April 5, 1997

Axing workers — a legal — smart art

I can recall being fired only once in my life. I was part of a crew of teen-age males hired by an agribusiness firm to yank tassels from the tops of 10-foot stalks of hybrid corn to prevent them from cross-pollinating with lesser varieties.

Not counting the razor-sharp corn leaves, the job came with three immediate problems: the pay was 60 cents an hour, 6-foot adolescents cannot easily reach the tops of 10-foot cornstalks and a crew of teen-age females was detasseling corn in a field adjacent to ours.

So what's a hormone-laden teen-age boy to do?

Yup.

Suffice it to say management did not take kindly to independent forays by its employees into possible cross-pollination — as clumsy, laughable and ineffectual as they were. We all got sacked.

That little memory-maker came to mind recently when I was handed an advertising flier that began, "HOW TO LEGALLY FIRE EMPLOYEES WITH ATTITUDE PROBLEMS . . . A STEP-BY-STEP GUIDE . . . One-Day Seminar."

I thought it was a joke. It wasn't. The seminar, sponsored by the Padgett-Thompson Division of the American Management Association, will be held in Louisville Oct. 7. Be the first on your block to wave a pink slip with a certain legal authority.

The advertising flier was as crisp, confident and cheerful a document on giving people the ax as I ever hope to read:

"Susan seems to work in only two speeds — slow and stop. She performs the minimum amount of work required, complains . . . and rushes out of the office at five o'clock on the dot. . . . Can you dismiss her for being a foot dragger?

"Tom is sharp as a tack and performs like gangbusters. The only problem is he knows everything. He always insists on doing things his way.... Can you terminate Tom for being so cocky?

"Lisa has been whining since the day she was transferred into your department.... when you counsel Lisa about her negative attitude, she complains to your boss about you.... Can you legally fire Lisa for being a whiner?

"The answer is YES, you can. After you attend this one-day seminar and learn the skills and techniques you need to turn an employee's poor attitude into a concrete reason for termination, you'll be able to fire employees legally, safely and confidently."

I don't know about you, but, after reading that, I sort of felt like a piker for not having fired anybody all week.

Actually, the flier is just as notable for the things it tap dances around — or just leaves dangling between its lines like a 10-ton legal brief: *Hey employers, in this age of ageism, racism, sexism, handicappedism and me-first-ism, you better nail down your case with real big staples or the fired employee will soon own your BMW.*

To avoid that, or other embarrassing situations, your $125 seminar entry fee will allow you to join group discussions in these highly sensitive areas:

Stop Trying To Deal With Employees Who Drive You Crazy: finally, a way to catch and document employees who bad-mouth you behind your back.

Handle Firing Sessions With More Confidence: a tried-and-test-ed technique for silencing employees who want to argue about being let go.

Build a "Litigation-Smart" Termination Case: three rules for dealing with hypochondriacs who abuse — but don't violate — your sick-leave policy.

I realize there are employees we all wish would take the last bus to the Bering Strait. The American Management Association also packages hundreds of more upbeat seminars that do not necessarily adhere to the Ebenezer Scrooge School of Communication. Yet I detected such a religious enthusiasm for behind-the-back documentation and employee firings in this seminar that I've already begun cleaning out my desk.

I relayed my fears to a Don Gura, a service representative for Padgett-Thompson, who made me feel much better:

"There's more regulation than there used to be. You have to deal with things like handicapped laws. You have to document your case and back it up. You can't just fire people anymore."

The man has a point. Firing people just ain't what it used to be. There is hope for malcontents. But please check your telephone for electronic bugs, quit sending silly computer messages to the new mail clerk and salute the air conditioning ducts at every opportunity.

Forty-five people already have signed up for the Louisville seminar. Big Brother is watching you.

Aug. 14, 1993

Despite the death of Highland Park, the spirit of community lives on

Their morning ritual was unchanged: Bill Gatton met Alvin Walters about 4:30 a.m. Saturday to give him a ride to Highland Park Masonic Lodge 865 to prepare fish for its weekly fry. Walters, 89, has been married to his wife, Katie, for 70 years and has rarely missed a fish fry in 36 years. This one was especially important.

This was the final gathering. This was — after 104 years — the death of Highland Park.

Highland Park was incorporated on May 14, 1890, a city one mile wide and three-fourths of a mile long, mostly settled by country people and immigrants who worked for the mighty L&N Railroad. Lots were 125 feet long and 25 feet wide, and could be had for $125; $10 down and $1 a week. The houses were plain, solid, workmanlike. The inhabitants were neighborly, close-knit.

In its boom years, Highland Park had schools, stores, saloons, barbershops, a bank, a post office and a movie theater. The Watterson Expressway divided Highland Park in the 1950s, and then Standiford Field expansion ate away at its eastern edge. Finally — in actions ruled illegal by the Kentucky Supreme Court long after the damage was done — more than 1,000 residents, many of them elderly who'd lived in Highland Park all their lives, were forced out. The city — and its people — were sacrificed to airport expansion and economic development.

The fish fries continued during the struggle. The masonic lodge, at 4473 Park Blvd., had always been a social center, and now it served as a rallying place. The fight was futile; where 800 people might have gathered on Saturdays 30 years ago, there were barely 200 in the early 1990s. The brick, two-story building — built by member contributions and opened in 1925 — also went to airport expansion. The fish fries will continue next Saturday — uninterrupted — in the new lodge hall at 4100 Pinecroft Drive in Okolona.

"Lord willing," said Paul Stearman, a longtime member. Hundreds of former Highland Park residents joined in the final gathering last Saturday. They came three and four generations deep, great-grandparents to small children. The old people sat on folding chairs in a cleared field next to the lodge, talking about the way things were, a brittle afternoon sunlight casting long shadows on the green grass.

The ghosts and man-made decay of Highland Park were all around them: silent, boarded-up houses; overgrown yards; weeds pushing up through asphalt; ramplike, 60-foot piles of dirt; a few big rocks spilling onto the streets.

Late in the afternoon, lodge members and their families went upstairs to honor past officers and longtime members. The names of nine men eligible for 25-year pins were read; none was present. The names of 12 men eligible for 40-year pins were read; two were present.

Three men were given 50-year pins and gold cards; four others could not make it. When asked to speak, one honoree began crying, gathered his composure, and said, "I have a heavy heart in the respect that I don't have another 50 years to be a member of the Highland Park Lodge."

One by one, 14 past masters of the lodge were asked to say something. Few were practiced speakers, but they spoke from their hearts — simply, directly, powerfully.

"This was a community of common people, good people who cared for each other, watched after each other," said Melvin Strange. "We need to keep the spirit of Highland Park alive in our hearts."

Alvin and Katie Walters were called forward. Alvin was given a plaque for his years of fish-fry service. His key to the lodge building was attached. He was asked if he wanted to speak. "I'm scared to death now," he said.

The ceremony ended about 7:31 p.m.; the lodge lights turned off at 7:57. Members gathered in twos and threes on the front sidewalk, then drifted away. In the distance, a train whistle sounded in the night.

Sept. 27, 1994